A Progressive's Guide

to the

New Testament

T.Collins Logan

First Edition, March 21, 2011
ISBN 0-9770336-7-8

Cover design assistance from Mollie Kellogg. Cover art includes a detail of Hieronymous Bosch's *St. John the Baptist in the Wilderness*, and Papyrus 46 text (circa 175-225 A.D.) from 2 Corinthians 11:33-12:9.

Published by the Integral Lifework Center
PO Box 221082
San Diego, CA 92192
www.integrallifework.com

For the Curious, the Skeptical

And the Confidently Certain

Other Books by T.Collins Logan:

Memory: Self

True Love: Integral Lifework Theory & Practice

Essential Mysticism

The Vital Mystic: A Guide to Emotional Strength & Spiritual Enrichment

Please also visit www.integrallifework.com for articles, updates and additional information about the work of T.Collins Logan.

SPECIAL THANKS

A very special thanks to Steve G. for introducing me to the New Testament and encouraging my initial exploration of Christian ideas; to Mark F. for modeling progressive-minded Christianity and insisting that I put my thoughts in writing some thirty years ago; to Rhonda E. for welcoming me into her world of festive Christian fellowship and enthusiastic faith; to Everett G. for teaching me what courageous honesty and humility really look like; to Lisa D. for imparting her wisdom, insight and *agape;* to Milo H. for sharing his research tools and substantial knowledge, introducing me to the Greek texts, and patiently answering all those questions; to Melissa M. for sticking with me through my many evolutions and joyfully participating in some of my wackiest ideas; to Riley R. for always being true to himself, even when he didn't realize it; to Greg M. for his infectious laugh and generous spirit in every situation; to Norm H. and John E. for their steadfast willingness to engage in thoughtful dialogue around conservative viewpoints; and to the many other believers over the years who wafted the aroma of Christ into my life and out into the world. I also would like to offer heartfelt gratitude to Robin B. for so readily discussing anything under the sun and his timely insights into the nature of faith; to Curt M. and Lee P. for their invaluable feedback on this book; to Larry P. for his care in balancing ineffable truths with rigorous skepticism; and of course to Mollie K., who continues to exhort me to follow through on my best ideas – many of which come from her.

Table of Contents

So much the rather thou, celestial Light,
Shine inward, and the mind through all her powers
Irradiate; there plant eyes, all mist from thence
Purge and disperse, that I may see and tell
Of things invisible to mortal sight.

– from Milton's *Paradise Lost*, Book III, 51-55

INTRODUCTION

When I was eighteen years old, I read the New Testament for the first time. As with many staples of that phase of my life, this was a tattered paperback I picked up at a thrift store. Having no idea how to approach the text, I began reading from the beginning. Soon my head was full of more questions than answers, so I asked a coworker of mine who professed to be a Christian for some recommendations on how I might tackle the content. Steve was studying to be an MD, drawing patient blood in the room next door at the hospital where we worked. My position was aptly named "blood runner," for my sole purpose was to transport any biological samples extracted from patients up to the pathology lab. The building we occupied on the University of Washington campus was undergoing remodeling, and one casualty of the construction was the pneumatic tube system used to transport things from one floor to the next. Not all of the samples were blood, of course – sometimes there were other fluids or tissues, and once there was even a live, pearlescent slug taken from someone's lung. And although I was left to myself most of the time, I took my job very seriously.

For his part, Steve was delighted to introduce me to the New Testament. He was also a little surprised. In our few interactions outside of the workplace, I had communicated my skeptical disdain for most things religious, as well as my decidedly existential approach to life – and even there I preferred Gide and Sartre to the more spiritually oriented Kierkegaard. Steve was delighted enough in my interest to purchase a copy of the New Testament for me. He apologized for the version, which he said wasn't his first choice in translation (at the time I had not known that multiple translations even existed), and encouraged me to start by reading through all the "red letters" in the text; that is, all the sayings purported to be from Jesus himself. So that's what I did.

In the many hours I had to myself at work, and when riding the bus to and from my job, I absorbed all of the red-lettered passages – and as much of the surrounding text as I could to provide context for what Jesus was saying. As I read, a number of things occurred to me, some more forcefully than others. For one, I found myself agreeing with everything I understood Jesus to be saying. Sometimes this was more of an intellectual agreement, and sometimes it was a feeling of rightness, a conviction that something deep, abiding and true was saturating those red letter verses. In parallel to this agreement, I was also struck by how contradictory the example of Christianity had been throughout history as I knew it, and indeed in the lives of many people I personally knew to be Christians. If more people actually followed the red letters of the New Testament, I reasoned, human society would be greatly improved, and Christianity would certainly have a much better reputation than it did among its skeptics.

And what about me? Was I willing to follow what I understood Jesus to be teaching? I knew that would be a question Steve would ask, because I knew that's what Christians did: they proselytized. To his credit, however, Steve never pressured me on this point, and never plied me with questions about my experience of the book he had given me. Our interactions remained light and friendly, and whenever I volunteered my opinions, he was an interested and patient listener with a ready laugh and a careful mind, but he did not set himself up as an authority on scripture or a gateway to Christendom. He did invite me to some events at his church, of course, and my experience of that caring community impressed my heart as much as the words of Jesus. But it would still be nearly a year before I committed in any way to serious exploration of my own beliefs.

Twenty-eight years have come and gone since that first exposure to the New Testament, and my understanding has undergone many evolutions. Yet those first two observations have endured, simmering in my unconscious: I still believe that Jesus' teachings – and indeed much of the New Testament – have a wealth of useful insight for individuals and society as whole, and I still believe that people who profess to follow those teachings often fall woefully short, sometimes even championing approaches antithetical to the ideals Jesus embodied. And so these sentiments will frame the discourse of the following pages. How can we understand the New Testament these two millennia after it was written? What were Jesus' values, and what was Christianity intended to look like as individual life choices and communal effort? What implications might these models have on modern institutions, traditions and culture? And why might it be that so few individuals or groups who claim to be Christian actually align themselves with Christ-like values?

Such questions surface frequently among established Christian organizations, where the intent is often to align each answer with the doctrine of a specific school of thought. As for me, I have no such affiliations and no desire to encourage conformance to a particular brand of Jesus Christ. Instead, I am deliberately departing from past traditions rather than conserving them, hence I offer an inherently progressive view. Further, my idea of progressive spirituality is one in which spiritual ideologies and practices improve over time to the benefit of everyone; that in fact individual and collective spirituality can and should evolve. I describe myself as an integral mystic who encourages spiritual self-nourishment because I believe we all have a spiritual dimension that requires regular exercise and care. I both appreciate and have participated in several faith traditions, and embrace mystical practice as the shared root of nearly all branches of spirituality. In this sense, I am a Perennialist who holds that most exoteric manifestations of religion issue from the same esoteric ocean of experience. I further hold that this esoteric experience, this *gnosis,* is accessible to everyone regardless of their beliefs. At the same time, Christianity was my first exposure to disciplined spirituality, has been a dominant force in my surrounding culture and upbringing, and continues to inform my spiritual life. I am still drawn to the wisdom of the Bible, still enamored of the person of Jesus, and still passionate about opportunities to apply these teachings to my life and the modern world. It is within these currents that I navigate the New Testament and offer a few tools to help comprehend this compelling and complex document.

In addition to spiritual progressivism, I am also socially, economically and governmentally progressive in most of my thinking, so this defines my approach to the New Testament as well. What I mean by "progressive" in these instances is that I advocate policies and practices that continually improve the well-being of individuals and society as a whole, and which, in seeking such positive change, often depart from oppressive, divisive and self-limiting traditions and institutions that have already been established. I want to emphasize that this also includes historically progressive positions and practices; that is, whenever I believe something is no longer in the best interest of personal or collective well-being, I will encourage transformation and evolution instead of clinging to approaches that may have seemed progressive at one time, but which are now outmoded. All of this is in stark contrast to a conservatism that seeks to maintain established customs regardless of their negative consequences, opposing innovation out of a sense of loyalty to the past.

With all of this said, it is extremely difficult to avoid emphasizing those parts of the Bible that agree with our worldview as we interpret its texts, regardless of what that worldview may be. This might explain why there are so many divergent interpretations of scripture, and why even the most fervent spiritual conversion often seems to lead most people back to many of the same attitudes, behaviors and convictions they had before they found religion. This seems to hold true for both individuals and entire cultures, where religion frequently conforms to dominant societal trends rather than the other way around. We will explore this theme in more detail in the coming chapters, but it begs the question of how we can approach the New Testament at all without such preexisting prejudices completely clouding our judgment. To be intellectually honest, we must develop some guidelines for how to interpret what we read, and apply them consistently to each new avenue of inquiry and discussion. In essence, we must develop a transparent hermeneutic and frequently check our assumptions against it. So this seems like the best place for us to begin.

In Search of a Simple Hermeneutic

"Where the scriptures speak, we speak; where the scriptures are silent, we are silent." This was a central tenet of the Churches of Christ I attended in my early twenties. I do not think the expression's author, Thomas Campbell, intended it to become a guideline for interpreting the Bible, but in my faith community at that time in the 1980s, Campbell's motto was often called upon to do just that. In fact, it was with some pride that anyone studying scripture in the Church of Christ could claim we had no need of complex hermeneutics or Biblical scholarship, because we were merely subscribing to this easy principle. Upon closer examination, however, what quickly becomes evident is that this supposedly simple approach to Biblical exegesis is itself an example of how misinterpretations can occur. When we assume that our current understanding of a word or phrase must mean exactly the same thing now that it did fifty, one-hundred or two thousand years ago, we unwittingly commit an egocentric error in formulating our understanding. Using some utterance in isolation, without any appreciation of the person who said it, the cultural backdrop of the times, the language in which it was written, what else the author wrote on the topic, etc. is to exclude critical information from our interpretive process.

There were of course several folks I knew personally in the Church of Christ who approached scriptural interpretation with much more discipline, scholarship and subtlety, so this experience is in no way an indictment of that community. It is, rather, a reminder that we must formulate some sort of structured, practical method of interpretation to consistently apply throughout our examination of any historical writings. Without such a guide, we will inevitably become mired in our own whims and prejudices – and the dominant beliefs and tendencies of our surrounding culture – without even knowing we have done so. Whether our primary exposure to Christianity has been through Sunday morning televangelists, teachers at a religious school, atheistic relatives, a bad experience at summer camp, college courses in comparative religion, a recently converted friend or a personal religious experience of our own, most of us have already become comfortable with conclusions that have little or no connection to the person of Jesus and the traditions of those earliest centuries of Christianity. Perhaps we can never fully comprehend those distant times, as our understanding of knowledge and even language itself are certainly a byproduct of our modern upbringing and enculturation, but at least we can become more conscious of how we are arriving at our conclusions, and thereby open our minds and hearts to fresh insights and experiences.

I tend to separate this process of discovery into two cognitive engines that work in unison. The first engine is the generalized set of beliefs we hold about the nature of the Bible. For example, do we believe the Bible is the revealed word of God, the literary efforts of human beings, or some combination of the two? Do we believe that we can fully comprehend scripture with intellect alone, or is there a spiritual intelligence we must call upon to explore its fullest meaning? Do we hold that Biblical interpretation is a solitary effort, or does our community have an important role? Is it possible that some external agent – a mentor, an angel, a religious leader, the holy spirit, etc. – can aid us, illuminating our understanding of the text? Or can our own conscience guide us if we listen carefully to that innermost voice? If the Bible is the transmission of God's mind, heart and will to humanity, has that transmission ended, or does it continue? Is the Biblical canon the only source of Divine revelation or spiritual understanding for Christendom, or are their other sources as well? And so on. Understanding our beliefs about the New Testament will dramatically alter the relevance, flexibility and power of our interpretations.

Therefore, the first part of an effective hermeneutic should be to invoke as neutral a disposition as possible when examining the New Testament texts. That is, to suspend to whatever degree we can our preexisting ideas about the nature of the Bible, its authors, Jesus, Christian history and so on. If we can begin with a relatively clean slate, then the process of applying the secondary tools described below will be much more powerful. If we are unable to temporarily shelve deeply held convictions about the New Testament, it will interfere with our reexamining it from multiple perspectives. This is a challenge, to be sure, but consider those times when you suspended your disbelief in order to enjoy a film, or become immersed in a work of fiction, or be caught up in a play or other live performance. It would not be very pleasurable to constantly remind ourselves that these are just fictional characters, or actors donning a role, or a made-up world, or a painted backdrop that a set designer dreamt up. Allowing ourselves to be swept up in a creative narrative and its reality-of-the-moment opens us to the meaning and import of that narrative as part of our personal experience. It encourages emotional involvement in story, identification with characters, surprise and delight at each turn of events. It is this quality of openness and interest that creates a fertile seedbed for new ideas, and a well-rounded appreciation of those ideas from multiple points of view.

Why is this so important? Mainly because, if we don't aim for a neutral disposition, our prejudices will almost always blind us to the truth. Closing our minds to things we don't like or can't explain just limits our understanding and hardens our heart. No matter how confusing, controversial or distasteful some information might seem at first, it may still be valid and constructive. This is itself a progressive-minded approach to investigation. However, along these lines, I don't think it is helpful to recast scripture as a modern progressive treatise by conforming its narrative to a 21st Century mindset. Instead, my goal will be to uncover whatever progressive themes natively exist there; that is, to identify readily observable progressive ideas that don't demand elaborate reworking or rationalization. When I have encountered scholars – both progressive and conservative – who try to explain away difficult passages with convoluted, ideological arguments, it only alienates me from their conclusions. So I will try my best not to duplicate this error, and I encourage readers to do the same. At the same time, it is also extremely difficult to place ourselves fully in the zeitgeist of first century Judea, so we must be humble about that as well. A perfectly neutral disposition may be a lofty goal, but it is a worthy one.

The second cognitive engine is our method of interpretation. The tools we are most comfortable with at first will of course be influenced by our beliefs. Viewing the Bible purely as literature or a mythology created by human beings will resist some methods, while viewing the Bible as the sacred and complete utterance of an infallible Deity will cause us to avoid others. Yet across a broad array of convictions, there are certain tools that lend themselves to being applied universally, and it is these we'll call upon in the coming chapters. These are grouped into four broad categories: the *analytical*, the *intuitive*, the *experiential* and the *participatory*. Each has its own strengths, but none of them stands complete on its own; mixing a little of each into our own method of interpretation will strengthen that interpretation. Then, to whatever extent we are able to combine them with a neutral disposition free of prejudice, we can welcome revised information from all these different input streams into our ongoing assessment.

Combining Analytical, Intuitive, Experiential & Participatory

Analytical methods rely upon traditional historical, literary and logical approaches to the text. These might include the following:

- **Author's Intent** – What do the other writings attributed to this same author reveal about the intent of a particular passage or a group of texts?

- **Context** – What is the cultural, historical and situational context of what has been written, as far as we can discover?

- **Language** – What hints can the original language, grammar and usage convey to us about intended meaning?

- **Cumulative NT References** – Are there other places in the New Testament where the same topic is addressed? If so, is the cumulative, consistent meaning when all such references are taken as a whole?

- **Early Christian Acceptance & Application** – As far as can be determined, how was the passage accepted and integrated in Christian teachings in the early Church?

In addition to analytical methods, intuitive methods rely on other processing centers to approach interpretation. For example, an attempt to feel our way through scripture, or rely on abstract, subtle, mystical or metaphorical explorations of meaning and import. Here we are able to appreciate and integrate additional content beyond what we can logically conclude. Intuitive methods might include the following:

- **Inner Inquiry** – Through meditation, mystic activation, silent contemplation or other deliberate and disciplined focus, we patiently invite the underlying meaning of a particular passage to percolate up into conscious awareness. That is, we deliberately suspend analytical aspects of our interpretive process, and instead create an open, spacious receptivity for emotional, intuitive, creative and spiritual forms of information.

- **Invocation** – Through prayer, divination or other supplication, we request the assistance of an external agent – for example, the holy spirit, angels, Jesus, God, (Catholic) saints, spirit guides, etc. – to provide guidance, insight and illumination about the nature and application of scripture. Once again, we create a relaxed, interior spaciousness to receive this assistance rather than rushing to analyze what occurs. Within a carefully maintained interior quiet, we invite insights to be revealed to us.

We also have experiential methods of expanding our understanding. Here we put Biblical teachings into practice with the hope of increasing our comprehension and insight through application. In essence, we learn by doing. For example:

- **Discernment through Practice** – Here we adhere to certain principles, practices and disciplines outlined in scripture in the hope that they will reveal their true meaning to us over time. For example, practicing forgiveness of our enemies until we understand experientially why this is a constructive response. Or practicing prayer until we sense some sort of connection with the Divine. Or revisiting the same passage of scripture all day long, keeping it in our consciousness and observing how it affects our thoughts and behavior. And so on. The essence of this practice is to increase our insight through consciously acting on what we may not completely understand in order that we may eventually comprehend it more holistically through application and felt experience.

- **Discipleship** – Here we allow ourselves to be guided by a mature spiritual example, so that we can gain knowledge and training in spiritual principles through imitation. This could be achieved by observing the attitudes and actions of a more experienced practitioner of the Christian faith, and then emulating that model. Or we might accept and follow the instruction such a mentor provides us, seeking their counsel when we need help with difficult issues, and so forth. The essence of a discipleship relationship is the subjugation of our own will through the modeling of someone we trust, so that we gain appreciation and understanding of challenging and perhaps otherwise incomprehensible patterns of thought and behavior.

And finally we have the *participatory* element of insight. This relies on exchanges about a given topic in a group setting that results in a synergy of insight that might not otherwise be possible as an individual. Examples of this include:

- **Dialogue** – Whether this is a formal discussion in an educational setting, a meditation group, a debate among spiritual peers or an informal gathering of friends, the idea here is to explore nuances of meaning by comparing experiences, learning and wisdom that relate to a given theme. For such dialogue to be most fruitful – that is, to be additive and synergistic – it should take place in a participatory, egalitarian context where everyone is encouraged to share and benefit equally.

- **Communal Insight** – Through practices like *inner inquiry* or *invocation* into a given subject in a group setting, a deeper comprehension of the subject can be achieved.

- **Communal Experience** – Engaging in *discernment through practice* or *discipleship* as part of a larger, interdependent community likewise can broaden and strengthen our insight and understanding.

If we synthesize some combination of analytical, intuitive, experiential and participatory methods to examine two-thousand-year-old text, it is almost certain our comprehension will be more multifaceted than relying on just one approach. So this is the hermeneutic I will rely upon as we explore each topic, and I encourage readers to utilize it as well. There will be references to the Koine Greek in which the earliest surviving manuscripts of New Testament texts were written. There will be copious attention paid to cumulative references on the same or similar topics. There will be some examination of a particular author's patterns of discourse. There will be my own intuitive explorations of certain themes, my experiences of the Christian faith relating to those issues, and contributions to my learning that were facilitated by community. I will encourage readers to try exercises intended to stimulate a deeper understanding of the text. All of this can then be synthesized in a spirit of neutral judgment in an attempt to allow the New Testament to speak for itself and permit us to be fully immersed in its language and mindset. Taken altogether, I hope we will gain more discernment into the spirit of these early Christian writings as they relate to modern-day spiritual and sociopolitical concerns.

It is important to emphasize that readers need not be Christian or even religiously inclined to apply all elements of this hermeneutic. I am not asking anyone to believe in God or have faith in New Testament veracity to guide their interpretation, but rather to have faith in a particular method of interpretation, a method that can reveal rare depths of insight for anyone willing to put it into practice. As you read through each chapter, it will become more evident how this approach works. But let's take on one controversial issue to examine ways this hermeneutic can create a consistent baseline for interpreting ancient texts. Throughout the New Testament, there are many references to miracles performed by Jesus and his apostles, including healings, casting out demons, resurrecting the dead and so forth. For one person, miraculous events may already align with their personal experience, observations and worldview. For another, anything smacking of the supernatural might be reflexively rejected because their experience, observations and beliefs do not support it. But what if, using our analytical tools, the writers of the New Testament seem to have placed great stock in these events? What if miracles seem to have occurred quite frequently in the early Church? What if there is much matter-of-fact discussion about the importance of these incidents in the development of the Christian religion?

This is where we can rely on the combined elements of our hermeneutic while suspending our preexisting conceptions. For example, we can broaden our communal dialogue to include others whose perspective on the miraculous, inexplicable, synchronistic or supernatural is different from our own, delaying judgment as we consider many different viewpoints. We can also look inside ourselves for guidance, calling upon our creative and intuitive faculties to the explore meaning and relevance of the miraculous; in doing so, we may find a way to incorporate seemingly supernatural events into our understanding that is not logically evident at first. The experiential component of this hermeneutic can also aid us. For example, what if we went about our daily life *as if* the miraculous could be accepted at face value? What if we were to trust in the possibility of spiritual power in order to see how such trust shapes our experience? How might entertaining the supernatural from a neutral standpoint change our interactions with others? Does it induce stress and undermine our well-being? Or does it strengthen our relationships in positive ways, enhancing our sense of wholeness and happiness? In imitating patterns of thought and action described in the New Testament with an open mind and heart – as guided by our analytical, participatory and intuitive assessment tools – we can come to appreciate those patterns more holistically.

Using this process, we don't accept or reject the concept of miracles in some sort of absolute sense, but instead learn to hold unknowns lightly in our minds and hearts, allowing them to gestate into conclusions and possibilities we haven't yet considered. By attempting to maintain neutrality and openness while exploring perspectives that may at first seem foreign to us, we can feel our way through them so that they inform our understanding the New Testament. By temporarily investing in a mode of thought or being that diverges from our personal status quo and stretches our comfort zone, we can see beyond the horizon of our personal worldview, exceeding current limitations to perceive nuances and subtleties we would otherwise overlook. Once again, this does not mean we are emotionally or intellectually investing in a perspective that is alien to us, it means we are empathizing with it, testing its assumptions, trying it on for size, and suspending conclusive judgment. In effect, it does not matter whether we believe in miracles or not, only that we appreciate how New Testament authors related to the miraculous from their vantage point.

In order for these approaches to be most successful, I tend not to rely on any one translation of the New Testament, but often synthesize a rendering from my own attempts to grapple with the original Greek, interlinear translations, and the various versions of the New Testament currently available in English (NASB, NIV, ESV, ISV, ERV, WEB, NLT, NRSV, etc.). In this book I will quote from some of these versions verbatim, and I give translation credit accordingly before individual quotes or a series of passages; for example (NIV) for New International Version, etc. Where no credit is given, the passages will be my own translation. However, what is striking to me is how even subtle differences in word choice can introduce new shades of meaning – and quite possibly reveal the bias of the translators. Even how the text has been punctuated or separated into paragraphs can influence its meaning. I have discovered that some popular versions of the New Testament tend to obscure the original intent of the Greek, in what appears to be an effort to make the text either more palatable to modern readers, or perhaps more aligned with a particular theological position. So even if we don't want to parse the Greek ourselves, it still behooves us to compare different versions to gain a better feel for the original language. In the past, I have found the New American Standard Bible to be useful in my ongoing studies of the New Testament. In the process of researching this book, I encountered the English Standard Version as one I feel also does an exceptional job of accurately representing the Greek.

For those with the time and energy to do so, struggling with the peculiarities of each New Testament author's writing – their common concepts, idioms, vocabulary, etc. – in the original language can also be helpful in navigating these texts. In addition, how can we understand the meaning of a particular phrase or passage without appreciating the parlance of the time, to whatever degree possible? To that end, the

Resources section at the end of the book highlights some of my most-frequented avenues of wrestling with Koine Greek. Beyond translation, for an overview of different avenues of interpretation, I recommend reading Marcus Borg's *Reading the Bible Again for the First Time,* which clarifies contrasting approaches and outlines the "historical-metaphorical" approach that Borg favors. Still, without the aids of experiential testing, communal synergy, inner inquiry and neutral disposition to anchor and broaden my understanding, I would have no confidence at all that my interpretations of scripture were useful to my own spiritual nourishment. For me, meditating on a difficult passage, discussing it with my peers or spending a week trying to put it into practice are just as important as working through the Greek, comparing different translations or finding verses that speak to similar themes. So at every step, the analytical is balanced with the participatory, intuitive and experiential.

One final note regarding my own translations: I try to do my best to remain loyal to the original Greek, and modernize language mainly to clarify what would otherwise be unintelligible or distractingly obscure. Thus I tend to avoid both traditional and modern conventions that are not represented in the Greek. So on the one hand I may leave the gender non-neutrality of the text intact (for example, "brothers" does not become "brothers and sisters"). But on the other hand, I don't capitalize "holy spirit" or "lord" either. With these choices, I am not trying to exclude anyone, refute any religious doctrine, alienate any particular denomination, or make any definitive pronouncements at all…I am merely attempting to reflect what was originally written as accurately as I am able. Again, my goal is to offer what is native to the New Testament so you can draw your own conclusions, and trying to convey the original feel of the language – as much possible without being fluent in Koine Greek – is part of that effort. Of course, I do bow to convention in some respects. For example, I will capitalize "God" and instances of "Father" relating to the Divine, even though the Greek does not. I will also utilize contractions (don't, won't, etc.) to make the text more readable in some cases. So I do have my own quirky exceptions to every rule, which relate more to my fascination with language and the process of translation than to any religious or philosophical position. I hope you will bear with that quirkiness.

Transmission, Canonization & Veracity of New Testament Texts

The question of whether we can rely on the authenticity or transmission of New Testament texts over the centuries has been exhaustively expounded upon by influential scholars and writers – Eberhard Nestle, F.F. Bruce, Bruce Metzger, Kurt and Barbara Aland, and many others – and I recommend consulting those authors for a thorough exploration of the topic. Suffice it to say that there are thousands of partial and complete manuscripts from all around the globe, from successive epochs of Church history, which corroborate a fairly reliable consistency in iteration for many New Testament texts back to about the second century. I say "fairly reliable" of course because there were indeed scribal copying errors, revisions and deletions unique to each manuscript. These would include the earliest Greek texts (the papyri, uncials and miniscules); the first translations of the Greek into other languages (vernacular versions and lectionaries); and numerous references to scripture in writings of the Church Fathers (patristic quotations).

When such divergent sources are taken together and carefully compared and collated, it is possible to resolve many errors and variations, and to hypothesize about the content of commonly shared original manuscripts (autographs). If you have interest in the technical details of this history, I encourage you to consult a good translation of Kurt and Barbara Aland's book, *Der Text des Neuen Testaments* (*The Text of the New Testament).* As of this writing, a quick Internet search on "timeline of Christianity" produces several interesting articles on the topic as well. However, it is important to acknowledge that no New Testament autographs that we know of have survived into modernity – so the second century is really as far back as we can go with any certainty. Because of this fact, there are countless theories about when the books of the New Testament were actually written, if, how and why various source materials might have been altered over time, and who the original authors actually were.

As for canonization, the New Testament in its current form is generally held to have been assembled rather gradually over three centuries, with much dispute and diversity of opinion over what should and should not be included. Initially, there were hundreds of writings circulating in the early Church. The first effort that we know of to organize these writings into an authoritative canon was initiated by Marcion of Sinope in the mid second century A.D. We can also observe that critical reactions to Marcion's teachings at the time (as found in Tertullian's *Adversus Marcionem*) seem to have spurred the Church into formalized efforts to differentiate orthodoxy from heresy and establish a Church-sanctioned scriptural canon. The final inclusions and organization of content we see today was then finalized over the course of three Church councils: the council at Hippo in 393 A.D., the council at Carthage in 397 A.D., and the council at Carthage in 419 A.D.

To reiterate, prior to this final canonization, there were hundreds of writings circulating in the early Church that were considered by one group or other to be spiritually valuable if not authoritative. And despite the endurance of the current canon, there has always been – and continues to be – debate over who authored certain New Testament books and what should or should not be relied upon to defend orthodoxy or define authentic Christianity. It is important to remember that the councils of Hippo and Carthage represent a very small slice of Christian history, insight and opinion as influenced by the culture and politics of those times. This begs the question of whether we should rely on their decisions for our spiritual edification today, and I will address this later in the book as well.

Yet regardless of how the canon evolved, are the writings in the New Testament accurate accounts of events that actually happened, as recorded by eyewitnesses? Are they fabrications to bolster belief in a Divine savior or propagate specific doctrines? Were original documents altered to appeal to popular prejudices and beliefs? Does the New Testament perhaps contain a little of each of these? From the texts themselves, the writers seemed to believe they were being truthful, claiming to offer first-hand observations or accounts from people they considered reliable sources. But whether the authors confused facts, misunderstood concepts, misremembered events, or trusted sources they shouldn't have are all excellent questions we must continually ask. In addition, without autographs, it is impossible to be certain that New Testament texts weren't doctored or distorted during their earliest decades of existence. Even where we might find independent historical evidence that corroborates New Testament accounts – from Roman records, Jewish historians, etc. – there will always remain a gap in reliable information that either doubt or faith will fill. So, ultimately, we can only rely on our own insights, judgment and discernment to form conclusions.

Historically, although the evidences and analytical tools have changed over time, the specific authorship of the New Testament texts themselves has been debated for centuries. Were Matthew and Luke derived from Mark and perhaps an undiscovered "Q document?" We don't know. Was the Gospel of John written by the Apostle John or did it likewise expand on some earlier account? We don't know. Who wrote Hebrews? We don't know. Who is the Jude who wrote the epistle of that name? We don't know. What we do know is that a majority of New Testament content was circulated and venerated throughout the early Church, and that most of what we have today represents a fair approximation of many of those earliest and most cherished writings. We also know which texts were credited to which authors fairly consistently throughout Christian history, and which of them were more disputed, and we will touch on some of this later in the book. Our only real confidence is that many people – among them the Church Fathers and the Christians who met at those fourth century councils – seem to have trusted either in the truthfulness and authenticity of these accounts, or in their usefulness in supporting the orthodoxy of the time, or both. Beyond that, it again becomes a matter for us to evaluate and decide for ourselves.

How have I approached this evaluation? The issues of transmission, authorship and veracity can largely be resolved using the same set of hermeneutical tools already outlined. For example, are the language and intent of texts attributed to the same author fairly consistent? Is the overall sentiment we find in any given passage supported by cumulative references across several different texts? Does the historical and cultural context that shaped interpretation of one text inform others equally? Did the early Church embrace these texts and their teachings? In applying the principles of particular scripture to our lives, are we challenged to mature and grow through that application, or does our progress stall, stagnate or regress? Does our wisdom and compassion increase or decrease when we integrate particular scriptural instruction into our lives? When we seek clarity through invocation or inner inquiry, do we encounter barriers to understanding the text and resistance to its practice, or does our understanding deepen? And so on. When we weigh the outcome of critical analysis, the communal exchange of ideas, experiential testing and spiritual discernment together, we can synthesize solid and reliable convictions about the New Testament canon – and indeed any and all other spiritual resources we encounter. But even when we establish a modicum of certainty, our own conscience still remains the final arbiter of the truth, and our understanding will likely continue to change and evolve over time.

In my own voyage through Christianity, I have felt comfortable venturing outside of the established Biblical canon into other sources using similar tools and discernment. Consistently applying elements of the same hermeneutic to determine the edification value of various sources, I believe I have encountered the aroma of Christ among Christian mystics, poets and scholars of both ancient and modern eras, as well as among spiritual writings from other faiths. However, I will include a minimum of such external references here, restricting my focus to the New Testament as the title implies. I do this for a reason: to demonstrate buoyant support for progressive ideas among the New Testament's pages, we should confine a majority of our discussion to the internal logic and evidence of that document. The established canon can thereby offer us a baseline for critical analysis and intuitive comparison when we expand our reading to other sources. Even where I suspect certain New Testament texts may be of dubious authorship or intent, I will nevertheless include them as part of that baseline reference, because I trust that whatever is true and good will shine through almost anything if I weigh it carefully and listen to my heart.

With all of this in mind, I readily admit that one of my core beliefs regarding spiritual wisdom is that there is a font of powerful insight and authority within each and every person, easily accessible if we take time to listen. And if such wisdom is indeed inscribed in the essence of our being, then we need not be so concerned about the accuracy and transmission of any scripture over millennia, what has been included in a particular canon, or the endurance of any given interpretation over time. This is my bias, but I am also convinced that the question of how to uncover spiritually authoritative answers is answered by the New Testament itself, so let's begin our investigation there.

SPIRITUAL AUTHORITY

Over decades of interacting with Christians from many different religious sects and philosophical viewpoints, the divisions I have encountered over the nature and purpose of the New Testament canon are almost too numerous to count. We can, however, simplify this diverse debate into two broad camps. At one end of the spectrum are those who believe the Bible is a fixed record of instruction, made authoritative by the fulfillment of various prophecies, the performing of miraculous signs by its central figures, a trust in accurate first-hand accounts of events witness by the authors, and the sanctioning of its authors by prophets, miracle workers and the Messiah himself. In other words, the spiritual authority of the canon is verified either by miraculous signs and prophecy fulfillment, or by the immediate proximity and intimate relationship of the authors to those prophets and miracle workers. The reasoning often follows that the canon is therefore complete because such prophets and miracles are no longer readily apparent today.

At the other end of the spectrum are those who believe the scriptures offer us seeds of an ever-evolving spiritual journey, and that spiritual authority resides less in the text itself, and more within the heart of every believer who yearns to comprehend the mysteries of the Divine with the aid of the holy spirit. This, in turn, allows believers and spiritual communities not only to interpret the deepest contemporary meaning of scripture, but also to adapt to new questions and challenges without relying entirely on the written word. The Biblical canon in this context is therefore an enduring and informative example of how the holy spirit, the word of Christ and the laws of God manifest in the thoughts and deeds of believers, but it is not static, complete, or the sole source of spiritual authority. We might even say a large number of divisions in Christendom – perhaps even a majority over the centuries – have been the byproduct of these opposing views on spiritual authority, usually with respect to some hot topic of a particular era. Even current day rifts could be characterized the same way, where some groups wish to maintain the immutably codified supremacy of the written word along with its static interpretation, while others wish to evolve new ideas and solutions out of classic spiritual principles, processes and approaches they feel scripture embodies but does not dictate.

But how does the New Testament itself address this topic? Let's begin our exploration with a number of relevant passages. The passages will be listed out in the order they are already organized in the New Testament, and with these we can hopefully connect the dots to derive some overarching themes. As an exercise in drawing your own conclusions, see if you can discern any developing motifs that inform the source of instruction, wisdom and spiritual authority for Christianity. I would encourage you to apply elements of the hermeneutic described in the first chapter on your own – familiarizing yourself with the authors, evaluating language and context, meditating or praying over what you discover, dialoguing with others over themes you identify, and even attempting to put into practice whatever applies to your situation. Using these same methods, I will of course offer my own conclusions – but it is quite possible that, like so much of the exegesis of the past two thousand years, I may only be arranging the text to suit preexisting beliefs.

> "Don't think I came to destroy the law or the prophets; I didn't come to destroy but to fulfill. For I tell you truly, until heaven and earth pass away, not one iota, not one point will pass away from the law in any way until everything is accomplished. Anyone who breaks one of the least of these commandments – and teaches others to do the same – will be called least in the kingdom of heaven; but whoever practices and teaches them will be called great in the kingdom of heaven. For I tell you that unless your righteousness exceeds that of the scribes and Pharisees, you will not enter the kingdom of heaven by any means."
>
> *Matthew* 5:17-20

> Hearing them debating, one of the scribes approached, and because Jesus had answered them so well, he asked, "What is the foremost of all the commandments?" Jesus answered, "The foremost is: 'Hear, Israel,

the lord our God is one lord. You shall love the lord your God with all your heart and with all your soul and with all your mind and with all your strength.' The second is this: 'You shall love your neighbor as yourself.' There is no commandment greater than these."

Mark 12:28-31

"Why don't you judge for yourselves what is right?"

Luke 12:57

For everyone who does evil things hates the light, and does not come to the light because they could be reproved for their deeds. But someone practicing the truth comes to the light, so that their deeds may be manifested as having been wrought in God.

John 3:20-21

"Don't you believe that I am in the Father, and that the Father is in me? The words I say to you are not from me myself, but the Father remains in me to do His work. Believe me that I am in the Father and the Father is in me – or at least believe based on the works themselves. With complete certainty I tell you that anyone who has faith in me will do the works I have done – and even greater things – because I am going to the Father. And I will do whatever you ask in my name, so that the son may bring glory to the Father. You may ask me for anything in my name, and I will do it. If you love me, you will keep my commandments. And I will ask the Father, and he will give you another counselor to be with you forever— the spirit of truth…"

John 14:10-16

"I have much more to tell you, more than you can now bear. But when the spirit of truth comes, that one will guide you into all truth. He will not speak on his own, but will speak only what he hears, and he will announce to you what is to come. That one will bring glory to me by receiving what is mine and making it known to you. All things that belong to the Father are mine, and this is why I said the spirit will receive what is mine and make it known to you."

John 16:12-15

"Therefore let all Israel be assured of this: God has made this Jesus, whom you crucified, both lord and Christ." When the people heard this, their hearts were stung and they said to Peter and the remaining apostles, "Brothers, what shall we do?" Peter replied, "Repent and be baptized, every one of you, in the name of Jesus Christ for the forgiveness of your sins, and you will receive the gift of the holy spirit.

This promise is for you and your children and for everyone far away—for as many as the lord our God may call."

Acts 2:36-39

Stephen, full of grace and power, did great wonders and miraculous signs among the people. But opposition arose from members of the synagogue of so-called freedmen – from Cyrene and Alexandria as well as Cilicia and Asia. These men began to debate with Stephen, but they could not withstand the wisdom and the spirit with which he spoke.

Acts 6:8-10

They spent considerable time there, speaking boldly about the lord, who testified to the message of his grace by enabling miraculous signs and wonders through their hands.

Acts 14:3

Whenever the Gentiles – who do not have the law – do by nature the things required by the law, they are a law unto themselves, even though they do not have the law. They show that the work of the law is written on their hearts, their conscience bearing witness and their thoughts alternately accusing or even excusing them...

Romans 2:14-15

But you are not in flesh but in spirit, since God's spirit dwells in you. If someone doesn't have the spirit of Christ, then they are not of him. But if Christ is in you, on the one hand the body is dead because of sin, but on the other the spirit is life because of righteousness. If the spirit of the one who raised Jesus from the dead dwells in you, the one who raised Christ Jesus from the dead will also make your mortal bodies alive through his spirit dwelling in you.

Romans 8:9-11

Don't owe anything to anyone except to love one another, for those who love each other fulfill the law. The commandments "You shall not commit adultery," "You shall not murder," "You shall not steal," "You shall not covet" and any other commandments are summed up in these words: "You shall love your neighbor as yourself." Love perpetrates no evil on its neighbor, therefore love is the fulfillment of the law.

Romans 13:8-10

Or don't you now that your body is a temple of the holy spirit that is in you, which you have received from God? You are not your own – you were bought with a price – so glorify God in your body.

1 Corinthians 6:19-20

There are different kinds of gifts, but the same spirit. There are different kinds of ministry, but the same lord. There are different operations at work, but the same God operating all things in all people. But each one is given the most profitable manifestation of the spirit. One person is given the message of wisdom through the spirit, another the message of knowledge according to the same spirit, another faith by the same spirit, another gifts of healing by that one spirit, another miraculous powers, another prophecy, another the discerning of spirits, another speaking in different kinds of languages and another the interpretation of languages. And in all of these one and the same spirit operates, distributing separately to each according to his purpose.

1 Corinthians 12: 4-11

If I speak in the languages of men and of angels, but don't have love, I have become a noisy gong or a clanging cymbal. And if I have the gift of prophecy and know all mysteries and knowledge, and if I have the faith to remove mountains, but don't have love, I am nothing. If I give all I own to the poor and surrender my body to be burned, but don't have love, it profits me nothing. Love is longsuffering and kind. Love is not jealous. Love does not boast, is not proud, is not rude, does not seek things for herself, cannot be provoked, and keeps no record of wrongs. Love does not delight in injustice but rejoices with the truth. Love covers all things, believes all things, hopes all things, endures all things. Love never fails. But whether there are prophecies, they will be abolished; or other languages, they will cease; or knowledge, it will pass away. For we know in part and we prophesy in part, but when perfection comes, the imperfect will disappear. When I was a child, I spoke like a child, I thought like a child, I reasoned like a child; when I became a man, I did away with childish things. Now we see an enigma in the mirror, but then we shall see face to face. Now I know in part, but then I shall know fully, even as I am fully known. For now, three things remain: faith, hope and love – and the greatest of these is love.

1 Corinthians 13:1-13

What does a temple of God have in common with idols? For we are a temple of a living God, as God said: "I will dwell among them and walk among them; I will be their God and they will be my people."

2 Corinthians 6:16

But the fruit of the spirit is love, joy, peace, patience, kindness, goodness, faithfulness, meekness and self-control. Against such things there is no law. Those who belong to Christ Jesus have crucified the flesh with its passions and lusts. Since we live by the spirit, let's walk in the spirit. Let's not become conceited, provoking and envying one another.

Galatians 5:22-26

You were also included in Christ when you heard the word of truth, the gospel of your salvation, and having believed you were sealed with the holy spirit of promise, a deposit guaranteeing our inheritance until the redemption of those who are God's possession—to the praise of his glory. For this reason, ever since I heard about your faith in the lord Jesus and your love for all the saints, I have not stopped giving thanks for you and making mention of you in my prayers, in order that the God of our lord Jesus Christ, the glorious Father, may give you the spirit of wisdom and revelation – so that you may know him better. I pray that the eyes of your heart may be enlightened so that you may know the hope to which he has called you, the riches of his glorious inheritance in the saints, and the exceeding greatness of his power toward us who believe.

Ephesians 1:13-19

For the word of God is living and active, sharper than any two-edged sword, penetrating as far as the division of soul and spirit, of joints and marrow, and able to judge the thoughts and intentions of the heart. No creature is hidden from God's sight, but all things are naked and laid bare before the eyes of him to whom we must give account.

Hebrews 4:12-13

We have much to say about this, but it is hard to explain because your hearing has become dull. In fact, though by this time you ought to be teachers, you need someone to teach you the rudiments of God's oracle; you have come to need milk instead of solid food. Anyone who relies on milk is still an infant and hasn't experienced the word of righteousness. But solid food is for the mature, who have conditioned their faculties through training to distinguish both good and evil.

Hebrews 5:11-14

His divine power has given us all things pertaining to life and godliness – by recognizing him who called us to his own splendor and virtue, through which he has gifted us his greatest and most precious promises – so that through them you may become partners in divine essence…

2 Peter 1:3-4

And we have the word of the prophets made more certain, and you will do well to pay attention to it, as to a light shining in a dark place, until the day dawns and the morning star rises in your hearts. Above all, know that no prophecy of scripture interprets itself. For prophecy was never carried by the will of man, but men spoke from God as they were supported by holy spirit.

2 Peter 1:19-21

By this we know that we remain in him, and he in us: because he has given us his spirit.

1 John 4:13

But you, beloved, build yourselves up in your most holy faith and pray in holy spirit. Keep yourselves in the love of God as you wait for the mercy of our lord Jesus Christ into eternal life.

Jude 1:20-21

Before I summarize my own ideas, please take a moment to mull over these passages before reading any further. Maintaining as neutral a disposition as possible, what themes do you see emerging here? What threads of wisdom? Perhaps you could spend some time meditating or praying over your own understanding. Perhaps discussing them in a group would be helpful. Some of these verses can also be put into practice to facilitate experiential learning. Use all of the tools in the hermeneutical toolkit if you can. Ultimately, a synthesis of these techniques will lead to the most well-rounded interpretation possible.

There are a number of principles reflected in these passages that have been widely accepted across Christendom throughout most of its history. We might summarize them as follows:

1. Jesus promised his immediate disciples that although he himself was departing the earthly realm, they would receive the holy spirit as a counselor who would guide them into "all truth" not yet revealed. He further promised that this spirit would be with them forever.

2. Anyone who repented (i.e. recognized their past errors and felt contrition about them) and was baptized in the name of Jesus Christ received the holy spirit. Further, that spirit was considered a seal of their salvation – a guarantee of their

inheritance through God's mercy, with their physical body becoming a sacred temple in which God would dwell.

3. Certain miraculous abilities – "signs and wonders," spiritual gifts – were enabled by the indwelling of the holy spirit. These differed from one believer to the next, but they all issued from the same Divine breath and were intended for the good of everyone. Initially, such gifts established the spiritual authority of apostles, prophets and teachers, but spiritual gifts were increasingly relied upon for the ongoing edification and support of the Church through all members of the congregation.

4. The law of love (ἀγαπάω: to be concerned for, devoted to, and generous toward; to value, esteem and take delight in; to manifest the loving kindness of *agape* in effective action) was more important than any such signs and wonders, and was a primary evidence of holy spirit's presence in someone's life. Even if and when such spiritual gifts were to pass away, love would remain supreme.

Expanding on this, there has been far less breadth of agreement about the following additional principles, but I believe they are nevertheless represented in these passages as well:

1. The spiritual laws of God were written on the hearts of every person, whether they believed in God or not, and this was one reason the Light of Divine Truth is recognizable to all people, and why Jesus in fact challenged people to judge for themselves what was virtuous, righteous and just.

2. The expectation of the writers of the New Testament was that the holy spirit would guide believers into an increasingly mature understanding of a Christ-like existence – to the point of sharing in the Divine essence, nature and purpose. The Greek word used for maturity most often is τέλειος, which meant *complete, perfect, fully realized*. However, it is equally clear that, as of the writing of these epistles, this expected maturity had not yet manifested in the early Christian Church. A solid understanding of Jesus' message had not yet developed in the churches who

received the apostles' missives, but the apostles kept hoping, praying for and exhorting this evolution to occur with the aid of the holy spirit.

3. The *logos*, the word of God, was not considered a static or passive thing, nor was the holy spirit. These were perpetually active, infusing the very core of human beings with wisdom, expressing the will of God in the present. Further, Jesus expressed an expectation that future believers would perform even greater works than he did himself through the power of their faith.

4. Even if miraculous abilities were to attenuate – even if the gifts of the spirit abated – holy spirit was still present, still active, still able to guide and inform, still able to open the eyes of the human heart. What became more and more important with time was that Christians be able to increase their discernment through practicing what they knew to be right, maintaining their faith and hope in Christ, praying in holy spirit, and expressing the love of God in every thought and action.

Most of these points can be reasoned out of the passages already quoted. However, our exegesis is incomplete if we do not include intuitive, participatory and experiential approaches along with analytical ones. This is of course where things become more personal for each of us – where our understanding is customized to whatever stage of spiritual development we happen to be passing through at a given time. At this point in my journey, the conclusions I intuit about the nature and sources of spiritual authority grow congruently from the fertile intersection of my life experiences, the wisdom of spiritual traditions, open sharing with others, and a felt connection with my own spiritual ground through mystical practice. And what are those conclusions? That reliance upon external signs and wonders to establish sources and authorities may facilitate the beginning of wisdom, but such reliance is left behind as we mature. What remains is much more subtle, more complicated, and in many ways more powerful. To be a partner in Divine essence is to radiate a love that does not conform to fixed ideals, but fosters a radically transformative activism that is both fierce in its compassion and completely at peace with itself. And although these scriptures still serve as an important litmus test or touchstone for a Christian's spiritual growth, they were in fact never intended to restrict that growth solely to the holy spirit's manifestation in the early Church or in the canonized texts.

We can in fact see this principle echoed everywhere around us. In the evolution of life into more and more complex systems, with ever more delicate gradations of interdependence. In the evolution of human culture into greater diversity, subtlety and complexity. In the evolution of human knowledge about the physics of the Universe to finer and finer degrees of differentiation. In the development of a child's extreme, reactive, black-and-white reasoning into the more nuanced, multifaceted and measured appreciations of adulthood. And all of these evolutions find parallels in progressive spiritual understanding, where complex qualities of loving intention overtake eye-for-an-eye reasoning. Indeed, the message of the New Testament embodies this evolution: Jesus came to fulfill the law of God, and the fulfillment of that law was *agape*. All the granular do's and don'ts of the Old Testament were reduced to the principle of loving intentions and actions. And what informs those loving intentions and actions? Our own conscience, the law of love written within us, which may be amplified by the ministrations of the holy spirit, but which is really powerful enough on its own to comprehend the Light, embrace the Light, and live perpetually within the Light – once we come to accept that this is so.

Like children who need training wheels to learn how to ride a bike, canonized scripture helps Christians appreciate certain principles and limitations. Eventually, however, everyone must learn how to sense their own inner balance, how to keep themselves from crashing, and how to maintain enough forward momentum to sustain both progress and spiritual equilibrium. Like a loving parent, the holy spirit promises to catch Christians as they fall, to help right their course if they make a wrong turn along the way, or help prompt them in the most fruitful direction when they ask, but that spirit need only run along side someone for so long before spiritual discernment is embedded in their being. The holy spirit of the New Testament offers Christians freedom, not dependence, and though it is natural for people to cling to signs and wonders – to synchronicities and affirmations and other external reinforcements that they are on the right path – once we let go of such fearful neediness we will gain something much greater. For what parent would not rejoice in the self-sufficiency, competence and confidence of their child? And what prophet of God would not rejoice the fantastic potential of every believer to accomplish greater things than the Messiah himself, just as Jesus promised? It seems to me that this kind of growth-inducing freedom and support is one of the finest expressions of love people can experience in this life.

An intended purpose of the New Testament in this light is to convey spiritual authority to everyone who believes in the message of Jesus, recognizing that this inner authority, this font of spiritual wisdom, is already present within all people, but requires encouragement and a few guiding principles and practices to help it evolve more fully – to help it mature. In this sense, to follow Christ is simply to follow our better selves, our more enlightened insights and understanding, and to culminate that understanding in a perfect love of All that Is. And lest we delude ourselves into thinking some self-serving, malevolent or indifferent thought or action is a part of this love, the holy spirit is there to remind us of our error – through scripture, through our spiritual community, through disciplined spiritual practice, and through our own inner promptings. Eventually, so the promise goes, if we follow the Light within, the mud will settle, the waters will clear, and we will apprehend Divinity face to face.

But is there additional scripture to support this approach to an interior spiritual authority? Returning to the analytical aspects of our hermeneutic, consider the expressed intentions of Luke at the beginning of his gospel:

> Since many have undertaken to draw up a narrative of the things that have been fully carried out among us – matters handed down to us by those who from the beginning were eyewitnesses and servants of the word – it seemed good to me, who also investigated these things from the beginning, to write an accurate account for you, most excellent Theophilus, so that you may know the certainty of the things you have been taught.
>
> *Luke 1:1-4*

Luke makes no claim to being anyone or anything other than a historian of collected accounts. He does not say his record is inspired by God, or guided by holy spirit, or in any way spiritually authoritative. And yet it has been included in the Biblical canon. I think this lends itself to an interpretation that at least some portions of the New Testament were never intended to be anything more than a reference and guide for spiritual aspirants.

Along the same lines, in the Gospel of John, the author writes to explain the reasons for writing the account:

> And the one who has seen has borne witness, and his testimony is true; and he knows that he is telling the truth, so that you also may believe.
>
> *John 19:35*

> Jesus also performed many other signs in the presence of the disciples, which are not written in this book, but these have been written so that you may believe that Jesus is the Christ, the Son of God, and that believing you may have life in his name.
>
> *John 20:30-31*

> Peter turns and sees that the disciple whom Jesus loved is following them – the one who also reclined against Jesus' breast at the evening meal and said, "lord, who is going to betray you?" Upon seeing him, Peter says to Jesus, "lord, what about this one?" Jesus says to him, "If I want him to remain until I come, what is that to you? You follow me!" Therefore this saying went out among the brothers: that that disciple would not die. Yet Jesus did not say to him that he would not die, but only, "If I want him to remain until I come, what is that to you?" This is the disciple who is testifying to these things and wrote these things, and we know that his testimony is true. And there are also many other things which Jesus did, which if they were written in detail, I suppose that even the world itself could not contain all the scrolls to be written.
>
> *John 21:20-25*

Although the author does assert the primacy of a close relationship with Jesus, they still do not claim the holy spirit inspired their account. Instead they affirm they are bearing witness to these events and writing these them down with a confidence that they are true. Now let's contrast these two gospels to Revelation, where the writing is much more assertive about invoking the Divine inspiration to enhance the authority of that text:

> A Revelation of Jesus Christ, which God gave him to show to his bond-servants the things which of necessity must soon take place. And he made it known by sending his angel to his bond-servant John, who testified to the word of God, to the witness of Jesus Christ and to all that he saw. Blessed is the one reading and hearing the words of the prophecy – and the one attentively observing the things which are written in it – for the time is near.
>
> *Revelation* 1:1-3

> I, John, your brother and companion in the affliction and kingdom and perseverance that are in Jesus, came to be on the island called Patmos because of the word of God and the witness of Jesus. I was in the spirit on the lord's day, and I heard behind me a loud voice like the sound of a trumpet saying, "Write in a scroll what you see, and send it to the seven churches: to Ephesus and to Smyrna and to Pergamum and to Thyatira and to Sardis and to Philadelphia and to Laodicea."
>
> *Revelation* 1:9-11

> "I, Jesus, have sent my angel to testify these things to you in the churches. I am the root and the descendant of David, the bright morning star." The spirit and the bride say, "Come" And let the one who hears say, "Come." And let the one who is thirsty come; let whomever wishes take the water of life freely. I testify to everyone who hears the words of the prophecy of this scroll: if anyone adds to them, God will add to him the plagues which are written in this scroll; and if anyone takes away from the words of the scroll of this prophecy, God will take away his part from the tree of life and from the holy city, which are described in this scroll.
>
> *Revelation* 22:16-19

What a difference we find here. In this revelation, the author is stating that he was "in the spirit" when events occurred; that this is prophecy from God, the testimony of an angel and not the author's own memory or imagination; that in fact these words are so sacred that to add or subtract from them in any way is a spiritually dangerous offense. In reading the whole of Revelation, it is clear that its author intended it to be a prophetic document, inspired by the holy spirit, designed to spiritually edify its readers – rather than be an historical or persuasive account of events as the gospels of John and Luke define themselves to be.

We see this same sort of contrast elsewhere in the New Testament as well, especially the writings of the Apostle Paul, who differentiates between what he himself recommends and what he believes to be Divinely inspired instruction. For example:

> But to the married I give instructions, not I, but the lord, that a woman should not leave her husband (but if she does leave, she must remain unmarried, or else be reconciled to her husband), and that the husband should not leave his wife. But to the rest I say, not the lord, that if any brother has a wife who is an unbeliever, and she consents to live with him, he must not leave her.
>
> *1 Corinthians 7:10-12*

> I don't say this by way of command, but through the diligence of others to prove the reality of your love. For you know the grace of our lord Jesus Christ, that although he was rich, for your sake he impoverished himself so that through his poverty you might become rich. I give my opinion in this matter because this is to your advantage, who were the first to begin a year ago not only to do this, but also to desire to do it.
>
> *2 Corinthians 8:8-10*

In Romans 9:1, Paul uses an almost beseeching tone to promote his own authority: "I am telling the truth in Christ, I am not lying, my conscience testifies with me in holy spirit…" In these few words we see both the authority of innate conscience and the authority of holy spirit combined, bearing witness together that Paul believes his words to be the inspired instruction of God. And yet, as we encountered in the excerpts from his Corinthian missives, Paul clearly differentiates his own opinions from such inspiration. Taken with all of the other references in the New Testament regarding the purpose and presence of the holy spirit, it is difficult to avoid the conclusion that there are vast swathes of the canon that were never intended to be embraced as direct revelation – never meant to be viewed as a burning bush on Mount Horeb – but rather the research, recollections and opinions of fervent believers. Thus the internal logic and evidence of the New Testament itself speaks against embracing all of the canon as inspired by God.

Though it is true that the gospels provide accounts of the miraculous life of Jesus, thereby intending to imbue his words and deeds with Divine authority, the accounts themselves are described as either personal observations or the secondhand recollections of others. So instead of being fed a continuous course of prophetic utterances, we are encouraged to rely on reason, our human conscience and the power of holy spirit to illuminate Divine truth – indeed even the accuracy of these accounts. The Light is already part of our being, whether we believe in Jesus' message or not, but through belief in his message Christians are promised amplification and clarification of the Light in the power of the holy spirit. That is the assertion made throughout the New Testament, and what the writers expressed as being demonstrated in their accounts and insights. There is of course a primacy of spiritual authority vested in Jesus, in his apostles, in the prophets of God and in the gifted teachers of the early Church. But this authority seems to have been deliberately temporary, planting the initial seeds of the Christian religion and exhorting believers to grow and evolve, rather than establishing some sort of irrefutable reference for Christians to rigidly mimic over the following millennia.

This empowerment of individual believers is part of what made Jesus such a revolutionary, as over and over again he challenged those who relied too heavily on religious hierarchies or codified and externalized versions of spiritual guidance and truth. Consider this example from Luke 13:10-17:

> Jesus was teaching on the Sabbath in one of the synagogues, and a woman was there who had been crippled by a spirit for eighteen years. She was bent over and could not straighten all the way up. When Jesus saw her, he called her forward and said to her, "Woman, you are set free from your infirmity." Then he put his hands on her, and immediately she straightened up and glorified God. In answer, the synagogue ruler became angry that Jesus had healed on the Sabbath, and said to the people, "There are six days for work, so come and be healed on those days and not on the Sabbath." But the lord answered him, "Hypocrites! Doesn't each one of you untie his ox or donkey from the manger on the Sabbath and lead it out to give it a drink? Then doesn't this woman, a daughter of Abraham, whom Satan has kept bound for eighteen years, deserve to be set free on the Sabbath from what bound her?" When he said this, all those opposing him were humiliated, but the people rejoiced over the glorious things he was doing.

And even as he established his own spiritual authority with signs and wonders, Jesus was critical of this necessity. Consider these verses:

> Then some of the scribes and Pharisees answered him, "Teacher, we wish to see a miraculous sign from you." But he answered, "A wicked and adulterous generation seeks a miraculous sign, but none will be given to it except the sign of the prophet Jonas. For as Jonas was three days and three nights in the belly of a sea monster, so the son of man will be three days and three nights in the heart of the earth."
>
> *Matthew 12:38-40*

> The Pharisees and Sadducees approached Jesus and tested him by asking him to show them a sign from heaven. He replied, "When evening comes, you say, 'It will be fair weather, for the sky is red,' and in the morning, 'Today it will be stormy, for the sky is red and overcast.' You know how to interpret the face of the heavens, but you cannot interpret the signs of the times. An evil and adulterous generation seeks a miraculous sign, but none will be given it except the sign of Jonah." Jesus then left them and went away.
>
> *Matthew 16:1-4*

> Once more he came to Cana in Galilee, where he had turned water into wine. And there was a certain nobleman whose son was ailing in Capernaum. When this man heard that Jesus had arrived in Galilee from Judea, he went to him and begged him to come and heal his son, who was close to death. "Unless you people see miraculous signs and portents," Jesus told him, "you just won't believe." The nobleman said, "Sir, come down before my child dies." Jesus replied, "Go. Your son lives."
>
> *John 4:46-50*

Today, if Christians demand signs and portents to validate their beliefs and spiritual course, aren't they falling into the same error as the religious elite of Jesus' day? And in the same vein, if they become overly dependent on canonized scripture as an inflexible prescription for their spiritual journey, aren't they delaying their own spiritual maturity? If they are blindly subscribing to established traditions or relying on the directives of institutional hierarchies to guide their faith and its expression in the world, aren't they in fact denying both the true nature of God's law as described in the New Testament, and the power of holy spirit in their lives by doing so? The abiding font of spiritual wisdom and clarity is established by the previous passages as residing in every human being and accessible to all. This was a substantial part of Jesus' liberating message, and a repeated exhortation from early Church leaders to the Christian community. So where does spiritual authority reside for both believer and nonbeliever? Ultimately, it resides within each of us. As the conscience which alternately "convicts or defends" us and already fully recognizes good and evil, as the holy spirit which guides the anointed into all truth, and as the knowledge and wisdom that develop through spiritual maturation.

As a mystic and practitioner of Integral Lifework, my goal is to empower individuals to increasingly rely on their internal spiritual compass rather than on external guideposts. External guideposts – whether a Biblical canon, longstanding traditions, mentors and leaders, signs and wonders, or any other authority we perceive to be outside of ourselves – are invaluable reminders of how spiritual life may begin and unfold, but they are not the only source of spiritual edification available to us, and may in fact hinder our growth if we become too dependent on them. So my understanding of an authoritative spirituality falls squarely in the camp of inner knowing or *gnosis* as supported by established spiritual principles. The most important form of Divine guidance always issues from within. And the New Testament's advocacy of this approach is in fact one of its most progressive attributes, for by identifying the font of spiritual edification as residing within each individual, it further attenuates the importance of conserving tradition, the influence of Church leaders, and overdependence on imperfect historical documents. That is, it liberates Christians from enslavement to rigid dogma from any source. This is a critical theme in New Testament teachings, and we will be exploring it in more depth in later chapters. For now, let's examine one way the fruits of this spiritual authority manifest themselves in the world.

The Kingdom of God

The powerful reality of an indwelling Divine guidance is congruent with another important principle expressed throughout the New Testament: the existence of a kingdom of spiritual power that demands various dimensions of Christian activism. Sometimes this kingdom is called the "kingdom of God," and sometimes "kingdom of heaven." As we will see, most of time neither of these refers to a heavenly realm where God's throne is surrounded by angels, nor to some bucolic vision of an afterlife, but rather to a spiritual realm on earth. How this earthly spiritual kingdom is named depends mainly on which New Testament author is writing about it. Matthew tends to use the phrase "kingdom of heaven," where Mark, Luke, John and Paul lean more towards "kingdom of God;" but they are all referring to the same thing. Here are a few parallels to illustrate this interchangeability. To help test the consistency of this assumption, the following side-by-side comparisons are all taken from the New International Version (NIV) of the New Testament:

"Blessed are the poor in spirit, for theirs is the kingdom of heaven." *Matthew 5:3*	"Blessed are you who are poor, for yours is the kingdom of God." *Luke 6:20*
The disciples came to him and asked, "Why do you speak to the people in parables?" He replied, "The knowledge of the secrets of the kingdom of heaven has been given to you, but not to them." *Mathew 13:10-11*	When he was alone, the Twelve and the others around him asked him about the parables. He told them, "The secret of the kingdom of God has been given to you. But to those on the outside everything is said in parables…" *Mark 4:10-11*
He told them another parable: "The kingdom of heaven is like a mustard	Then Jesus asked, "What is the kingdom of God like? What shall I

seed, which a man took and planted in his field. Though it is the smallest of all your seeds, yet when it grows, it is the largest of garden plants and becomes a tree, so that the birds of the air come and perch in its branches."

Matthew 13:31-32

compare it to? It is like a mustard seed, which a man took and planted in his garden. It grew and became a tree, and the birds of the air perched in its branches."

Luke 13:18-19

Jesus said, "Let the little children come to me, and do not hinder them, for the kingdom of heaven belongs to such as these."

Matthew 19:14

People were bringing little children to Jesus to have him touch them, but the disciples rebuked them. When Jesus saw this, he was indignant. He said to them, "Let the little children come to me, and do not hinder them, for the kingdom of God belongs to such as these."

Mark 10:13-14

Then, almost as if he was putting this specific question to rest, Matthew himself eventually equates the two phrases (NIV):

> Then Jesus said to his disciples, "I tell you the truth, it is hard for a rich man to enter the kingdom of heaven. Again I tell you, it is easier for a camel to go through the eye of a needle than for a rich man to enter the kingdom of God."
>
> *Matthew 19:23-24*

Although some doctrinal differences among Christian denominations encourage differentiation between the "kingdom of heaven" and the "kingdom of God" (for example, in millennialism vs. postmillennialism debates), there is really no spiritually profitable reason to overcomplicate this issue. Perhaps the gospels were meant for different audiences, so different terms were used. Perhaps Jesus himself used the terms interchangeably. Perhaps there is no definitive rationale. In order to understand what this spiritual kingdom really represents, however, it seems reasonable to examine New Testament references to both terms. Here are a few more of those for you to consider:

> From then on Jesus began to proclaim, "Repent, for the kingdom of heaven has drawn near."
>
> *Matthew 4:17*

"Not everyone saying, 'lord, lord,' to me will enter the kingdom of heaven, but those doing the will of my Father in heaven."

Mathew 7:21

"From the days of John the Baptist until now, the kingdom of heaven has advanced with force, and forceful men seize it."

Matthew 11:12

But Jesus knew their thoughts and said to them, "Every kingdom divided against itself is brought to desolation, and every city or household divided against itself will not stand. And if Satan expels Satan, he is divided against himself – so how can his kingdom stand? If I expel demons by Beelzebub, by whom do your people drive them out? Therefore, they will be your judges. But if I expel demons by the spirit of God, then the kingdom of God has come upon you."

Matthew 12:25-28

"The kingdom of heaven is like treasure hidden in the field: when a man finds it he hides it again, and in his joy sells all he has and buys that field."

Matthew 13:44

"Woe to you, scribes and Pharisees, hypocrites because you shut the kingdom of heaven in men's faces. You do not enter, nor do you allow those to enter who are making the effort."

Matthew 23:13

And taking a cup and giving thanks he offered it to them, saying, "Drink from it, all of you, for this is my blood of the covenant, the blood being shed for many for the forgiveness of sins. I tell you, by no means will I drink this fruit of the vine again, until that day when I drink it anew with you in my Father's kingdom."

Matthew 26:27-29

And after John had been taken into custody, Jesus came into Galilee, proclaiming the gospel of God and saying, "The time is fulfilled, and the kingdom of God has drawn near; repent and believe in the gospel."

Mark 1:14-15

And he said to them, "I tell you the truth, some who are standing here will not taste death until they see the kingdom of God arriving with power."

Mark 9:1

"Very well, teacher," the scribe replied, "in truth you say that God is one and there is no other beside him, and to love him with all your heart, with all your understanding and with all your strength – and that to love one's neighbor as yourself is greater than all the burnt offerings and sacrifices." Seeing that he had answered sensibly, Jesus said to him, "You are not far from the kingdom of God."

Mark 12:32-34

"And they will come from east and west, and from north and south, and will recline at the table in the kingdom of God. And behold there are those who are last who will be first, and first who will be last."

Luke 13:29-30

Being questioned by the Pharisees about when the Kingdom of God would come, Jesus answered them, saying, "The kingdom of God does not come through intent watchfulness, nor will people say, 'Here it is,' or 'There it is,' for the kingdom of God is within you."

Luke 17:20-21

"I tell you truly, whoever does not receive the kingdom of God like a child will not enter it by any means."

Luke 18:17

In addition, while they were listening, he told them a parable – because he was near Jerusalem and they thought that the kingdom of God was going to appear at once.

Luke 19:11

And when the hour came, Jesus and his apostles reclined at the table. And he said to them, "I have fervently desired to eat this Passover with you before I suffer. For I tell you, I will not eat it again until it is fulfilled in the kingdom of God." And taking the cup and giving thanks he said, "Take this and divide it among yourselves; for I tell you I will not drink the fruit of the vine again until the kingdom of God comes."

Luke 22:14-18

One of the hanging criminals reviled him: "Aren't you the Christ? Save yourself and us!" But another rebuked him and said: "Don't you fear God, since you are under the same judgment? For we justly got what we deserved, but this man did no harm." Then he said, "Jesus, remember me when you come into your kingdom." And Jesus said to him, "I tell you truly, you will join me in paradise today." It was now about the sixth hour, and darkness came over the whole land until the ninth hour as the sun failed. And the curtain of the temple was torn down the middle.

And Jesus cried out in a loud voice, "Father, into your hands I commit my spirit!" Uttering this, he breathed his last.

Luke 23:39-46

Behold, a man named Joseph, a councilmember and a good and righteous man, did not agree with their advice and action. He came from the Judean town of Arimathea and was awaiting the kingdom of God; this man approached Pilate and asked for Jesus' body. He took it down, wrapped it in linen, and placed it in a tomb cut from rock, where no one had yet been laid. It was the Day of Preparation, the Sabbath was about to begin, and the women following after – who had come with him from Galilee – saw the tomb and how his body was laid in it. They returned to prepare spices and ointments.

Luke 23:50-55

As they were saying these things, Jesus himself stood in their midst and said, "Peace to you." But they were startled and terrified, thinking they saw a spirit. He said to them, "Why are you troubled, and why do doubts arise in your hearts? See my hands and my feet, that I am myself. Touch me and see – a spirit has no flesh and bones, as you behold I have." After he had said this, he showed them his hands and feet. And while they still disbelieved from joy and amazement, he asked them, "Do you have anything to eat here?" They handed him a piece of broiled fish, and he took it and ate it before their eyes.

Luke 24:36-43

Now there was a man of the Pharisees named Nicodemus, a ruler of the Judeans. He came to Jesus at night and said to him: "Rabbi, we know you are a teacher who has come from God, for no one could do these signs that you are doing without God being with him." Jesus answered and said to him: "With complete certainty I tell you that unless a person is born from above, he cannot see the kingdom of God." Nicodemus says to him: "How is a man able to be born when he is old? He cannot enter a second time into his mother's womb to be born?" Jesus answered: "I tell you with certainty that unless a person is born of water and spirit, he cannot enter into the kingdom of God. Anything born of the flesh is flesh, and anything born of the spirit is spirit. Don't marvel that I said, 'It is necessary for you to be born from above.' The spirit breathes where it wishes and you hear its utterance, but you can't tell where it comes from or where it goes. It is the same with everyone born of the spirit."

John 3:1-8

The other disciples followed in the little boat, dragging the net full of fish, for they were not far from land – about a hundred yards. When they disembarked, they saw a fire of coals with fish lying on it, and some bread. Jesus said to them, "Bring some of the small fish you've just caught." Simon Peter went up and hauled the net to land, full of large fish (a hundred and fifty-three), and even though there were so many the net wasn't torn. Jesus said to them, "Come and have breakfast." None of the disciples dared to ask him, "Who are you?" for they knew it was the lord. Jesus came, took the bread and gave it to them, and the fish likewise. This was now the third time Jesus demonstrated to his disciples that he had been raised from the dead. When they had finished breakfast, Jesus said to Simon Peter, "Simon son of John, do you love me more than these…?"

John 21:8-15

I know and have been persuaded by lord Jesus that nothing is profane in itself – except when someone considers something to be profane, then to them it is profane. If your food causes your brother grief, you are no longer walking in love. Do not let your food destroy someone for whom Christ died. Do not let your good be spoken of as evil. For the kingdom of God is not about eating and drinking, but about righteousness, peace and joy in holy spirit…

Romans 14:14-17

But if the lord wills, I will come to you soon, and then I will know what power these arrogant people have, not just their talk. For the kingdom of God is not made of talk, but of power.

1 Corinthians 4:19-20

Before reading further, I would again encourage you to reflect on the previous excerpts as a whole while delaying any definite conclusions. Meditate on them. Pray about them. Discuss them with others. Intuit your way to a possibility until you feel a sense of rightness regarding your convictions. Put any verses that speak to your current situation into practice for a few days, and carefully observe the results. Then compare your assessment with what is offered below.

Although not entirely beyond controversy and debate, here are some easily recognizable and widely accepted principles we can glean from these passages:

1. People during Jesus' life who heard his preaching assumed that the arrival of kingdom of God was imminent. Jesus reinforced this belief by assuring them that at least some of the people living at that time would witness the kingdom's arrival before they died.

2. Jesus claimed repeatedly that the arrival of kingdom of God was in fact actually occurring – that is, that the fulfillment of past prophecies regarding the kingdom of God were being fulfilled in the present at that time.

3. The kingdom of God described in these passages was not a physical kingdom or worldly rule as was likely expected by Jesus' followers of that era. It was instead an immanent kingdom within – a special state of heart, mind and spirit. At the same time, this kingdom within was expressed without as well, evidenced in a community and actions that brimmed with loving kindness, humble obedience to God, and the powerful evidences of an indwelling holy spirit.

4. According to Matthew, Mark and Luke, at the Passover meal before his crucifixion, Jesus claimed he would not partake of food or wine again until the kingdom of God had arrived. Then, explicitly in Luke 24 – and perhaps implicitly in John 21 – Jesus does take sustenance during post-resurrection appearances to his disciples. Perhaps, then, this was meant to be a further verification of the kingdom's arrival.

So the kingdom of God described here was neither heaven itself nor a worldly kingdom, but a synthesis of both: a kingdom of spiritual power on earth, made up of faithful believers christened with the holy spirit. And how was that kingdom initiated? By Jesus first laying down his life for his friends – thus demonstrating that critical necessity of humility, obedience and love – and returning from the grave and appearing to his disciples as evidence of spiritual power and liberation.

However, with that said, there are other passages that offer stark contrast to these conclusions. They refer to Jesus' eventual return, after a number of ominous signs have occurred, to establish a tangible kingdom that would have been more recognizable to the messianic expectations of his time. We hear a description first from Jesus himself in Matthew 24 and 25, which is echoed here in Luke 21:20-33. I quote this passage from World English Bible (WEB) translation, using bold text to highlight elements that challenge the idea that Christ's kingdom arrived with his resurrection:

> "But when you see Jerusalem surrounded by armies, then know that its desolation is at hand. Then let those who are in Judea flee to the mountains. Let those who are in the midst of her depart. Let those who are in the country not enter therein. For these are days of vengeance, that all things which are written may be fulfilled. Woe to those who are pregnant and to those who nurse infants in those days! For there will be great distress in the land, and wrath to this people. They will fall by the edge of the sword, and will be led captive into all the nations. Jerusalem will be trampled down by the Gentiles, until the times of the Gentiles are fulfilled. There will be signs in the sun, moon, and stars; and on the earth anxiety of nations, in perplexity for the roaring of the sea and the waves; men fainting for fear, and for expectation of the things which are coming on the world: for the powers of the heavens will be shaken. Then they will see the Son of Man coming in a cloud with power and great glory. But when these things begin to happen, look up, and lift up your heads, because your redemption is near." He told them a parable. "See the fig tree, and all the trees. When they are already budding, you see it and know by your own selves that the summer is already near. **Even so you also, when you see these things happening, know that the Kingdom of God is near.** Most certainly I tell you, this generation will not pass away until all things are accomplished. Heaven and earth will pass away, but my words will by no means pass away."

A similar prediction is greatly expanded upon in Revelation, where John describes a series of cataclysmic events that must occur before the kingdom of the world can "become the kingdom of our lord and of his Christ" (Revelation 11:15) after Jesus' return. Among those events are the resurrection of the dead, plagues and pestilence, signs in the heavens, earthquakes, a mountain hurtling into the ocean, the appearance of a beast from the sea, a dragon with seven heads, and so forth. In addition to this account in Revelation, we also hear similar sentiments in some of the epistles, where the kingdom of God is clearly described as a future event. For example, Paul discusses the resurrection of the dead extensively in 1 Corinthians 15, and in verses 40 through 50 elaborates on the state of being that will inherit that future kingdom of God:

> There are heavenly bodies and earthly bodies, but indeed heavenly splendor is one kind, and earthly splendor is another. There is one splendor of the sun, and another splendor of the moon, and another splendor of the stars – for star differs from star in splendor. It is the same with the resurrection of the dead: it is sown in the perishable, it is raised in the imperishable; it is sown in dishonor, it is raised in glory; it is sown in weakness, it is raised in power; it is sown a natural body, it is raised a spiritual body. If there is a natural body, there is also a spiritual one. So also it has been written, "The first man, Adam, became a living soul; the last Adam a life-giving spirit." The spiritual isn't first, but the natural, and afterward the spiritual. The first man from the dust of the earth; the second man from heaven. Those of the earth are like the dust of the earth; and those of heaven are like the heavens. Just as we wore the image of dust, we will also wear the image of the heavens. **Now I say this, brothers: that flesh and blood aren't able to inherit the kingdom of God, and the perishable isn't able to inherit the imperishable.**

Such verses reinforce the view that this particular 'kingdom of God' will not in fact arrive until Jesus' second coming, and that such a future event is the spiritual inheritance of those who put their faith in Christ. I think anyone who has studied the New Testament and the early Christian Church has encountered not only this apparent contradiction, but also evidence that there was confusion in early Christendom over this issue. Many among the first generation of believers seemed to have expected Jesus to return during their lifetime. This conviction was so pervasive that, when it became clear that this first generation was dying off, the belief morphed into an assumption that certain people would live an unnaturally long time in order to witness the prophesied last days. As explained in John 21:20-23:

> Peter turns and sees that the disciple whom Jesus loved is following them – the one who also reclined against Jesus' breast at the evening meal and said, "lord, who is going to betray you?" Upon seeing him, Peter says to Jesus, "lord, what about this one?" Jesus says to him, "If I want him to remain until I come, what is that to you? You follow me!" **Therefore this saying went out among the brothers: that that disciple**

> **would not die.** Yet Jesus did not say to him that he would not die, but only, "If I want him to remain until I come, what is that to you?"

In the opening lines of Revelation, the writer hints that the second coming was nevertheless drawing near: "Blessed is the one who reads the words of this prophecy, and blessed are those who hear it and take to heart what is written in it, because the time is near." The Apostle Paul likewise uses language indicating a belief on his part that at least some people of his generation would live to see Jesus' return, for he writes in 1 Corinthians 15:51-52: "Behold, I tell you a mystery: We will not all sleep, but we will be changed – in an instant, in the blink of an eye, at the last trumpet. For a trumpet will sound, the dead will be raised imperishable, and we will be changed." And again in 1 Thessalonians 4:15: "For this we say to you by word of the lord: that we who live and remain until the coming of the lord will not precede those who have fallen asleep by any means." Here the term "sleep" was a common euphemism for death, and if not all of the Christians of his era would sleep until Jesus' return as Paul suggests, he must have expected at least some to remain alive until that prophesied event.

What does this apparent contradiction mean? The Greek doesn't aid us, as "kingdom" is translated consistently from the same word, βασιλεία, throughout the text. Perhaps there has always been unresolved confusion among Christians about when and how Jesus would return. However, I think that taken as a whole with the passages quoted in the first half of this chapter, there may be a reasonable explanation: that there are actually multiple iterations of the same kingdom being described here. The first would be the spiritual kingdom established by Jesus' in-the-flesh visit to the earthly plain, where he left behind the good news regarding redemption, a community of believers, and a holy spirit to help establish and expand that message and community. The second iteration would then occur during his dramatic return in the end times to establish a more transparent and irrefutable dominion over the earth – a more worldly spiritual kingdom, if you will. This interpretation of these two iterations or phases of the same kingdom is in fact supported by two of the authors who helped introduce confusion over the issue. As Paul writes in 1 Corinthians 15:20-26:

> But now Christ has been raised from the dead, the first fruits of those who have fallen asleep. For since death came by man, the resurrection

> of the dead also came through man. For as in Adam all died, so also in Christ all will be made alive. But each one in his own order: the first fruit Christ, then those who are Christ's in his presence, **then the completion, when he delivers the kingdom to God the Father – when he will abolish all rule and all authority and power.** It is necessary for him to reign until he has put all his enemies under his feet. The last enemy to be abolished is death.

And John also helps clarify a transition of kingdoms, a "handing over of the kingdom of God," in Revelation. For he writes of the first kingdom, the kingdom that preexists Jesus' triumphant return, in the following verses. These are taken from the New American Standard Bible (NASB), with my added emphasis in bold:

> John to the seven churches that are in Asia: Grace to you and peace, from Him who is and who was and who is to come, and from the seven Spirits who are before His throne, and from Jesus Christ, the faithful witness, the firstborn of the dead, and the ruler of the kings of the earth. To Him who loves us and released us from our sins by His blood—**and He has made us to be a kingdom, priests to His God and Father**—to Him be the glory and the dominion forever and ever. Amen.
>
> *Revelation* 1:4-6

> And He came and took the book out of the right hand of Him who sat on the throne. When He had taken the book, the four living creatures and the twenty-four elders fell down before the Lamb, each one holding a harp and golden bowls full of incense, which are the prayers of the saints. And they sang a new song, saying, "Worthy are You to take the book and to break its seals; for You were slain, and purchased for God with Your blood men from every tribe and tongue and people and nation. **You have made them to be a kingdom and priests to our God; and they will reign upon the earth."**
>
> *Revelation* 5:7-10

So the kingdom of God, or the kingdom of heaven, is both right here on earth, right now in this life, and promises to become something more at the end of days. These kingdoms appear to be phases of the same continuous event. As with the iterations of God's spiritual law on earth, the prophesied second coming of Christ pledges the fulfillment of the new covenant, just as Jesus, during his first appearance on the earthly plain, claimed he fulfilled the first covenant God had made with his people under the Law of Moses. Then, later in Revelation, the prophecy speaks of a thousand-year reign (Revelation 20) followed by a new heaven and a new earth (Revelation 21). Could these be additional iterations or phases of the kingdom of God, recasting yet again the transformative interplay between mortal and immortal, Earth and heaven, humans and Deity? I think it is a reasonable assumption.

But what does all this really mean, and why have I focused on this topic? I believe each kingdom described in the New Testament represents an advancing level of refinement in spiritual principles, which in turn facilitates and evidences a more complex, conscious and inclusive relationship between humanity and the Divine. On the one hand the concept of progressive kingdoms reinforces the idea that Christendom was not intended to be a static place, but a transformative one. Successive iterations of spiritual kingdoms not only implies spiritual evolution, but scripture explicitly demands the participation of Christians in ongoing preparation of themselves and the Church in anticipation of each kingdom. The progression of God's kingdoms requires an ongoing spiritual maturation process from believers. In addition, some potentially confusing Christian traditions can also be clarified. For example, consider the Lord's Prayer:

> "Our Father, the one in heaven, may your name be holy.
> May your kingdom come,
> may your will be done upon the Earth, as it is in heaven.
> Give us today the bread that sustains us,
> and forgive us our debts, just as we forgive our debtors.
> And lead us not into temptation, but deliver us from evil."
>
> *Matthew 6:9-13*

At the time Jesus gave this instruction, the first iteration of the Kingdom had not yet occurred – that is, Jesus had not yet undergone his transformation and the holy spirit had not yet descended on believers. So it made perfect sense in that context – "your kingdom come, your will be done" simply advocated that first phase. Then, after the Church was established and Christians anticipated the second coming of Christ, the prayer took on new meaning. It became an advocacy of the second coming of Jesus; that is, of phase two of Christ's ever-expanding dominion. We could even observe that God's will being done on Earth is the primary component of each and every kingdom, a continuous manifestation. As equal parts of that manifestation are God's forgiveness, the Christian's responsibility to forgive, deliverance from evil, true and reliable sustenance, and honoring the Divine above all else. Whether as a mantra or a meditation, an invocation or an inspiration to act, the Lord's Prayer offers us a template for what the kingdom of God is intended to look like. And when we view the many references to the kingdom of heaven or kingdom of God in this light, some distracting differentiations begin to evaporate. That Divine realm becomes both internal and external, both past and future, both heavenly and earthly, both established and perpetually coming into being, a fulfillment of Divine will in concert with the devoted efforts of believers in Christ.

And finally, what also arises from this study is how easily misconceptions can propagate about a particular religious idea. How often I have heard people ask: "Why are Christians so preoccupied with the afterlife and getting into heaven? What about the here-and-now?" In fact, the New Testament instructs Christians to be concerned with the kingdom of God in the here-and-now, with perpetual anticipation of Christ's second coming as part of that awareness – but worrying about the afterlife, or even the existence of heaven and hell, isn't really on the radar at all. We could even say that the concepts of heaven and hell themselves are mostly irrelevant to the spiritual framework of the New Testament, in the same way that references to unicorns in the Old Testament are mostly irrelevant to the spiritual framework of that document. Certainly neither of these ideas were intended to shape Christ-like character or motivate Christian faith-in-action. Unfortunately, ignorance about the contextual meaning of the "kingdom of heaven" has led to gross misinterpretations of the express focus of Christian intentions and efforts. For the kingdom of heaven in the verses we've covered so far is an evolving kingdom of God on earth, a kingdom that expects ongoing, continually maturing participation from its believers in every moment.

As the recurring emphasis in the New Testament scripture indicates, Christians should primarily be committed to actualizing this kingdom above anything else. In part this actualization is extremely personal, involving the transformation of heart, mind, body and spirit as the result of faith, love and spiritual practice. In part this actualization is communal, in the expression of this interior transformation in every action and interaction. And in part this actualization is the anticipation of a global inevitability – that is, living in harmony with the expectation that Jesus could return at any moment to rule the planet; as Jesus says in Matthew 24:42, "So remain watchful, for you don't know in what moment your lord will come." When verses relating to the kingdom of God or the kingdom of heaven are absorbed through this orientation, a whole new landscape of spiritual activism springs into being, an activism that becomes the essential purpose of Christendom. And thus we arrive at the heart of the matter, for as we will see in the following chapters, much of the spiritual activism promoted in the New Testament is unquestionably both culturally and spiritually progressive in its orientation. As we will see, the successive iterations of the kingdom of God demand progressive attitudes and actions from the Church and all its members in order to sustain that defining spiritual trajectory.

Sociopolitical Activism

For an historical overview of Judea, the Roman Empire, and both Jesus and early Christianity's place in them, I recommend Gerd Theissen and Annette Merz's book, *The Historical Jesus*, James Ermatinger's *Daily Life of Christians in Ancient Rome*, and Martin Goodman's *Rome and Jerusalem: The Clash of Ancient Civilizations*. At the time of publication, a web search on the phrase "historicity of Jesus" generated some excellent resources as well. According to these and other sources, Jesus and his followers lived under what could best be described as a military dictatorship. With all of its deliberate imitation of ancient Greece and its early attempts to maintain a Republic, by the first century the Roman Empire had left representative democracy behind almost entirely, favoring instead the rule of a despotic emperor and a wealthy aristocracy – backed by the might of the most effective army on the planet. In the meantime, Rome had conquered Judea early in the first century B.C., and seems to have offered the Judeans a fair amount of freedom to manage their own affairs.

From both the New Testament and what few independent historical accounts we have of that time, at the onset Jesus was likely viewed by the Romans as just one of many messianic agitators who sought to disrupt the social order of the Judeans. As his followers grew in numbers, however, the minor irritation became more of a pressing concern. Christianity began to be viewed with increasing mistrust and suspicion, and ultimately was violently persecuted under Emperor Nero. As the historian Tacitus characterizes in his *Annals* (circa 109 A.D.) in reference to the Great Fire of Rome in 64 A.D.:

> To get rid of the report, Nero fastened the guilt and inflicted the most exquisite tortures on a class hated for their abominations, called

> Christians by the populace. Christus, from whom the name had its origin, suffered the extreme penalty during the reign of Tiberius at the hands of one of our procurators, Pontius Pilatus, and a most mischievous superstition, thus checked for the moment, again broke out not only in Judæa, the first source of the evil, but even in Rome, where all things hideous and shameful from every part of the world find their centre and become popular. Accordingly, an arrest was first made of all who pleaded guilty; then, upon their information, an immense multitude was convicted, not so much of the crime of firing the city, as of hatred against mankind. Mockery of every sort was added to their deaths. Covered with the skins of beasts, they were torn by dogs and perished, or were nailed to crosses, or were doomed to the flames and burnt, to serve as a nightly illumination, when daylight had expired.
>
> *Annals XV (translated by Alfred Church & William Brodribb)*

Yet even as Christianity was suffering persecution, unrelated social unrest in Judea blossomed into outright rebellion in 66 A.D., eventually ending Roman rule there, and also culminating in the destruction of the Judean temple in Jerusalem in 70 A.D. It could be said of that time that relations between Roman rulers and both Christians and Jews were rather tense. And it was under these circumstances that most of the texts of the New Testament began to take shape.

Keeping this historical framework in mind, how do any sociopolitical themes we might glean from the New Testament translate for Christians living in democracies of today, and especially in the U.S. where there are both ample civil liberties and influential Christian populations? Are there spiritual principles that can help define Christian participation in modern sociopolitical institutions? Are there passages that might support what legislation to advocate, what institutions to support, what parties to join or what candidate to vote for? At the current time, a majority of voters in the U.S. who self-identify as Christian tend to lean toward the social, economic, religious and governmentally conservative end of the political spectrum. This has been documented by exit polls in the 2000, 2004 and 2008 presidential elections, which showed that among all Christians who voted, voting leaned two-to-one in favor of the Republican candidate, while among evangelical Christians the ratio was over three-to-one in favor of Republicans. Additionally, according to the 2000 exit polls, some 14% of all voters identified as belonging to the "Christian Right." All of this data is readily available at www.pewforum.org.

Although it is widely known as of this writing that Republicans of the last forty years have generally leaned conservative, I'll also offer some data to back this up. As one snapshot, a 2009 Gallup study showed 72% of Republicans identified themselves as either conservative or very conservative, compared to 35% of independents and 22% of Democrats. When Gallup surveyed the same group on individual issues (abortion rights, labor unions, government regulation, gun control, global warming, same-sex marriage, the death penalty, etc.), 66% of Republicans expressed more conservative views, as did 44% of independents and 22% of Democrats. Gallup statistics in 2008 showed a similar distribution of conservatives between these three groups, as did surveys in previous years. This data is readily available at www.gallup.com. To fully appreciate how intimate Republican politics have become with conservative Christianity, we needn't look far. For a revealing peek at the symbiotic relationship between the Republican political machine and conservative evangelical Christianity, David Kuo's *Tempting Faith: An Inside Story of Political Seduction* is a must read. As a more anecdotal snapshot of this instrumental linkage, Rachel Grady and Heidi Ewing's 2006 film, *Jesus Camp*, offers some compelling insights as well.

Of course, what "conservatism" really represents in the U.S. fluctuates depending on the area of focus. In economics, Libertarian and neoliberal ideals – where an efficient market unfettered by government intrusion or regulation reigns supreme – tend to dominate what defines conservative ideology. In foreign policy, neoconservative agendas to actively propagate a U.S. brand of democracy and capitalism around the globe became a pervasive force under the George W. Bush administration. Paleoconservatives, another fairly recent identification, stress the conserving of cultural and religious traditions, limited government and the centrality of family life. And of course there are also those who base their conservatism solely on what they claim are Christian beliefs, and thus among other things advocate prayer and creationism in schools, opposition to federal funding of science, the preservation of the nuclear family and opposition to abortion. In the Gallup studies, the surveying of hot-button issues that have traditionally defined these conservative outlooks and values has helped clarify a more amalgamated definition, and allows us to conclude that most, if not all, conservative valuations have found a political home in the Republican Party.

So is there a natural resonance between the flavor of social, economic, religious and governmental conservatism offered by the Republican party – and favored by a majority of voting Christians – and what we find in the New Testament? Let's begin by looking at the example Jesus offers us in New Testament accounts. To make this overview more manageable, I have grouped excerpts under various themes. This method of selective organization and analysis mirrors how I believe we organize information in *semantic containers* of cognitive function, and therefore lends itself to the conclusions I have already drawn and wish to propagate. However, we need to organize our approach in some fashion, and to counter any inherent bias I will offer contrasting themes whenever they are readily available. After examining a number of such themes, we will then be able to begin to assemble what a modern model of Christ-like values and activism might look like as derived from the scriptural record.

The Role of Government

What were Jesus' teachings and attitudes regarding government? How would we characterize his interactions with government? Here are a few excerpts of scripture to chew upon, quoted from the New American Standard Bible (NASB):

> And when Jesus entered Capernaum, a centurion came to Him, imploring Him, and saying, "Lord, my servant is lying paralyzed at home, fearfully tormented." Jesus said to him, "I will come and heal him." But the centurion said, "Lord, I am not worthy for You to come under my roof, but just say the word, and my servant will be healed. For I also am a man under authority, with soldiers under me; and I say to this one, 'Go!' and he goes, and to another, 'Come!' and he comes, and to my slave, 'Do this!' and he does it." Now when Jesus heard this, He marveled and said to those who were following, "Truly I say to you, I have not found such great faith with anyone in Israel. I say to you that many will come from east and west, and recline at the table with Abraham, Isaac and Jacob in the kingdom of heaven; but the sons of the kingdom will be cast out into the outer darkness; in that place there will be weeping and gnashing of teeth." And Jesus said to the centurion, "Go; it shall be done for you as you have believed." And the servant was healed that very moment.
>
> *Matthew 8:5-13*

"But beware of men, for they will hand you over to the courts and scourge you in their synagogues; and you will even be brought before governors and kings for My sake, as a testimony to them and to the Gentiles. But when they hand you over, do not worry about how or what you are to say; for it will be given you in that hour what you are to say. For it is not you who speak, but it is the Spirit of your Father who speaks in you."

Matthew 10:17-20

Immediately Jesus, aware in His spirit that they were reasoning that way within themselves, said to them, "Why are you reasoning about these things in your hearts? Which is easier, to say to the paralytic, 'Your sins are forgiven'; or to say, 'Get up, and pick up your pallet and walk'? But so that you may know that the Son of Man has authority on earth to forgive sins"—He said to the paralytic, "I say to you, get up, pick up your pallet and go home." And he got up and immediately picked up the pallet and went out in the sight of everyone, so that they were all amazed and were glorifying God, saying, "We have never seen anything like this."

Mark 2:8-12

Hearing this, the ten began to feel indignant with James and John. Calling them to Himself, Jesus said to them, "You know that those who are recognized as rulers of the Gentiles lord it over them; and their great men exercise authority over them. But it is not this way among you, but whoever wishes to become great among you shall be your servant; and whoever wishes to be first among you shall be slave of all. For even the Son of Man did not come to be served, but to serve, and to give His life a ransom for many."

Mark 10:41-45

And he led Him up and showed Him all the kingdoms of the world in a moment of time. And the devil said to Him, "I will give You all this domain and its glory; for it has been handed over to me, and I give it to whomever I wish. Therefore if You worship before me, it shall all be Yours." Jesus answered him, "It is written, 'YOU SHALL WORSHIP THE LORD YOUR GOD AND SERVE HIM ONLY.'"

Luke 4:5-8

"And why do you not even on your own initiative judge what is right? For while you are going with your opponent to appear before the magistrate, on your way there make an effort to settle with him, so that he may not drag you before the judge, and the judge turn you over to the officer, and the officer throw you into prison. I say to you, you will not get out of there until you have paid the very last cent."

Luke 12:57-59

So they watched Him, and sent spies who pretended to be righteous, in order that they might catch Him in some statement, so that they could deliver Him to the rule and the authority of the governor. They questioned Him, saying, "Teacher, we know that You speak and teach correctly, and You are not partial to any, but teach the way of God in truth. "Is it lawful for us to pay taxes to Caesar, or not?" But He detected their trickery and said to them, "Show Me a denarius. Whose likeness and inscription does it have?" They said, "Caesar's." And He said to them, "Then render to Caesar the things that are Caesar's, and to God the things that are God's."

Luke 20:20-25

Jesus answered, "My kingdom is not of this world. If My kingdom were of this world, then My servants would be fighting so that I would not be handed over to the Jews; but as it is, My kingdom is not of this realm." Therefore Pilate said to Him, "So You are a king?" Jesus answered, "You say correctly that I am a king. For this I have been born, and for this I have come into the world, to testify to the truth. Everyone who is of the truth hears My voice."

John 18:36-37

The Jews answered him, "We have a law, and by that law He ought to die because He made Himself out to be the Son of God." Therefore when Pilate heard this statement, he was even more afraid; and he entered into the Praetorium again and said to Jesus, "Where are You from?" But Jesus gave him no answer. So Pilate said to Him, "You do not speak to me? Do You not know that I have authority to release You, and I have authority to crucify You?" Jesus answered, "You would have no authority over Me, unless it had been given you from above; for this reason he who delivered Me to you has the greater sin."

John 19:7-11

Please take a moment to consider these excerpts together from a neutral standpoint. Meditate or pray about them. Discuss them with others.. Try putting any verses that apply to your current situation into practice. Intuit your way to a tentative interpretation, feeling the rightness of your convictions. Then compare your conclusions with those offered below.

We have only glimpses among the gospels into the mind of Christ regarding the purpose of government and a faithful believer's relationship with it, but these glimpses are nonetheless telling. Here are a few of the principles we can glean:

1. Jesus tells his disciples not to be like the rulers of the Gentiles who exercise positional power over others. Instead, they should excel in service to each other with self-sacrifice. In addition, they should submit to governing authorities with the expectation of an opportunity to testify about their beliefs.

2. Jesus recognizes worldly authority in worldly matters, and asserts his own authority in spiritual matters. This is a critical distinction, and one that is demonstrated repeatedly throughout the gospels. Jesus even admires the faith of the centurion who seems to appreciate this difference, while at the same time understanding the parallels of authoritative hierarchy between the spiritual and material realms. Jesus emphasizes that his own authority, and his kingdom, are not of this world, and exhorts his followers to respect this differentiation. In this sense, the separation of Church and state is explicit.

3. When Jesus is given the opportunity to have worldly power and authority, he rejects it in favor of worshipful obedience to God. And he advises people not to become overly dependent on the secular rule of law as well – for example, instead of relying on the arbitration of a magistrate or judge, that they work things out with their adversaries before going to court.

Is this pattern amplified elsewhere in the New Testament? Do we have more evidence to support this seeming lack of direct involvement with government and emphasis on dedication to a spiritual life and relationships? Let's take a look. The following verses are quoted from the New Living Translation (NLT):

> A mob quickly formed against Paul and Silas, and the city officials ordered them stripped and beaten with wooden rods. They were severely beaten, and then they were thrown into prison. The jailer was ordered to make sure they didn't escape. So the jailer put them into the inner dungeon and clamped their feet in the stocks. Around midnight

Paul and Silas were praying and singing hymns to God, and the other prisoners were listening. Suddenly, there was a massive earthquake, and the prison was shaken to its foundations. All the doors immediately flew open, and the chains of every prisoner fell off! The jailer woke up to see the prison doors wide open. He assumed the prisoners had escaped, so he drew his sword to kill himself. But Paul shouted to him, "Stop! Don't kill yourself! We are all here!" The jailer called for lights and ran to the dungeon and fell down trembling before Paul and Silas. Then he brought them out and asked, "Sirs, what must I do to be saved?" They replied, "Believe in the Lord Jesus and you will be saved, along with everyone in your household." And they shared the word of the Lord with him and with all who lived in his household. Even at that hour of the night, the jailer cared for them and washed their wounds. Then he and everyone in his household were immediately baptized. He brought them into his house and set a meal before them, and he and his entire household rejoiced because they all believed in God. The next morning the city officials sent the police to tell the jailer, "Let those men go!" So the jailer told Paul, "The city officials have said you and Silas are free to leave. Go in peace." But Paul replied, "They have publicly beaten us without a trial and put us in prison—and we are Roman citizens. So now they want us to leave secretly? Certainly not! Let them come themselves to release us!" When the police reported this, the city officials were alarmed to learn that Paul and Silas were Roman citizens. So they came to the jail and apologized to them. Then they brought them out and begged them to leave the city. When Paul and Silas left the prison, they returned to the home of Lydia. There they met with the believers and encouraged them once more. Then they left town.

Acts 16:22-40

Three days after Paul's arrival, he called together the local Jewish leaders. He said to them, "Brothers, I was arrested in Jerusalem and handed over to the Roman government, even though I had done nothing against our people or the customs of our ancestors. The Romans tried me and wanted to release me, because they found no cause for the death sentence. But when the Jewish leaders protested the decision, I felt it necessary to appeal to Caesar, even though I had no desire to press charges against my own people. I asked you to come here today so we could get acquainted and so I could explain to you that I am bound with this chain because I believe that the hope of Israel—the Messiah—has already come."

Acts 28:17-20

Everyone must submit to governing authorities. For all authority comes from God, and those in positions of authority have been placed there by God. So anyone who rebels against authority is rebelling against what God has instituted, and they will be punished. For the authorities do not strike fear in people who are doing right, but in those who are doing wrong. Would you like to live without fear of the authorities? Do what is right, and they will honor you. The authorities are God's servants, sent for your good. But if you are doing wrong, of course you should be afraid, for they have the power to punish you. They are God's servants, sent for the very purpose of punishing those who do what is wrong. So you must submit to them, not only to avoid punishment, but also to keep a clear conscience. Pay your taxes, too, for these same reasons. For government workers need to be paid. They are serving God in what they do. Give to everyone what you owe them: Pay your taxes and government fees to those who collect them, and give respect and honor to those who are in authority.

Romans 13:1-7

Christ is the visible image of the invisible God. He existed before anything was created and is supreme over all creation, for through him God created everything in the heavenly realms and on earth. He made the things we can see and the things we can't see — such as thrones, kingdoms, rulers, and authorities in the unseen world. Everything was created through him and for him.

Colossians 1:15-16

You have died with Christ, and he has set you free from the spiritual powers of this world. So why do you keep on following the rules of the world, such as, "Don't handle! Don't taste! Don't touch!"? Such rules are mere human teachings about things that deteriorate as we use them. These rules may seem wise because they require strong devotion, pious self-denial, and severe bodily discipline. But they provide no help in conquering a person's evil desires.

Colossians 2:20-23

I urge you, first of all, to pray for all people. Ask God to help them; intercede on their behalf, and give thanks for them. Pray this way for kings and all who are in authority so that we can live peaceful and quiet lives marked by godliness and dignity. This is good and pleases God our Savior, who wants everyone to be saved and to understand the truth.

1 Timothy 2:1-4

Remind the believers to submit to the government and its officers. They should be obedient, always ready to do what is good. They must not slander anyone and must avoid quarreling. Instead, they should be gentle and show true humility to everyone.

Titus 3:1-2

For the Lord's sake, respect all human authority—whether the king as head of state, or the officials he has appointed. For the king has sent them to punish those who do wrong and to honor those who do right. It is God's will that your honorable lives should silence those ignorant people who make foolish accusations against you. For you are free, yet you are God's slaves, so don't use your freedom as an excuse to do evil. Respect everyone, and love your Christian brothers and sisters. Fear God, and respect the king.

1 Peter 2:13-17

Once again, before continuing, please take a moment to reflect on these excerpts with an impartial mindset, meditating or praying about them, discussing and applying them if possible, then comparing your conclusions with my own.

There is more scripture along these same lines, but these verses are certainly sufficient to reinforce a prominent component of New Testament teaching: that the Christian's responsibility is to focus on the humility and kindness of their own heart, on their own inner obedience to God, on their outer obedience to worldly authorities, and to instigate good deeds in service to others. Even during the occasions in Acts where Paul and Silas hold local authorities accountable for mistreatment, they are relying on the existing laws of the land to do so – not rebelling against those laws or authorities. And just as Jesus exhorted his followers to do, Paul later uses the laws of Rome to create an opportunity to spread the gospel there. In 1 Timothy we also read that Christians should pray for governing authorities so that the good news can be spread in peace and quiet. Yet no matter how oppressive the laws of the land were at that time, no matter how Christians might be persecuted or imprisoned, no matter what suffering they endured, rebelling against the governing authorities, usurping them or in any way competing with them was never part of the spectrum of Christ-like responses.

And why was this so? Because, according to Paul and Peter, those authorities exist to exalt those who do good, and punish those who do evil, and ultimately to fulfill God's will. In the case of Jesus, the gospels claim secular authorities fulfilled Old Testament prophecies regarding the messiah. In the case of the apostles, later accounts show how these authorities fulfilled New Testament prophecies regarding the propagation of Jesus' message. Clearly, worldly government had an important role in God's kingdom, but the authority of that government was never intended to be placed in the hands of Christians, or even be aspired to by Christians. In fact, Christ himself and those who followed him in the early Church seem to have set aside any desires for such worldly power in favor of humble and sacrificial service to the world. At the same time, we have many examples in the New Testament of Jesus and his Apostles speaking truth to government, holding it accountable to the rule of law, and capitalizing on such interactions to share the gospel. Jesus and his early followers may have enjoyed challenging misguided religious laws, but they readily conformed to the laws of Rome.

The Liberation of Women

The Roman and Jewish cultures of Jesus' time were dominated by men, and women had very little power and even fewer rights. Consider the following insights about Roman women, gleaned in part from Jo-Ann Shelton's *As the Romans Did,* and from *Women's Life in Greece and Rome* by Mary Lefkowitz and Maureen Fant. Unlike many contemporaries of their day, Roman women of the first century could own their own property and manage their own finances, but they could not vote or hold political office. They might have influence as the dutiful wife of a wealthy Roman with social standing, or by engineering political careers for their sons, but they were not allowed to wield power directly. Women were under the authority of their father until they married, at which point that authority transferred to their husband. Roman women did not receive the same level of education as men, and only a handful of documents written by Roman women have survived into modernity. However, women were considered important transmitters of Roman culture in preparing children for participation in society. Unlike some other cultures of the day, Roman women were not sequestered away from men or public view; they were expected to participate in religious festivals, and there is even evidence that female gladiators competed in Rome.

In Jewish culture, women likewise passed from the authority of their father to their husband, but had far fewer rights, freedoms or privileges. Under Levitical law, they were considered little more than slaves, and according to the Mishnah (a record of the oral traditions that would have pervaded Judea in the time of Jesus), women could be "obtained by intercourse, money or writ" (*Qidd.* 1.1). They could not hold positions of power in a synagogue, could not be disciples of a rabbi, did not receive religious education, and were not expected to participate in religious festivals (*Qidd.* 1.7). They did not have the right to divorce, and a woman's testimony in court was considered less reliable than a man's – if it was allowed at all (*Ned.* 11.10). Not only were women considered impure during menstruation, but they could not ask for sex, and they could be stoned to death for committing adultery – a fate seemingly exclusive to women and not men. Women were, in effect, spiritually, socially and sexually oppressed to a much greater degree than their Roman counterparts. In both Roman and Jewish culture, however, it is not too strong a statement to claim that women were, at best, second-class citizens.

One other item of note regarding first century women is that, according to Roman census statistics of the time, there seem to have been far fewer of them than men. Among Romans, this may have been the result of the practice of *exposure*, where newborn children were placed before the pater familias, the male head of the household, who then either excepted them into the family by lifting them into his arms, or rejected them by leaving them lying on the ground. And, of course, because they were less desirable due to expensive dowries and their inability to increase the family's social status, rejected children were most often girls. Any child who was rejected in this way was frequently left outside to die.

Sadly, we can see many of the attitudes and practices of both of these ancient cultures carried forward into modern times – not just in exceptional cases, but in vast populations around the globe. Consider rural China, where female newborns may be abandoned because they cannot provide in the same way for the family – that is, in socioeconomic terms they are considered less valuable. This is not a religious doctrine, but a cultural standard. In many other cultures, such as those in sub-Saharan Africa and South Asia, the forced marriage of young girls to older men has been common for centuries. In fact, we can use this practice as a litmus test for the level of female oppression throughout a given culture – for where young girls are treated as reproductive chattel, they do not escape the mindset of enslavement when they become adult women. In these same cultures, we also find other heinous practices such as female genital mutilation, bride abduction and a high incidence of rape and brutality against women. And although such fear, hatred and prejudice towards female human beings may be sustained by the ultraconservative doctrines of various religions, in reality we find such propensities are first and foremost deeply rooted in cultural traditions. Like a cycle of emotional and physical abuse that is passed from one generation to the next, the oppression of women is a symptom of longstanding and profound cultural failure. Even when religious institutions reinforce these patterns out of conformance to dominant cultural memes, we often can find little or no justification for them in the primary spiritual source materials of the faith traditions themselves. To better understand the extent of suffering women must bear around the globe, I recommend consulting websites like www.vday.org, www.unwomen.org, and www.womankind.org.uk. In particular, take a moment to view the statistics available on these sites regarding human rights violations against women.

A particularly potent example of the oppression of women are Arab societies where strict Shari'a law is observed, its practice paralleling Jewish Levitical law in the belittling and contemptuous strictures regarding women. Here, too, that oppression is often a perpetuation of cultural attitudes masquerading as religion to justify themselves. Wael Hallaq's book, *The Origins and Evolution of Islamic Law*, gives a detailed account of how Shari'a evolved out of pre-Islamic Arab customs, concretizing into a formal legal system long after the Prophet Muhammad's death. Along these lines, there is the example of traditional clothing meant to conceal feminine features (see: hijab; jilbāb, burqa, abaya, etc.), which is a mainly cultural invention, but which has come to represent religious obedience among some Muslims. As I understand it, the Qur'an does convey moderate instructions regarding women's clothing – such as covering private parts (sura 24:31) and covering the body in such a way as to discourage harassment in public (sura 33:59). But within this venerated text, there are no commands to hide every hint of sexuality in order to avoid the wrath of religious leaders or prevent violent reactions from male family members. And even where the Qur'an and the later Hadith Qudsi might condemn sexual impropriety for men and women alike – and very harshly so – it is mainly women who suffer "honor killings" and other extreme punishments, thus belying purely religious justifications for these judgments. Just as within Christianity and Judaism, it is cultural conservatism – bolstered by dogmatic religious legalism that evolved after those religions were institutionalized – that perpetuates fear, hate, prejudice and violence; and in such cases it is women who suffer the most.

This sort of discrimination, objectification and indeed alienation of the feminine is present in some form nearly everywhere. Even in the most progressive cultures of the world, women are still a minority in positions of power and privilege, and still struggle to earn wages equal to a man's. This is true in the U.S., where we still see a staggering level of rape and domestic violence towards women, rampant sexism in workplaces, the military and on college campuses, wage inequality, and other indications that America still has a very long way to go to embrace equal value of the sexes. Take a moment to view the evidence gathered at www.now.org/issues/violence/stats.html to appreciate the depth and breadth of this problem. It is also easy to forget that women did not have the right to vote in the U.S. until 1920, some fifty years after freed male slaves were given the same right.

So when we add all these populations and chauvinistic attitudes together across vast swaths of time and geography, we discover there to be hundreds of millions of human beings around the globe from the past and in the present who have been and are being oppressed and devalued solely because of their gender. We could even presume that this marginalized population includes the vast majority of women alive today. With what we know of ancient times, we can surmise that it was the same or worse in first century Judea. So, against such a backdrop of extreme prejudice, how does the New Testament portray Jesus' response to women in his day, and how might this inform what Christians can do to respond to this injustice and inequality in modern times? Here are some accounts to consider, this time from the International Standard Version (ISV):

> So Jesus went with him. A huge crowd kept following him and jostling him. Now there was a woman who had been suffering from chronic bleeding for twelve years. Although she had endured a great deal under the care of many doctors and had spent all of her money, she had not been helped at all but rather grew worse. Since she had heard about Jesus, she came up behind him in the crowd and touched his robe, because she had been saying, "If I can just touch his robe, I will get well." Her bleeding stopped at once, and she felt in her body that she was healed from her illness. Immediately Jesus became aware that power had gone out of him. So he turned around in the crowd and asked, "Who touched my clothes?" His disciples asked him, "You see the crowd jostling you, and yet you ask, 'Who touched me?'" But he kept looking around to see the woman who had done this. So the woman, knowing what had happened to her, came forward fearfully, fell down trembling in front of him, and told him the whole truth. He said to her, "Daughter, your faith has made you well. Go in peace and be healed from your illness."
>
> *Mark 5:24-34*

> Now one of the Pharisees invited Jesus to eat with him. So he went to the Pharisee's home and took his place at the table. There was a woman who was a notorious sinner in that city. When she learned that Jesus was eating at the Pharisee's home, she took an alabaster jar of perfume and knelt at his feet behind him. She was crying and began to wash his feet with her tears and dry them with her hair. Then she kissed his feet over and over again, anointing them constantly with the perfume. Now the Pharisee who had invited Jesus saw this and said to himself, "If this man were a prophet, he would have known who is touching him and what kind of woman she is. She's a sinner!" Jesus said to him, "Simon, I have something to say to you." "Teacher," he replied, "say it." "Two men were in debt to a moneylender. One owed him 500 denarii, and the other 50. When they couldn't pay it back, he generously canceled the debts for both of them. Now which of them will love him more?" Simon answered, "I suppose the one who had the larger debt canceled." Jesus said to him, "You have answered correctly." Then, turning to the woman, he said to Simon, "Do you see this woman? I came into your house. You didn't give me any water for my feet, but this woman has washed my feet with her tears and dried them with her hair. You didn't give me a kiss, but this woman, from the moment I came in, has not stopped kissing my feet. You didn't anoint my head with oil, but this

woman has anointed my feet with perfume. So I'm telling you that her sins, as many as they are, have been forgiven, and that's why she has shown such great love. But the one to whom little is forgiven loves little." Then Jesus said to the woman, "Your sins are forgiven!"

Luke 7:36-48

A Samaritan woman came to draw water, and Jesus said to her, "Please give me a drink," since his disciples had gone off into town to buy food. The Samaritan woman asked him, "How can you, a Jew, ask for a drink from me, a Samaritan woman?" Because Jews do not have anything to do with Samaritans. Jesus answered her, "If you knew the gift of God, and who it is who is saying to you, 'Please give me a drink,' you would have been the one to ask him, and he would have given you living water." The woman said to him, "Sir, you don't have a bucket, and the well is deep. Where are you going to get this living water? You're not greater than our ancestor Jacob, who gave us the well and drank from it, along with his sons and his flocks, are you?" Jesus answered her, "Everyone who drinks this water will become thirsty again. But whoever drinks the water that I will give him will never become thirsty again. The water that I will give him will become a well of water for him, springing up to eternal life." The woman said to him, "Sir, give me this water, so that I won't get thirsty or have to keep coming here to draw water." He said to her, "Go and call your husband, and come back here." The woman answered him, "I don't have a husband." Jesus said to her, "You are quite right in saying, 'I don't have a husband,' because you have had five husbands, and the man you have now is not your husband. What you have said is true." The woman said to him, "Sir, I see that you are a prophet! Our ancestors worshiped on this mountain. But you Jews say that the place where people should worship is in Jerusalem." Jesus said to her, "Believe me, dear lady, the hour is coming when you Samaritans will worship the Father neither on this mountain nor in Jerusalem. You don't know what you're worshiping. We Jews know what we're worshiping, because salvation comes from the Jews. Yet the time is coming, and is now here, when true worshipers will worship the Father in spirit and truth. Indeed, the Father is looking for people like that to worship him. God is spirit, and those who worship him must worship in spirit and truth." The woman said to him, "I know that Messiah is coming, who is being called 'Christ'. When that person comes, he will explain everything." Jesus said to her, "I am he, the one who is speaking to you." At this point his disciples arrived, and they were amazed that he was talking to a woman. Yet no one said, "What do you want from her?" or, "Why are you talking to her?" Then the woman left her water jar and went back to town. She told people, "Come, see a man who told me everything I've ever done! Could he possibly be the Messiah?" The people left the town and started on their way to him.

John 4:7-30

Jesus, however, went to the Mount of Olives. At daybreak he appeared again in the temple, and all the people came to him. So he sat down and began to teach them. But the scribes and the Pharisees brought a woman who had been caught in adultery. After setting her before them, they said to him, "Teacher, this woman has been caught in the very act of adultery. Now in the law, Moses commanded us to stone such women to death. What do you say?" They said this to test him, so that they might have a charge against him. But Jesus bent down and began to write on the ground with his finger. When they persisted in questioning him, he straightened up and said to them, "Let the person among you who is without sin be the first to throw a stone at her." Then he bent down again and continued writing on the ground. When they heard this, they went away one by one, beginning with the oldest, and he was left alone with the woman standing there. Then Jesus stood up and said to her, "Dear lady, where are your accusers? Hasn't anyone condemned you?" She said, "No one, sir." Then Jesus said, "I don't condemn you, either. Go home, and from now on do not sin any more."

John 8:1-11

Now a certain man was ill, Lazarus from Bethany, the village of Mary and her sister Martha. Mary was the woman who anointed the Lord with perfume and wiped his feet with her hair. Her brother Lazarus was the one who was ill. So the sisters sent word to Jesus, saying, "Lord, the one whom you love is ill." But when Jesus heard it, he said, "This illness is not meant to end in death. It is for God's glory, so that the Son of God may be glorified through it." Now Jesus loved Martha and her sister and Lazarus. Yet, when he heard that Lazarus was ill, he stayed where he was for two more days. After this he said to the disciples, "Let's go back to Judea." The disciples said to him, "Rabbi, the Jews were just now trying to stone you to death, and you are going back there again?" Jesus replied, "There are twelve hours in the day, aren't there? If anyone walks during the day he does not stumble, because he sees the light of this world. But if anyone walks at night he stumbles, because the light is not in him." These were the things he said. Then after this he told them, "Our friend Lazarus has fallen asleep, but I am leaving to wake him up." So the disciples said to him, "Lord, if he has fallen asleep, he will get well." Jesus, however, had been speaking about his death, but they thought that he was speaking about resting or sleeping. Then Jesus told them plainly, "Lazarus has died. For your sake I am glad that I was not there, so that you may believe. But let's go to him." Then

Thomas, who was called the Twin, said to his fellow disciples, "Let's go, too, so that we may die with him!" When Jesus arrived, he found that Lazarus had already been in the tomb for four days. Now Bethany was near Jerusalem, about two miles away, and many of the Jews had come to Martha and Mary to console them about their brother. As soon as Martha heard that Jesus was coming, she went and met him, while Mary stayed at home. Martha said to Jesus, "Lord, if you had been here, my brother would not have died. But even now I know that whatever you ask of God, he will give it to you." Jesus told her, "Your brother will rise again." Martha said to him, "I know that he will rise again in the resurrection on the last day." Jesus said to her, "I am the resurrection and the life. The person who believes in me, even though he dies, will live. Indeed, everyone who lives and believes in me will never die. Do you believe that?" She said to him, "Yes, Lord, I believe that you are the Messiah, the Son of God, the one who was to come into the world." When she had said this, she went away and called her sister Mary and told her privately, "The Teacher is here and is calling for you!" As soon as Mary heard this, she got up quickly and went to him. Now Jesus had not yet arrived at the village but was still at the place where Martha had met him. When the Jews who had been with her, consoling her in the house, saw Mary get up quickly and go out, they followed her, thinking that she had gone to the tomb to cry there. As soon as Mary came to where Jesus was and saw him, she fell down at his feet and said to him, "Lord, if you had been here, my brother would not have died." When Jesus saw her crying, and the Jews who had come with her crying, he was greatly troubled in spirit and deeply moved. He asked, "Where have you put him?" They said to him, "Lord, come and see." Jesus burst into tears.

John 11:1-35

Before reading further, please take some time to consider the previous excerpts of scripture as a whole. Meditate on them. Pray about them. Discuss them with others who can keep an open mind. Try to enact some of the principles that apply to your situation. Intuit your way to a conclusion, feeling the rightness of your convictions from a place of neutrality. Then compare what you have concluded with the following thoughts.

As framed by the context of his times, Jesus' attitudes and actions towards women in these stories are for me beyond radical. To begin with, the chronically bleeding woman was almost certainly hemorrhaging from her uterus. Although a different Greek term is used in Matthew's account than in Mark's and Luke's, they all refer to a "flow of blood" that is used euphemistically elsewhere in the Bible to represent menstruation (for example, albeit in Hebrew, Leviticus 15 and 20:18). Under Levitical law, this condition would have made the woman ritually unclean. In fact, she would have remained unclean for seven days even after the flow ceased. This meant that, among other things, she would not be allowed entry to the temple, and could not atone for her sins – ever. It is no small wonder, then, that the woman in this account was terrified of revealing her intentions to Jesus and the crowd. And for Jesus to praise her faith, not rebuke her in any way for touching him, and bless her with peace and relief from her suffering not only amplifies the quality of his compassion, but annihilates the negative Levitical dogma of the time regarding menstruation and its shameful stigma in Jewish culture. From the perspective of the people of that day, Jesus was acting as if the female reproductive cycle was a normal and natural thing – something many modern cultures still seem to struggle with.

We then see that Jesus' liberating attitude towards women extended beyond the acceptance of their physiology. When he allowed the "sinful woman" to anoint him with perfume in the Pharisee's house, and then praised her for the act and forgave her sins, his actions flew in the face of contemporary Jewish attitudes. Adding insult to injury, Jesus asserted that the woman's love proved more important in God's eyes than the actions of a Pharisee – a fastidious observer of Jewish religious laws. Imagine the shock of such a statement. It would be like elevating the social status of a poor, uneducated slave laborer above a wealthy, aristocratic powerbroker with a PhD. What is also interesting about this account is that Jesus described how any person's love would be proportionate to the forgiveness they received. But this woman lavished her tearful affections on Jesus *without having received any forgiveness first.* What might this mean? Why would she do this? Taken with the other accounts in the New Testament texts, I think this is a clear indication that word had spread among the people that Jesus' accepting and compassionate mindset towards women strongly contradicted the cultural values of his time.

One of the more significant accounts in the New Testament of Jesus' honoring the feminine is the story of the Samaritan woman at the well. As the text describes, relations between Judeans and Samaritans were fairly alienated at the time. Yet this woman was not only a Samaritan, she was also an adulteress living with her lover. How does Jesus react to this? He offers her living water, the salvation of God, and the opportunity to be the first to share the message of salvation with her community. And, as if that weren't enough, according to John's account this Samaritan alien, this sinner, this random woman whom Jesus' own disciples are surprised to see him conversing with, is also the first person in John's account to whom Jesus confirms he is the Messiah! This must have been stunning to the people of Jesus' day, and a clear confirmation that this particular Messiah esteemed women greatly. If we imagine the voice from the burning bush delivering Yahweh's commandments to, say, a Canaanite prostitute instead of Moses, I think we can begin to appreciate the depth and impact of Jesus' actions at the well.

And then we come to one of the best known passages in the New Testament, where Jesus forgives the adulteress who is about to be stoned. By encouraging introspection about the mistakes they themselves have made in the past, Jesus uses the consciences of the woman's accusers to derail their self-righteous wrath. But I think it is even more significant that Jesus forgives the woman outright. She herself does not demonstrate contrition or repentance. She does not pass some religious test of righteousness or demonstrate the depth of her love for God. In this account, Jesus dismisses the whole situation while scribbling in the dirt. As we see in many other stories throughout the New Testament, religious legalism simply had no place in the kingdom of God. And, quite apparently from the sum of these passages, women had just as important a place in that kingdom as any man.

But for me, the most impressive of all New Testament stories involving women is Lazarus' death and resurrection. If we read this carefully, all sorts of eye-opening insights percolate to the foreground. First, we learn that Jesus changed his travel plans in response to a letter from Mary and Martha. Then we learn that he had a special affection for these two sisters and their brother, an affection we only find elsewhere in reference to the "disciple whom Jesus loved" in the Gospel of John. Then we see Martha alternately rebuking and debating with Jesus regarding her brother's death, and Jesus patiently and lovingly answering her. Then, according to Martha, Jesus requests that Mary come to him. And after that? One of only two places in the New Testament where Jesus weeps openly is here, in response to Mary's grief. Remember that this is the Mary whom Jesus praised for her devoted attention (Luke 10), and the Mary whom Jesus defended when she anointed him with expensive perfumed, saying "I tell you truly, wherever the gospel is proclaimed in all the world, what this woman has done will be told in memory of her." (Mark 14:9). Lazarus' death is of course a pivotal event in Jesus' life, for, according to John, it is after Jesus' resurrection of Lazarus that a plot is hatched to take Jesus' life. But for me it is Jesus' interactions with the women he loved that make this pivotal in a feminist sense. Taken altogether, it is impossible to overlook the pronounced love and respect Jesus holds for these female disciples, and indeed the unique place they hold in his heart and in his life according to these accounts.

There are many other examples of similar sentiments. Jesus performed many miracles on women and lauded their faith (Matthew 9:34 & 15:21-28; Luke 8:1-3 & 13:10-13). He included women in his parables (Matthew 13:33 & 25:1-13). According to the Gospels of Matthew, Mark and John, Jesus first appeared to women following his resurrection, and it was women who then announced the miracle to his male disciples. It was Mary Magdalene whom the Gospels credit with this first encounter; she was the first to physically touch Jesus when he reappeared, and first to speak with him and bear his words back to the other disciples. The inescapable conclusion here is that Jesus valued women much more highly than the cultures of first century Judea and Rome. Again and again he rebukes men – even his own disciples – who are critical of the love, faith and worshipful actions of women. To claim that Jesus intended to aggressively liberate women is an understatement. And to fully follow Jesus' example today would mean releasing women from centuries of oppression into an equal and venerated status.

Now, for anyone who has studied the history of the Christian religion, or familiarized themselves with contemporary Christian doctrines about a number of women's issues, one question rapidly percolates to the fore: *what the heck happened to this radically liberating attitude?* Whether during centuries of the Roman Catholic tradition, or the puritanical restrictions of early America, or the actions and attitudes of modern day evangelicals, Christian women have most often not been treated with the equality, privilege and esteem that Jesus exemplified. In part, I believe this is the result of the principle I've already alluded to: that religion tends to conform to culture rather than changing it in fundamental ways. So, for example, the propagation of Christianity across a rigidly patriarchal Roman civilization did not change that society as much as conform to it. But this is not the only reason.

One argument I have heard from some of my Christian friends is that the spirit of Jesus' emancipation of women did not propagate throughout Christendom because the Apostle Paul did not always embrace this spirit in his writing. We will examine some of the passages that have inspired that conclusion in a moment; but first I'd like to offer you Romans 16:1-16 (ISV):

> Now I commend to you our sister Phoebe, a servant in the church at Cenchreae. Welcome her in the Lord as is appropriate for saints, and provide her with anything she may need from you, for she has assisted many people, including me. Greet Prisca and Aquila, who work with me for the Messiah Jesus, and who risked their necks for my life. I am thankful to them, and so are all the churches among the gentiles. Greet also the church in their house. Greet my dear friend Epaenetus, who was the first convert to the Messiah in Asia. Greet Mary, who has worked very hard for you. Greet Andronicus and Junias, my fellow Jews who are in prison with me and are prominent among the apostles. They belonged to the Messiah before I did. Greet Ampliatus, my dear friend in the Lord. Greet Urbanus, our co-worker in the Messiah, and my dear friend Stachys. Greet Apelles, who has been approved by the Messiah. Greet those who belong to the family of Aristobulus. Greet Herodion, my fellow Jew. Greet those in the family of Narcissus, who belong to the Lord. Greet Tryphaena and Tryphosa, who have worked hard for the Lord. Greet my dear friend Persis, who has toiled diligently for the Lord. Greet Rufus, the one chosen by the Lord, and his mother, who has been a mother to me, too. Greet Asyncritus, Phlegon, Hermes, Patrobas, Hermas, and the brothers who are with them. Greet Philologus and Julia, Nereus and his sister, and Olympas and all the saints who are with them. Greet one another with a holy kiss. All the churches of the Messiah greet you.

Of particular note here is that many of the women Paul praises and honors here clearly had prominent positions in the early Church. Among them is Prisca (Priscilla), who together with her husband Aquila travelled with Paul during his missionary journeys (see Acts 18), and whom Paul viewed as a "coworker" (συνεργός) in Christ. As we can see in the following account, this reference to Priscilla as an associate, a fellow laborer in Christ, is supported by other evidence in scripture as well (ISV):

> Meanwhile, a Jew named Apollos arrived in Ephesus. He was a native of Alexandria, an eloquent man, and well versed in the Scriptures. He had been instructed in the Lord's way, and with spiritual fervor he kept speaking and teaching accurately about Jesus, although he knew only about John's baptism. He began to speak boldly in the synagogue, but when Priscilla and Aquila heard him, they took him home and explained God's way to him more accurately.
>
> *Acts 18:24-26*

It is also interesting to note that in all but one of the instances in the New Testament where Priscilla and Aquila are named together, Priscilla's name precedes her husband's. And then we have Junias (Junia), whom Paul claims is "prominent among the apostles." Whether her notability (επίσμος) was in being an apostle herself or in how she was viewed by other apostles – in the Greek it is unclear – it still places Junias in a highly esteemed position according to Paul's estimation. It is also interesting that Paul elevates her even more by reminding his readers that she became a believer in Christ before he did. And of course there is Phoebe, whom Paul commends to the Church in Rome with specific instructions for her honored reception, naming her a "servant" (διάκονος) in her own congregation. This term, sometimes translated "deacon" and sometimes "minister," was utilized by Paul to describe a pivotal role of service in the early Church. In addition to these three, in this brief greeting Paul names no less than seven other women whose contributions to the Church he felt were praiseworthy.

This is not an isolated instance, of course. Similar accolades and status attributions for women can be found in Phillipians 4:2-3 and 1 Corinthians 1:11. But then, as we examine Paul's other references to sisters in Christ, a dichotomy begins to intrude on the writing attributed to him. Let's take a look at some of those contrasts (ISV):

> A man should not cover his head, because he exists as God's image and glory. But the woman is man's glory. For man did not come from woman, but woman from man; and man was not created for woman,

but woman for man. This is why a woman should have authority over her own head: because of the angels. In the Lord, however, woman is not independent of man, nor is man of woman. For as woman came from man, so man comes through woman. But everything comes from God. Decide for yourselves: Is it proper for a woman to pray to God with her head uncovered? Nature itself teaches you neither that it is disgraceful for a man to have long hair nor that hair is a woman's glory, for hair is given as a substitute for coverings.

1 Corinthians 11:7-15

As in all the churches of the saints, the women must keep silent in the churches. They are not allowed to speak out, but must place themselves in submission, as the oral law also says. If they want to learn anything, they should ask their own husbands at home, for it is inappropriate for a woman to speak out in church.

1 Corinthians 14:33-35

For all of you are God's children through faith in the Messiah Jesus. Indeed, all of you who were baptized into the Messiah have clothed yourselves with the Messiah. Because all of you are one in the Messiah Jesus, a person is no longer a Jew or a Greek, a slave or a free person, a male or a female.

Galatians 3:26-28

Wives, submit yourselves to your husbands as to the Lord. For the husband is the head of his wife as the Messiah is the head of the church. It is he who is the Savior of the body. Indeed, just as the church is submissive to the Messiah, so wives must be submissive to their husbands in everything. Husbands, love your wives as the Messiah loved the church and gave himself for it, so that he might make it holy by cleansing it, washing it with water and the word, and might present the church to himself in all its glory, without a spot or wrinkle or anything of the kind, but holy and without fault. In the same way, husbands must love their wives as they love their own bodies. A man who loves his wife loves himself. For no one has ever hated his own body, but he nourishes and tenderly cares for it, as the Messiah does the church.

Ephesians 5:22-29

Wives, submit yourselves to your husbands, as is appropriate for those who belong to the Lord. Husbands, love your wives, and do not be harsh with them.

Colossians 3:18-19

Remember that Paul differentiates between what he considers to be his own advice, and what he believes to be from holy spirit or "in the lord." In 1 Corinthians 11, when he speaks with the inspiration of the spirit, he admits that men and women are equal in the eyes of God; but when he reverts to his own observations and logic or defers to Levitical law, women are placed in a different category – a subordinate category – to men. We see this tension repeated in the other passages as well: on the one hand there is no difference between males and females in Christ, but on the other women should submit to their husbands. Women are praised as ministers, teachers and coworkers in Christ, but then are told they should remain silent at church and learn from their husbands at home. And so on. Perhaps this tension was simply a result of the patriarchal influence of the times – the enveloping sexism of the surrounding culture. Perhaps it was the vestigial conditioning of Paul's Pharisaic training (Acts 23:6, Philippians 3:5). Perhaps, as scholars like Gordon Fee suggest regarding 1 Corinthians 14:33-35, certain contradictions are actually the result of textual interpolation; that is, additions incorporated into the text long after Paul's death. But when we take the lion's share of the New Testament into account, Paul's vacillation does indeed seem to reflect a tug-of-war between what holy spirit guided Paul to perceive and relate, and old habits of thought that lingered into his spiritual renewal.

Then, most unfortunately, in 1 Timothy we discover even more abrasive and condescending attitudes towards women. Over the centuries, and despite the wealth of scripture that contradicts it, this epistle has become the guiding dark for oppressing women in the Church (ISV):

> A woman must learn quietly and submissively. Moreover, I do not allow a woman to teach or to usurp authority over a man. Instead, she is to be quiet. For Adam was formed first, then Eve. And it was not Adam who was deceived. It was the woman who was deceived and became a lawbreaker. However, women will be saved by having children, if they continue to have faith, love, and holiness, along with good judgment.
>
> *1 Timothy 2:11-15*

Rather than taking up the cause of women's emancipation that Jesus so carefully demonstrated, this Pastoral Epistle rather violently extinguishes it. Where Jesus empowers women to preach his message, testify to his resurrection, be relieved of tainted conceptions of their own bodies, physically worship his person and be freed from the judgments of Levitical law, 1 Timothy revives legalistic constrictions, declaring that women should never have authority over men, should keep their mouths shut, should be perceived as spiritually inferior, and should pursue their salvation through childbearing – a vitriolic concentration of attitudes, proscriptions and prescriptions unique to 1 Timothy. Compared with the rest of the New Testament, this seems to be truly regressive instruction. And when such hateful prejudice is then combined selectively with Paul's apparent vacillation and similar proscriptions elsewhere, the denigration of women within the Church becomes that much easier to sustain.

And the result? As of this writing, many U.S. denominations still resist allowing women prominent roles in the Church. In most fundamentalist denominations, women are still encouraged to submit to their husbands without question – just as a literal interpretation of selective epistles might promote. Even in the more mainstream evangelical churches I attended for many years, chauvinistic attitudes, disparagement of a woman's importance in spiritual matters, emotional and physical abuse of women and girls, and a generally dismissive attitude regarding any female contributions to society beyond childbearing and family responsibilities were common. Friends and acquaintances who were raised Roman Catholic also report to me that, in their experience of that denomination in the U.S., women were treated as second-class citizens in almost every respect. Those I know who have attended Free Methodist, Mormon, Lutheran, Southern Baptist and many other congregations for most of their lives report much the same. In fact, only a relatively small fraction of Christendom in the U.S. – communities of Quakers, Anglicans and Presbyterians, the United Church of Christ, etc. – have openly embraced the spiritual equality of women that Jesus promoted, allowing women greater leadership in those congregations.

Despite the strong evidence in favor of the equality and importance of women found in the New Testament – and especially in the example Jesus provides – a majority of Christian denominations still "conserve" the view that women are somehow relegated to a lower or different status than men in the Church and society. Yet we can't blame Paul or the Pastoral Epistles for all of this; no matter how much weight we give those authors, they simply don't trump the words and deeds attributed to Jesus. So once again we return to individual behaviors and religious institutions conforming to surrounding culture. The Christianity to be found in the United States is the product of centuries of male-dominated social hierarchies. In largest part I think we have the Angles, Saxons and Romans to thank for our individual and collective chauvinism; the vestiges of Levitical law carried forward in Judeo-Christian dogma are just icing on a well-baked cake of tribal inheritance.

But let's take a look at some of the other New Testament evidence that supports a championing of feminist issues. In addition to Jesus' example in the Gospels, we find many powerful contradictions to the misogyny of 1 Timothy and the other Pastoral Epistles, and to the waffling, incomplete understanding and possible interpolation in some of Paul's epistles. Perhaps the most persuasive examples are the instances where women are cited as having received the gift of Divine prophecy (ISV):

> Now Anna, a prophetess, was also there. She was a descendant of Phanuel from the tribe of Asher. She was very old, having lived with her husband for seven years after her marriage, and then as a widow for 84 years. She never left the temple, but continued to worship there night and day with times of fasting and prayer. Just then she came forward and began to thank God and to speak about Jesus to everyone who was waiting for the redemption of Jerusalem.
>
> *Luke* 2:36-38

> The next day we left and came to Caesarea. We went to the home of Philip the evangelist, one of the Seven, and stayed with him. He had four unmarried daughters who could prophesy.
>
> *Acts* 21:8-9

> Every man who prays or prophesies with something on his head dishonors his head, and every woman who prays or prophesies with her head uncovered dishonors her head, which is the same as having her head shaved.
>
> *1 Corinthians* 11:4-5

So we have clear evidence that women not only were prophets but were expected to prophesy. And what is the purpose of prophecy? According to Paul, to edify the Church in a public way:

> Pursue love, but earnestly desire spiritual gifts – and especially that you may prophesy. For someone speaking in another language doesn't speak to men, but to God; for in the spirit he speaks mysteries that no one understands. But the one who prophesies speaks to men for edification, encouragement, and consolation. The one speaking in another language edifies himself, but the one prophesying before the assembly edifies them. I want all of you to speak in other languages, but even more that you may prophesy. For the one who prophesies is greater than the one who speaks in other languages – unless he interprets, so that the assembly may be edified.
>
> *1 Corinthians 14:1-5*

So how could it be that women were to remain "silent and submissive" if they had the gift of prophecy? Wasn't it their responsibility to contribute to the edification of the assembly? Isn't that in fact what Paul exhorted believers to do? And isn't their ample evidence in scripture that women in fact performed this vital function in the early Church? In this light, the condemnation and restrictions regarding women in 1 Timothy – and echoed in 1 Corinthians 14:33-35 – really make no sense at all. So why are there such as strongly worded contradictions in the Pastoral Epistles? For now, I'll simply offer that I think they represent grievous errors on the part of the writer; however, in the chapter *Beyond the New Testament* we will explore in greater detail why 1 Timothy and the other Pastoral Epistles may have gone so astray.

In other writings of the early Church, such as the *Shepherd of Hermas,* we encounter a powerful, supernatural woman who imparts Divine wisdom to the shepherd in visions. In the *Gospel of Mary,* we learn of Jesus' teachings from the first person account of a woman, and witness a female disciple's special relationship with Christ that imbues her with spiritual leadership. In the *Gospel of Thomas* we encounter female disciples asking Jesus questions in the same manner as the male disciples. In Elaine Pagel's book, *The Gnostic Gospels,* she describes how the writing of Valentinian Christian Gnostics in the second century showed that women were treated as equals, allowing them to be prophets, teachers, healers and evangelists within that community. And although these other early writings were not included in the New Testament canon we have today, they certainly reinforce Jesus' liberating sentiments toward the daughters of his kingdom. All-in-all, it is difficult to escape the conclusion that, at its inception, Christianity offered women a striking and empowering departure from the oppression of male-dominated cultures. But once prevailing culture took root in more institutionalized versions of Christianity, one of the most sweeping and progressive ideas Christ advocated was, for the most part, quickly forgotten.

Inclusion, Harmony & Service vs. Righteous Anger & Judgment

We see that Jesus' attitudes towards women, Gentiles, prostitutes, tax collectors and social outcasts in many different situations tended to be much more tolerant and inclusive than judgmental, and especially so when contrasted to the religious and political leaders of his day as reported in the New Testament and other historical accounts. We find these same loving attitudes and intentions in countless situations, towards many different kinds of people, regardless of their race or religious affiliations and beliefs. Here are some of those other examples. These verses are quoted from the English Standard Version (ESV):

> "You have heard that it was said, 'An eye for an eye and a tooth for a tooth.' But I say to you, Do not resist the one who is evil. But if anyone slaps you on the right cheek, turn to him the other also. And if anyone would sue you and take your tunic, let him have your cloak as well. And if anyone forces you to go one mile, go with him two miles. Give to the one who begs from you, and do not refuse the one who would borrow from you. "You have heard that it was said, 'You shall love your neighbor and hate your enemy.' But I say to you, Love your enemies and pray for those who persecute you, so that you may be sons of your Father who is in heaven. For he makes his sun rise on the evil and on the good, and sends rain on the just and on the unjust."
>
> *Matthew 5:38-45*

> And as Jesus reclined at table in the house, behold, many tax collectors and sinners came and were reclining with Jesus and his disciples. And when the Pharisees saw this, they said to his disciples, "Why does your teacher eat with tax collectors and sinners?" But when he heard it, he said, "Those who are well have no need of a physician, but those who are sick. Go and learn what this means, 'I desire mercy, and not sacrifice.' For I came not to call the righteous, but sinners."
>
> *Matthew 9:10-13*

> And from there he arose and went away to the region of Tyre and Sidon. And he entered a house and did not want anyone to know, yet he could

not be hidden. But immediately a woman whose little daughter had an unclean spirit heard of him and came and fell down at his feet. Now the woman was a Gentile, a Syrophoenician by birth. And she begged him to cast the demon out of her daughter. And he said to her, "Let the children be fed first, for it is not right to take the children's bread and throw it to the dogs." But she answered him, "Yes, Lord; yet even the dogs under the table eat the children's crumbs." And he said to her, "For this statement you may go your way; the demon has left your daughter." And she went home and found the child lying in bed and the demon gone.

Mark 7:24-30

John said to him, "Teacher, we saw someone casting out demons in your name, and we tried to stop him, because he was not following us." But Jesus said, "Do not stop him, for no one who does a mighty work in my name will be able soon afterward to speak evil of me. For the one who is not against us is for us. For truly, I say to you, whoever gives you a cup of water to drink because you belong to Christ will by no means lose his reward."

Mark 9:38-41

"If you love those who love you, what benefit is that to you? For even sinners love those who love them. And if you do good to those who do good to you, what benefit is that to you? For even sinners do the same. And if you lend to those from whom you expect to receive, what credit is that to you? Even sinners lend to sinners, to get back the same amount. But love your enemies, and do good, and lend, expecting nothing in return, and your reward will be great, and you will be sons of the Most High, for he is kind to the ungrateful and the evil. Be merciful, even as your Father is merciful. Judge not, and you will not be judged; condemn not, and you will not be condemned; forgive, and you will be forgiven; give, and it will be given to you. Good measure, pressed down, shaken together, running over, will be put into your lap. For with the measure you use it will be measured back to you."

Luke 6:32-38

And he said to his disciples, "Temptations to sin are sure to come, but woe to the one through whom they come! It would be better for him if a millstone were hung around his neck and he were cast into the sea than that he should cause one of these little ones to sin. Pay attention to yourselves! If your brother sins, rebuke him, and if he repents, forgive him, and if he sins against you seven times in the day, and turns to you seven times, saying, 'I repent,' you must forgive him."

Luke 17:1-4

> He also told this parable to some who trusted in themselves that they were righteous, and treated others with contempt: "Two men went up into the temple to pray, one a Pharisee and the other a tax collector. The Pharisee, standing by himself, prayed thus: 'God, I thank you that I am not like other men, extortioners, unjust, adulterers, or even like this tax collector. I fast twice a week; I give tithes of all that I get.' But the tax collector, standing far off, would not even lift up his eyes to heaven, but beat his breast, saying, 'God, be merciful to me, a sinner!' I tell you, this man went down to his house justified, rather than the other. For everyone who exalts himself will be humbled, but the one who humbles himself will be exalted."
>
> *Luke 18:9-14*

> A new commandment I give to you, that you love one another: just as I have loved you, you also are to love one another. By this all people will know that you are my disciples, if you have love for one another."
>
> *John 13:34-35*

And is this same generous, loving, accepting and serving attitude continued by Jesus' disciples and exemplified in the various stories involving them? Let's take a look (ESV):

> And Peter went down to the men and said, "I am the one you are looking for. What is the reason for your coming?" And they said, "Cornelius, a centurion, an upright and God-fearing man, who is well spoken of by the whole Jewish nation, was directed by a holy angel to send for you to come to his house and to hear what you have to say." So he invited them in to be his guests. The next day he rose and went away with them, and some of the brothers from Joppa accompanied him. And on the following day they entered Caesarea. Cornelius was expecting them and had called together his relatives and close friends. When Peter entered, Cornelius met him and fell down at his feet and worshiped him. But Peter lifted him up, saying, "Stand up; I too am a man." And as he talked with him, he went in and found many persons gathered. And he said to them, "You yourselves know how unlawful it is for a Jew to associate with or to visit anyone of another nation, but God has shown me that I should not call any person common or unclean. So when I was sent for, I came without objection. I ask then why you sent for me." And Cornelius said, "Four days ago, about this hour, I was praying in my house at the ninth hour, and behold, a man stood before me in bright clothing and said, 'Cornelius, your prayer has been heard and your alms have been remembered before God. Send therefore to Joppa and ask for Simon who is called Peter. He is lodging in the house

of Simon, a tanner, by the sea.' So I sent for you at once, and you have been kind enough to come. Now therefore we are all here in the presence of God to hear all that you have been commanded by the Lord." So Peter opened his mouth and said: "Truly I understand that God shows no partiality, but in every nation anyone who fears him and does what is right is acceptable to him."

Acts 10:21-35

What shall we say, then? That Gentiles who did not pursue righteousness have attained it, that is, a righteousness that is by faith; but that Israel who pursued a law that would lead to righteousness did not succeed in reaching that law. Why? Because they did not pursue it by faith, but as if it were based on works. They have stumbled over the stumbling stone, as it is written, "Behold, I am laying in Zion a stone of stumbling, and a rock of offense; and whoever believes in him will not be put to shame."

Romans 9:30-33

For with the heart one believes and is justified, and with the mouth one confesses and is saved. For the Scripture says, "Everyone who believes in him will not be put to shame." For there is no distinction between Jew and Greek; for the same Lord is Lord of all, bestowing his riches on all who call on him. For "everyone who calls on the name of the Lord will be saved."

Romans 10:10-13

For consider your calling, brothers: not many of you were wise according to worldly standards, not many were powerful, not many were of noble birth. But God chose what is foolish in the world to shame the wise; God chose what is weak in the world to shame the strong; God chose what is low and despised in the world, even things that are not, to bring to nothing things that are, so that no human being might boast in the presence of God.

1 Corinthians 1:26-29

For though I am free from all, I have made myself a servant to all, that I might win more of them. To the Jews I became as a Jew, in order to win Jews. To those under the law I became as one under the law (though not being myself under the law) that I might win those under the law. To those outside the law I became as one outside the law (not being outside the law of God but under the law of Christ) that I might win those outside the law. To the weak I became weak, that I might win the weak. I have become all things to all people, that by all means I might save some. I do it all for the sake of the gospel, that I may share with them in its blessings.

1 Corinthians 9:19-23

And let us not grow weary of doing good, for in due season we will reap, if we do not give up. So then, as we have opportunity, let us do good to everyone, and especially to those who are of the household of faith.

Galatians 6:9-10

I therefore, a prisoner for the Lord, urge you to walk in a manner worthy of the calling to which you have been called, with all humility and gentleness, with patience, bearing with one another in love, eager to maintain the unity of the Spirit in the bond of peace.

Ephesians 4:1-3

Put on then, as God's chosen ones, holy and beloved, compassionate hearts, kindness, humility, meekness, and patience, bearing with one another and, if one has a complaint against another, forgiving each other; as the Lord has forgiven you, so you also must forgive. And above all these put on love, which binds everything together in perfect harmony.

Colossians 3:12-14

Walk in wisdom toward outsiders, making the best use of the time. Let your speech always be gracious, seasoned with salt, so that you may know how you ought to answer each person.

Colossians 4:5-6

Now concerning brotherly love you have no need for anyone to write to you, for you yourselves have been taught by God to love one another, for that indeed is what you are doing to all the brothers throughout Macedonia. But we urge you, brothers, to do this more and more, and to aspire to live quietly, and to mind your own affairs, and to work with your hands, as we instructed you, so that you may walk properly before outsiders and be dependent on no one.

1 Thessalonians 4:9-12

I thank him who has given me strength, Christ Jesus our Lord, because he judged me faithful, appointing me to his service, though formerly I was a blasphemer, persecutor, and insolent opponent. But I received mercy because I had acted ignorantly in unbelief, and the grace of our Lord overflowed for me with the faith and love that are in Christ Jesus. The saying is trustworthy and deserving of full acceptance, that Christ Jesus came into the world to save sinners, of whom I am the foremost.

But I received mercy for this reason, that in me, as the foremost, Jesus Christ might display his perfect patience as an example to those who were to believe in him for eternal life.

1 Timothy 1:12-16

Strive for peace with everyone, and for the holiness without which no one will see the Lord. See to it that no one fails to obtain the grace of God; that no "root of bitterness" springs up and causes trouble, and by it many become defiled…

Hebrews 12:14-15

By this we know love, that he laid down his life for us, and we ought to lay down our lives for the brothers. But if anyone has the world's goods and sees his brother in need, yet closes his heart against him, how does God's love abide in him? Little children, let us not love in word or talk but in deed and in truth. By this we shall know that we are of the truth and reassure our heart before him; for whenever our heart condemns us, God is greater than our heart, and he knows everything.

1 John 3:16-20

If anyone thinks he is religious and does not bridle his tongue but deceives his heart, this person's religion is worthless. Religion that is pure and undefiled before God, the Father, is this: to visit orphans and widows in their affliction, and to keep oneself unstained from the world.

James 1:26-27

Keep your conduct among the Gentiles honorable, so that when they speak against you as evildoers, they may see your good deeds and glorify God on the day of visitation.

1 Peter 2:12

Above all, keep loving one another earnestly, since love covers a multitude of sins. Show hospitality to one another without grumbling. As each has received a gift, use it to serve one another, as good stewards of God's varied grace: whoever speaks, as one who speaks oracles of God; whoever serves, as one who serves by the strength that God supplies—in order that in everything God may be glorified through Jesus Christ. To him belong glory and dominion forever and ever. Amen.

1 Peter 4:8-11

Once again take some time to meditate, pray, or reflect upon these verses and discuss them with others from a position of suspended judgment. Apply some of the concepts to your situation. What do these verses tell us about Christ-like intentions of inclusion, harmony and service? Synthesize your own conclusions and compare them to my own ideas.

On the other hand, such accepting attitudes are only one side of the equation. In these same accounts and missives, we also find sentiments brimming with accusation, condemnation, indignation and even wrath. Here are some of those, first from the gospels regarding Jesus' actions and teaching (ESV):

> Then Pharisees and scribes came to Jesus from Jerusalem and said, "Why do your disciples break the tradition of the elders? For they do not wash their hands when they eat." He answered them, "And why do you break the commandment of God for the sake of your tradition? For God commanded, 'Honor your father and your mother,' and, 'Whoever reviles father or mother must surely die.' But you say, 'If anyone tells his father or his mother, "What you would have gained from me is given to God," he need not honor his father.' So for the sake of your tradition you have made void the word of God. You hypocrites! Well did Isaiah prophesy of you, when he said: "'This people honors me with their lips, but their heart is far from me; in vain do they worship me, teaching as doctrines the commandments of men.'"
>
> *Matthew 15:1-9*

> "Woe to you, blind guides, who say, 'If anyone swears by the temple, it is nothing, but if anyone swears by the gold of the temple, he is bound by his oath.' You blind fools! For which is greater, the gold or the temple that has made the gold sacred? And you say, 'If anyone swears by the altar, it is nothing, but if anyone swears by the gift that is on the altar, he is bound by his oath.' You blind men! For which is greater, the gift or the altar that makes the gift sacred? So whoever swears by the altar swears by it and by everything on it. And whoever swears by the temple swears by it and by him who dwells in it. And whoever swears by heaven swears by the throne of God and by him who sits upon it. Woe to you, scribes and Pharisees, hypocrites! For you tithe mint and dill and cumin, and have neglected the weightier matters of the law: justice and mercy and faithfulness. These you ought to have done, without neglecting the others. You blind guides, straining out a gnat and swallowing a camel! Woe to you, scribes and Pharisees, hypocrites! For

you clean the outside of the cup and the plate, but inside they are full of greed and self-indulgence. You blind Pharisee! First clean the inside of the cup and the plate, that the outside also may be clean. Woe to you, scribes and Pharisees, hypocrites! For you are like whitewashed tombs, which outwardly appear beautiful, but within are full of dead people's bones and all uncleanness. So you also outwardly appear righteous to others, but within you are full of hypocrisy and lawlessness."

Matthew 23:16-28

"When the Son of Man comes in his glory, and all the angels with him, then he will sit on his glorious throne. Before him will be gathered all the nations, and he will separate people one from another as a shepherd separates the sheep from the goats. And he will place the sheep on his right, but the goats on the left. Then the King will say to those on his right, 'Come, you who are blessed by my Father, inherit the kingdom prepared for you from the foundation of the world. For I was hungry and you gave me food, I was thirsty and you gave me drink, I was a stranger and you welcomed me, I was naked and you clothed me, I was sick and you visited me, I was in prison and you came to me.' Then the righteous will answer him, saying, 'Lord, when did we see you hungry and feed you, or thirsty and give you drink? And when did we see you a stranger and welcome you, or naked and clothe you? And when did we see you sick or in prison and visit you?' And the King will answer them, 'Truly, I say to you, as you did it to one of the least of these my brothers, you did it to me.' Then he will say to those on his left, 'Depart from me, you cursed, into the eternal fire prepared for the devil and his angels. For I was hungry and you gave me no food, I was thirsty and you gave me no drink, I was a stranger and you did not welcome me, naked and you did not clothe me, sick and in prison and you did not visit me.' Then they also will answer, saying, 'Lord, when did we see you hungry or thirsty or a stranger or naked or sick or in prison, and did not minister to you?' Then he will answer them, saying, 'Truly, I say to you, as you did not do it to one of the least of these, you did not do it to me.' And these will go away into eternal punishment, but the righteous into eternal life."

Matthew 25:31-46

And the Pharisees and the scribes asked him, "Why do your disciples not walk according to the tradition of the elders, but eat with defiled hands?" And he said to them, "Well did Isaiah prophesy of you hypocrites, as it is written, "'This people honors me with their lips, but their heart is far from me; in vain do they worship me, teaching as doctrines the commandments of men.' You leave the commandment of God and hold to the tradition of men."

Mark 7:5-8

> And he began to teach them that the Son of Man must suffer many things and be rejected by the elders and the chief priests and the scribes and be killed, and after three days rise again. And he said this plainly. And Peter took him aside and began to rebuke him. But turning and seeing his disciples, he rebuked Peter and said, "Get behind me, Satan! For you are not setting your mind on the things of God, but on the things of man."
>
> *Mark 8:31-33*

> The Passover of the Jews was at hand, and Jesus went up to Jerusalem. In the temple he found those who were selling oxen and sheep and pigeons, and the money-changers sitting there. And making a whip of cords, he drove them all out of the temple, with the sheep and oxen. And he poured out the coins of the money-changers and overturned their tables. And he told those who sold the pigeons, "Take these things away; do not make my Father's house a house of trade."
>
> *John 2:13-16*

> "I do not receive glory from people. But I know that you do not have the love of God within you. I have come in my Father's name, and you do not receive me. If another comes in his own name, you will receive him. How can you believe, when you receive glory from one another and do not seek the glory that comes from the only God? Do not think that I will accuse you to the Father. There is one who accuses you: Moses, on whom you have set your hope."
>
> *John 5:41-45*

> Jesus said, "For judgment I came into this world, that those who do not see may see, and those who see may become blind." Some of the Pharisees near him heard these things, and said to him, "Are we also blind?" Jesus said to them, "If you were blind, you would have no guilt; but now that you say, 'We see,' your guilt remains."
>
> *John 9:39-41*

And here are some additional echoes and clarifications of these more angry and condemning attitudes that we find later in the New Testament (ESV):

> Some are arrogant, as though I were not coming to you. But I will come to you soon, if the Lord wills, and I will find out not the talk of these arrogant people but their power. For the kingdom of God does not

consist in talk but in power. What do you wish? Shall I come to you with a rod, or with love in a spirit of gentleness?

1 Corinthians 4:18-21

I wrote to you in my letter not to associate with sexually immoral people— not at all meaning the sexually immoral of this world, or the greedy and swindlers, or idolaters, since then you would need to go out of the world. But now I am writing to you not to associate with anyone who bears the name of brother if he is guilty of sexual immorality or greed, or is an idolater, reviler, drunkard, or swindler—not even to eat with such a one. For what have I to do with judging outsiders? Is it not those inside the church whom you are to judge? God judges those outside. "Purge the evil person from among you."

1 Corinthians 5:9-13

For we cannot do anything against the truth, but only for the truth. For we are glad when we are weak and you are strong. Your restoration is what we pray for. For this reason I write these things while I am away from you, that when I come I may not have to be severe in my use of the authority that the Lord has given me for building up and not for tearing down.

2 Corinthians 13:8-10

I am astonished that you are so quickly deserting him who called you in the grace of Christ and are turning to a different gospel— not that there is another one, but there are some who trouble you and want to distort the gospel of Christ. But even if we or an angel from heaven should preach to you a gospel contrary to the one we preached to you, let him be accursed. As we have said before, so now I say again: If anyone is preaching to you a gospel contrary to the one you received, let him be accursed.

Galatians 1:6-9

O foolish Galatians! Who has bewitched you? It was before your eyes that Jesus Christ was publicly portrayed as crucified. Let me ask you only this: Did you receive the Spirit by works of the law or by hearing with faith? Are you so foolish? Having begun by the Spirit, are you now being perfected by the flesh? Did you suffer so many things in vain—if indeed it was in vain? Does he who supplies the Spirit to you and works miracles among you do so by works of the law, or by hearing with faith—?

Galatians 3:1-5

Look: I, Paul, say to you that if you accept circumcision, Christ will be of no advantage to you. I testify again to every man who accepts circumcision that he is obligated to keep the whole law. You are severed from Christ, you who would be justified by the law; you have fallen away from grace. For through the Spirit, by faith, we ourselves eagerly wait for the hope of righteousness. For in Christ Jesus neither circumcision nor uncircumcision counts for anything, but only faith working through love.

Galatians 5:2-6

Therefore let no one pass judgment on you in questions of food and drink, or with regard to a festival or a new moon or a Sabbath. These are a shadow of the things to come, but the substance belongs to Christ. Let no one disqualify you, insisting on asceticism and worship of angels, going on in detail about visions, puffed up without reason by his sensuous mind, and not holding fast to the Head, from whom the whole body, nourished and knit together through its joints and ligaments, grows with a growth that is from God.

Colossians 2:16-19

For though by this time you ought to be teachers, you need someone to teach you again the basic principles of the oracles of God. You need milk, not solid food, for everyone who lives on milk is unskilled in the word of righteousness, since he is a child.

Hebrews 5:12

Therefore I intend always to remind you of these qualities, though you know them and are established in the truth that you have. I think it right, as long as I am in this body, to stir you up by way of reminder, since I know that the putting off of my body will be soon, as our Lord Jesus Christ made clear to me. And I will make every effort so that after my departure you may be able at any time to recall these things.

1 Peter 1:12-15

Bold and willful, they do not tremble as they blaspheme the glorious ones, whereas angels, though greater in might and power, do not pronounce a blasphemous judgment against them before the Lord. But these, like irrational animals, creatures of instinct, born to be caught and destroyed, blaspheming about matters of which they are ignorant, will also be destroyed in their destruction, suffering wrong as the wage for their wrongdoing.

2 Peter 2:10-13

Those whom I love, I reprove and discipline, so be zealous and repent.
Revelations 3:19

Take a moment to reflect upon the contrast between this last group of excerpts and the more tolerant attitudes expressed earlier. Why does this contrast exist? Meditate, pray, or mull over these, and discuss and apply them if possible with a neutral, open disposition. Then compare your conclusions to my own.

The Defining Difference

What is the defining difference between the instances when Jesus and his apostles are forgiving, magnanimous and empowering of others, and those in which they seem to be bursting with righteous anger and condemnation? Is there a contradiction here? On the contrary, these reactions are consistent, and the difference can be simply stated. Those who are arrogantly proud of their own spiritual righteousness – and who then magnify that arrogance by rejecting the law of love and ignoring the needs of others – are harshly judged. Those who acknowledge God with humility and serve others out of gratitude and compassion are embraced, forgiven and rewarded – regardless of any other faults they might have, their race or social status, or their religious pedigree. In the former we find the hardened heart of willfulness, indifference and pride, and in the latter we find the open heart of kindness, willingness and faith. Condemnation is reserved for those who proclaim that they can see the truth, who insist that they know the mind of God, who have set themselves in the position of holiness and sitting in judgment of others, but who cleave to tradition and don't reflect the love of Christ in any of their actions. For those who recognize their incompleteness and the shortcomings of human institutions, but who nonetheless draw near to the Light in devotion and love, the inclusiveness of Jesus' message seems to be all-encompassing. The only people who are excluded are those who exclude; the only people who are judged are those who judge; the only believers who are chastised are the self-righteous elite who chastise others.

There is some judgmental language to be found in New Testament scripture that appears to fall outside of this generalization. For example, Mark 3 and Luke 12 intimate that whoever blasphemes against the holy spirit will not be forgiven. This seems directed against the religious elite of the time disbelieving the miracles they were witnessing. But in nearly every other instance where we have such strong language, the emphasis is obvious. Where 1 Corinthians 5:5 (ESV) gives instruction regarding believers who are particularly depraved in their immorality: "You are to deliver this man to Satan for the destruction of the flesh, so that his spirit may be saved in the day of the Lord." Where 1 John 3:14 (ESV) says: "We know that we have passed out of death into life, because we love the brothers. Whoever does not love abides in death." When James 2:17 (ESV) conveys that "So also faith by itself, if it does not have works, is dead." In Revelation 3:16, when Jesus threatens to spit out those who are lukewarm in their actions. Wherever disciplinary or condemning language is invoked, it almost always relates to being in the presence of Divine Light and grace, and either doing little or nothing in response to that gift, rejecting it outright, or defiling it with depraved, uncompassionate or self-serving actions. Yet even within each seemingly harsh judgment the emphasis remains on doing good, on holding believers accountable to their beliefs, and on reminding those who have drifted from the loving path how they can return. The underlying intention here is the discipline of fierce compassion rather than wrathful vengeance, fear, prejudice or arbitrary punishment.

Perhaps most importantly of all, such discipline does not apply to those outside the community of God's chosen. Jesus was critical of the Judean religious leaders who proclaimed their holiness without being holy. Paul was critical of Christians who denigrated the gift of grace they received. But nowhere in the New Testament do we find accounts of Gentiles being similarly ridiculed for their lack of faith, or those outside of the early Christian Church being chastised for their noncompliance with the instructions of Church leaders. In fact, we see the opposite: a clear relaxation of rigid spiritual precepts for those outside of an expressed and committed spiritual course, and instead ample praise for those who attempt to understand and approach holiness with a simple, sincere faith devoid of religious legalism. We see this with the Italian centurion, the chronically bleeding woman, Cornelius, and others. Even Paul, who invokes judgmental language often as he writes to the city churches, clarifies in 1 Corinthians 5:12 that his rebukes and exhortations are meant only for those within the Christian community, not those outside of it.

So it is not human failing that is problematic for the writers of the New Testament; over and over again human failings are accepted and forgiven, especially when genuine humility, compassion and longing to draw near to the Divine are present in those who fall short. It is instead the willful rejection of compassion, humility, faith – and the plethora of other positive qualities that spring forth from anyone drawn to the Light – that becomes problematic. Belief in God is a requisite foundation for the Christian spiritual milieu, but that belief is irrelevant if it is not accompanied by fruits of the spirit – that is, by actions that demonstrate loving kindness, spiritual discipline, self-sacrifice and a willing obedience to Divine will. Jesus and his apostles repeatedly invoked a ferocious and dogged compassion when confronting those who professed belief, but who did not demonstrate their convictions in a transformed mind, heart and life. Yes, these confrontations were forceful, but that forcefulness was born out of intense and devoted affection. And all of this – all definitions and contrasts and encouragements – were once again not instructions for those outside of the Christian or Jewish faith, but for those who had already embraced them. In contrast to centuries of intolerance and strife between races and religious factions in and around Judea, Jesus and his followers cast aside such differences, focusing instead on embracing anyone and everyone in the known world as equals in the kingdom of God.

Interestingly, the more closely we examine these dynamics, the more demanding the choice to dedicate oneself to Christ appears to become. For the nonbeliever is treated with infinite graciousness and tolerance, but the believer who has embraced spiritual liberation is held accountable for their commitment with the heightened attentiveness of love. As Revelations 3:19 (ESV) reminds Christians, "Those whom I love, I reprove and discipline." A Christian has responsibilities they cannot shirk. But this accountability remains grounded in compassion, for its objective is to stimulate spiritual authenticity, growth and maturity. Rebukes in the New Testament aren't offered to those who inadvertently stumble and humbly seek their way back to the Light, but for those who stubbornly persist in their error while trumpeting their own rectitude. For them, as it says in 2 Peter 2:21 (ESV), "it would have been better for them never to have known the way of righteousness than after knowing it to turn back from the holy commandment delivered to them."

Christ-like Activism Defined for Modern Times

At this point, we have enough information to inform a few fundamentals about the intended quality of human relationships in the kingdom of God, and the types of activism that are supported by the New Testament. From the excerpts covered so far in this chapter, some distinct themes emerge. To contextualize this exploration, let's examine the kinds of relationships Christians are encouraged to have with each other, their government and society at large:

- **What responsibility do Christians have to each other?** To love and empower each other fervently and self-sacrificially, without bias, hierarchy or prejudice – regardless of gender, wealth, social status, past mistakes, etc. This includes reminding each other of Christ's message and purpose, holding each other accountable to professed beliefs, caring for one other without grumbling or complaint, being unfailingly generous in emotional and material support, edifying each other with spiritual truth, and maintaining unity and mutual devotion within the Church.

- **What is the civic responsibility of Christians?** To recognize the established rule of law, to submit to governing authorities, to accept the Divinely sanctioned role of government to punish evildoers, to pay taxes without misgivings, to compassionately serve society in whatever way possible, to pray that civic leaders maintain a society that allows the message of Christ to propagate unhindered, and to utilize the facilities and protections of government to share the gospel whenever possible. At the same time, Christians should not rely too heavily on the secular rule of law to adjudicate disputes, but rather use their own judgment.

- **When is it acceptable for Christians to challenge or rebel against governing authorities?** Very narrowly, when it serves the purpose of furthering Christ's message and expanding his kingdom, yet even here this is restricted to working within the established rule of law, and appealing to existing authorities rather than usurping them or competing with them. It is clear that speaking truth to power and seeking justice through the established rule of law is part of the Christian toolkit for sharing the good news of Christ.

- **How should Christians act towards those outside the Church?** To demonstrate their faith with loving, self-sacrificing actions that help non-Christians, to pray for them, to never judge, rebuke or even resist the actions of non-believers, and to always show compassion, forgiveness, generosity and tolerance. Once again this is to occur without bias, hierarchy or prejudice. The aim of this demonstrated faith is to remain above reproach within secular communities, to live in harmony with non-believing segments of society, and thereby both exemplify Christ to outsiders and provide opportunities to share Jesus' message.

- **What kinds of service should Christians perform in society?** The simplest answer seems to be to serve anyone who is in need. For those who are hungry, homeless, widowed, orphaned, imprisoned, sick, thirsty, poor, strangers and so on, meeting basic physical and material needs is part of the high art of Christian faith-in-action. To offer hospitality, comfort, monetary support and so on to those who – for whatever reason – cannot provide for themselves are the chief expressions of Christ-like love, both within the Church community and in society as a whole.

- **Should Christians aspire to political office?** None of the scripture we have cited so far indicates that political aspiration is a wise or spiritually profitable course. In fact, any desire for worldly power seems contrary to everything Jesus taught and everything his apostles exemplified. Believers should instead devote their efforts to the spiritual kingdom of God, not

> material kingdoms or positional authority. In this sense, the separation of Church and state is implicit if not explicit. That is not to say that holding political office is somehow forbidden to Christians, but according to the New Testament, pursuing such worldly authority was not an avenue promoted within the early Church.

In U.S. history, we occasionally hear these general principles advocated by narrow slices of the Christian community and a smattering of influential historical figures. More often, however, and quite notably within the last few decades, Christian religion has been used by rightwing conservatives as a tool to justify political causes at odds with the principles of the New Testament itself. For example, one traditional conservative argument for exotic gun ownership (assault weapons, etc.) is the constitutional right to bear arms and maintain a state militia in self-defense against unlawful governmental action (i.e. the Second Amendment to the Constitution in the 1791 Bill of Rights). This is usually characterized as being in the spirit of the initial American resistance to the oppressions of King George II. And yet this foundation of a free America, a freedom highly valued by the conservative right, was just the sort of rebellion that Jesus and his apostles never sanctioned or participated in. Such disputes over worldly kingdoms are largely irrelevant to the kingdom of God, and the right to bear arms in order to resist governing authorities would have been a gross anathema to first century Christians.

Along the same lines, the desire for lower taxes and a smaller, less intrusive government also contradicts New Testament principles. For those today who view the Boston Tea Party as an example of unfair taxation, and who hold that an ongoing American duty is to resist the repeat of any similar taxation, the dissonance with Jesus' pronouncement on this very topic is obvious. Giving Caesar his due is an unquestionable reflexive in Christ's view. And what if all levels of government were truly reduced in scope and size as radically as many conservative ideologues propose? Such a government would no longer have the capacity to enforce the rule of law against powerful evildoers – not against well-funded special interests, not against organized crime, not against the efforts of other nations to harm America or its citizens, and certainly not against multinational corporations whose incomes and influence rival those of whole countries. That such Libertarian sentiments are so pervasive among many Christian conservatives is, frankly, bewildering.

And then there are the judgmental, condemning and hateful attitudes and language frequently associated with these same conservative-leaning Christians. In the rhetoric of conservative talk show hosts who claim to believe in Christ, in the podium pounding of Republican political candidates who claim to be Christian, in the attack ads and deception campaigns funded by Christian organizations...what do we hear? Vicious critiques of any progressive U.S. President and that administration's policies. Angry denunciation of the civil rights and liberties of everyone from immigrants to homosexuals. Gleeful schadenfreude when "liberals" are somehow proven wrong, are publically embarassed or make some sort of mistake. Aggressive proposals to impose conservative values on non-believers through legislation and the courts. Loud complaints about the power and size of government, unfair taxes, and the horrible waste of government programs that help the sick and the poor. The reviling of anyone who does not agree with these extreme perspectives. And a combative, competitive spirit in seemingly every undertaking. It appears as if every plank in the conservative philosophical platform seeks to directly contradict specifically how the New Testament exhorts Christians to act.

But once again, how can we be sure these judgmental, anti-government, anti-tax, anti-service, pro free-market conservatives really think of themselves as Christian? In a September, 2010 "American Values Survey" by the Public Religion Research Institute, 81% of Tea Partiers self-identified as Christian, with 57% claiming to be conservative Christians. Here, at least, the rank-and-file of an ultraconservative movement are unabashed about their religious affiliation. And the methods and objectives of the Tea Party echo the conservative values already enumerated: vociferously disrespecting our current government, lobbying forcefully for tax repeals, aggressively advocating the imposition of conservative values on non-Christians, while acidly condemning those who disagree. Where is the forgiveness here? Where is the submission to governing authorities? Where is the inclusion and compassion? Where is the humble service to the needy? Waiving the banner of conservatism proudly overhead, the Tea Partiers eagerly drop their Bibles on the ground and grind the pages of scripture soundly into the dirt.

The question of Christians running for political office is an interesting issue. In the New Testament accounts, politics and worldly authority is not the primary provenance of Christian activism. Christians can serve such leaders, submit to them, pray for them, appeal to them and hold them accountable according to the law…but there is no basis in the New Testament for pursuing a career in politics. In the early Church, Christianity was not politicized and politics were not Christianized. There was of course no prohibition against this, either, other than perhaps Jesus' warning to his disciples that they should not lord it over others as the Gentile rulers did. And of course the obvious benefit of more effectively serving those in need through political office can be enticing. If such a committed intention to service can be sincerely maintained without self-deception or craving for power, then the opportunities to help others through political influence are vast. At the same time, effective politicians are most definitely both in this world and of this world, relying on wealth, the favor of the masses, quid pro quo dealings, misleading promises and deceptive campaign ads to succeed – so the dangers and temptations of political office are equally obvious.

With all of this said, Christians in the U.S. still live in democratic society and are empowered to influence political outcomes with their dollars and votes. If a good Samaritan passes a voting booth on the road, it seems likely Jesus would expect them to embrace their responsibility to vote – especially if it benefits the safety, healing and well-being of others. A Christian's participation in the democratic process, and their support for and expansion the good of All through government systems is, in this sense, a compassionate imperative. And yet the scriptures also exhort Christians not to impose their values or will on others, and above all to be at peace with everyone and perpetually above reproach. So this is quite a balancing act. I think that how each Christian votes must therefore be a matter of conscience, prayer and illuminated understanding in concert with holy spirit. As such, it should therefore be impossible to predict how any Christian should vote, and very likely that believers with different experiences and different levels of spiritual maturity would vote differently on the same issues.

However, when we look at the current cultural landscape in the U.S., it is clear that many Christians do not even try to adhere to these New Testament directives, and instead vote in lockstep with each other in a kind of irrational conservative groupthink. As a result, those who have lobbied hard for certain political causes in the guise of promoting Christian values have alienated vast swathes of the electorate rather than serving or inspiring them. Defending prayer in public schools, imposing restrictions on abortion funding and rights, oppressing other religions, opposing Darwinian theory and scientific research, attacking free speech and artistic expression, withdrawing funding of federal programs for the poor…all of these efforts have done nothing to sanctify God's kingdom, and everything to alienate nonbelievers from that kingdom. If instead Christians and Christian organizations focused these substantial energies on humble service and self-sacrifice within civil society, the impact could be profound. Instead of estranging people from Christ, they could astonish the world with love and become "all things to all people."

Frankly, I think much the confusion in the conservative Christian community around these issues in part stems from their desire to do what is right in the sight of other conservative Christians, rather than what is right in the sight of all people. That is, to win favor, praise and position within the conservative tribe rather than among non-believers. But that isn't the model or ideal the New Testament provides. Yes, it is clear that believers should live in harmony and unity with each other, and lavish spiritual brothers and sisters with love, forgiveness and material support; but this is not intended to achieve an insular, self-righteous "members-only" club that rejects or oppresses everyone and everything outside of the clubhouse or passes harsh judgment on the world. That is just recreating the Pharisees and Sadducees all over again. The examples of righteous anger we find in the New Testament are instead directed against those who are religious but not compassionate; against believers who are spiritually prideful and conceited in their dealings with other people. To their shame, many modern conservative Christians are effectively directing haughty spiritual indignation against the tax collectors, Gentiles, Roman centurions, and Samaritan women of today – just as the religious elite did in Jesus' time.

With all of this elaborated upon, and despite the complexity of the modern sociopolitical landscape, we can refine the chief elements of

Christ-like activism within that landscape into a few surprisingly simple ideas:

1. The primary tool of Christian activism is living a life of loving, self-disciplined and self-sacrificing example in the world and on behalf of the world. This does not require the cultivation of worldly influence or power, but rather the development of a personal faith and example that befriends and harmonizes with everyone outside of the Church. In all actions and interactions, the Christian objective is to live above reproach in the eyes of nonbelievers, and to tirelessly attend to the basic needs of those in crisis, poverty, illness and suffering.

2. Critical speech and corrective actions are reserved for those within the Christian community, and especially for Christians who puff themselves up with prideful arrogance, forsake the teachings and example of Christ, forget the gift of grace they have received, or reject the power of the holy spirit. However, there is never any call in the New Testament for such judgments to be made of non-Christians.

3. Secular government exists to enforce a rule of law that issues from the Divine, but which the New Testament never encourages to be controlled or overutilized by Christians. Indeed scripture suggests that the existing structure of government can be called upon to further God's will and kingdom on Earth within existing secular laws, to which Christians should willingly and joyfully submit. In the U.S., for example, this would mean that conforming to existing civil liberties, such as the right to free speech, allows Christians to discuss their beliefs with others. There is no need, however, for Christians to be concerned with creating new laws to further God's will, or to rebel against secular authorities in any way. In this sense, New Testament Christianity is distinctly apolitical. At the same time, Christians should not shy away from voting their conscience, speaking truth to power and holding secular government accountable for the rule of law, especially when this creates opportunities to share the love of Christ.

4. As exemplified by Jesus, Christians have an obligation to resist the cultural programming that runs counter to the principles of the kingdom of God. Some examples of this programming would be: the belief that women are somehow inferior to men, or that worldly wealth and power provide happiness, or that people who think or act differently than the mainstream should be feared and persecuted, or that might makes right, or that rebellion and revolution are necessary struggles against flesh and blood, or that proving I am in the right in a court of law is more important than promoting compassionate relationship, and so on. Christians also have an obligation to avoid making themselves into an exclusive and elitist priesthood that seeks to lord it over the world or pass judgment on non-believers – for this, too, is yet another tribal habit that destroys the transformative power of spirit.

There has of course been much cultural programming that has infected the Christian tradition over the last two thousand years, distorting it into what would be almost unrecognizable to believers of the first century. In many of Jesus' pronouncements, the contrast between the way the world works and the way the kingdom of God functions is strongly evident. An interesting exercise in this context is to distinguish, to whatever degree possible, the spiritual principles or *memes* that inspired the core values of the Christian religion from the social mores of its first century parent culture, and then to likewise separate the spiritual principles that have endured into the present day from modern cultural standards. In this way we can begin to differentiate what constitutes a spiritual approach from a worldly one. But this isn't always obvious or transparent, and sometimes a given set of responses or perceived outcomes might appear similar, with the main change occurring internally, with our intentions.

For example, living "above reproach" in the eyes of others can be accomplished many different ways, and can undoubtedly be found in various cultures as an important survival mechanism. For one person this might be accomplished through careful deception and avoiding being caught doing something that is offensive to others. For another person this could be achieved by deferring any and all risks that might place them in a compromising position. Another person might compulsively accede to any and all requests made of them, so that they can thereby avoid conflict or judgment. Another person would make themselves seem above reproach by frightening everyone around them into submission, so that no one dares to criticize or correct them. But if the underlying intention is guided by the many qualities and characteristics of the holy spirit's presence, then this confines the method of being "above reproach" to specific expressions of loving kindness. And without that loving intention, the hallmark characteristics of Christ-like behavior can become empty and meaningless. This process seems to be a carefully choreographed dance of yin-and-yang, of refining our intentions even as those intentions are expressed in new and creative ways.

What we have already uncovered as a unique and potent component of Christian activism is its guiding intentionality, the core reformation of mind and heart and the center of Christian practice in the New Testament. The single point from which all faith-in-action radiates is highly energized compassion. How this loving kindness manifests is guided by a maturation of wisdom, insight and confidence in the Divine, but its actions in and on the world are unceasing. Once a person grounds themselves in the guiding force of love, all that remains is to intuit the most spiritually profitable choice in each moment. That such governing intentionality might lead modern Christians beyond some of the definitions and examples of the New Testament is understandable – this is part of the progressive vision Jesus described when he said that his followers would achieve even greater works that he had done. At the same time, those scriptural definitions and examples provide a helpful baseline for ongoing individual and collective spiritual growth.

Once a person identifies the most spiritual profitable course of action – the most efficacious fulfillment of that guiding intentionality – this is really just the beginning of their efforts. For transitioning out of conformance to worldly ideals into Christ-like attitudes and behaviors is a lifelong journey. Living in *agape* is no easy task. As a healthy starting point, however, modern believers can examine the processes at work in their own minds and hearts, while at the same time carefully scrutinizing the New Testament, and thereby divine the most appropriate next steps for their own spiritual activism. However, it is difficult avoid concluding that the law of love seems to vanquish nearly every plank and supporting pillar of the economic, religious, social and governmentally conservative principles currently favored by roughly half of the U.S. electorate. As we will continue to explore, the good news is not just progressive-leaning, it actively opposes conservative ideology.

This observed contradiction between Christian conservatives and Biblical principles is not new. Indeed, I would like to note the efforts of others who have explored the incompatibility of authentic Christianity with modern conservative sociopolitical agendas. For some different characterizations of this topic, try *How Republicans Stole Religion* by Bill Press; *Jesus is Not a Republican,* a compilation of essays and excerpts edited by Clint Willis and Nate Hardcastle; and *Why the Christian Right is Wrong* by Robin Meyers. From the very beginning of Christendom until now, examination and criticism of Christian attitudes and behaviors via Biblical exegesis has required frequent and compassionate reiteration, so hopefully such efforts will continue.

At this point we have a loose framework that begins to define what personal, interpersonal and transpersonal activism looks like in the kingdom of God. So far, we have only the barest hints of a progressive philosophy. These include the encouragements to trust in governmental authority, pay taxes unflinchingly, help others in self-sacrificing ways, be as inclusive as possible, resist the entrapment of tradition and culture, and avoid striving for worldly power and control over others. The prioritization of goodwill towards everyone is explicit, with a primary mechanism for faith-in-action clearly defined as compassionate service backed by diligent self-examination and prayer. But what about specifics that relate to current conventions, institutions and concerns? What about waging war? What about environmentalism and civil liberties? What about corporate capitalism? In the following chapters, we'll explore these topics and more to reveal that the New Testament in fact promotes a progressive approach in nearly every one of these arenas, defining "compassionate service" itself in emphatically progressive ways.

Sex, Money & War

I think that the more time we spend exploring scripture, the more examples of progressive ideology we will find. But there are some important prerequisites to understanding the New Testament in this light. Foremost among these is disconnecting our interpretation and assumptions from the cultural backdrop of our times and – to whatever extent possible – the many previous assertions and associations that have been made regarding the Bible and Christianity throughout history. Considering the power and pervasiveness of these influences and prejudices, this is a tall order. However, if we allow the Divine Light within to guide us, we can liberate ourselves from the darkness of external programming, and effectively apply each component of our hermeneutic.

The process of freeing ourselves from the dominant memes of our society can often be solitary and self-isolating. Even Jesus himself sought solitary places to pray (Matthew 14:22-24, Mark 1:35-37, Luke 5:15-16), and withdrew from humanity for forty days and forty nights to confront his own temptations (Matthew 4:1-11). And I believe the intrusions of cultural programming are just that – a series of temptations and distractions from reliance on our inner voice and a clarity of communion with our conscience – in the Christian idiom: cultural programming drowns out the law of God written on our hearts and the promptings of holy spirit. So to separate ourselves for a time from all those external clamorings for attention and priority, and to learn how to listen to our innermost whisperings, is a mandatory practice that will help us discern the many liberating themes of scripture. In order to do this, we require solitude and voluntary isolation on a regular basis. We require time alone – apart from family, friends, our community of support, and other people – to acquaint ourselves with both angels and demons, to clearly differentiate the voice of the Divine from the many pressures and expectations of the world.

To gain the discernment required to appreciate the radically advanced tone of the New Testament, we will need to develop a strong practice of separation and involution. This intuitive component of our interpretive method requires careful and consistent application. We might call it prayer, or meditation, or simply quieting the clamoring of our mind, heart and body until we can clearly hear Divine murmurings. But the more subtle and nuanced our tools are, the more subtle and nuanced our observations will be. In a way, encouraging such practice is much more effective than elaborating upon its fruits in a book. But I also believe it is useful to capture those fruits on the page, to journal them for ourselves and even share them with others – mainly because they are so fleeting, and because the context of our lives and times is constantly changing. With that in mind, let's dive into some of the readily identifiable progressive themes in New Testament scripture, acknowledging that these are glimpses of a Light that only our innermost, spiritual self can fully comprehend.

Gradations of Celibacy

In recent years, the topic of celibacy has often been sullied by so many competing ideas and unfortunate tragedies that its original meaning has been obscured. In first century Judea, celibacy would not have been a completely foreign idea, but it would not have been associated with Jewish religious practices. Instead, it would have been observed historically more among Ethiopian, Greek, Egyptian and Roman culture, where male slaves were castrated to make them better suited to obedient service. It should be noted that this asexuality sometimes included sexual service, but with a much reduced sex drive. It would make sense, however, that such eunuchs would be used to exemplify the deprioritization of sexual activity. Perhaps some people were also familiar with the devotees of the Greek goddess Hestia and Roman goddess Vesta, women who pledged themselves to celibacy to better serve the Goddess. However, Jesus' disciples would certainly have been surprised to hear him offer the following:

> He said to them: "Not everyone can make room for this saying, but only those to whom it has been given. There are eunuchs who were born from their mother's womb that way. There are eunuchs were made eunuchs by men. And there are eunuchs who have made eunuchs of themselves on account of the kingdom of heaven. The one who is able to make room for this should do so."
>
> *Matthew 19:11-12*

Later on, the Apostle Paul takes up the topic in more detail in 1 Corinthians 7, making many pronouncements. He writes (WEB):

> Now concerning the things about which you wrote to me: it is good for a man not to touch a woman. But, because of sexual immoralities, let each man have his own wife, and let each woman have her own husband. Let the husband render to his wife the affection owed her, and likewise also the wife to her husband. The wife doesn't have authority over her own body, but the husband. Likewise also the husband doesn't have authority over his own body, but the wife. Don't deprive one another, unless it is by consent for a season, that you may give yourselves to fasting and prayer, and may be together again, that Satan doesn't tempt you because of your lack of self-control. But this I say by way of concession, not of commandment. Yet I wish that all men were like me. However each man has his own gift from God, one of this kind, and another of that kind. But I say to the unmarried and to widows, it is good for them if they remain even as I am. But if they don't have self-control, let them marry. For it's better to marry than to burn.
>
> *1 Corinthians 7:1-9*

> Now concerning virgins, I have no commandment from the Lord, but I give my judgment as one who has obtained mercy from the Lord to be trustworthy. I think that it is good therefore, because of the distress that is on us, that it is good for a man to be as he is. Are you bound to a wife? Don't seek to be freed. Are you free from a wife? Don't seek a wife. But if you marry, you have not sinned. If a virgin marries, she has not sinned. Yet such will have oppression in the flesh, and I want to spare you. But I say this, brothers: the time is short, that from now on, both those who have wives may be as though they had none; and those who weep, as though they didn't weep; and those who rejoice, as though they didn't rejoice; and those who buy, as though they didn't possess; and those who use the world, as not using it to the fullest. For the mode of this world passes away. But I desire to have you to be free from cares. He who is unmarried is concerned for the things of the Lord,

> how he may please the Lord; but he who is married is concerned about the things of the world, how he may please his wife. There is also a difference between a wife and a virgin. The unmarried woman cares about the things of the Lord, that she may be holy both in body and in spirit. But she who is married cares about the things of the world--how she may please her husband. This I say for your own profit; not that I may ensnare you, but for that which is appropriate, and that you may attend to the Lord without distraction.
>
> *1 Corinthians 7:25-35*

And, out of all the writings of the New Testament, this is pretty much all we have on the topic that is clear and unambiguous. We do have other hints, however, such as (WEB):

> Peter said, "Look, we have left everything, and followed you." He said to them, "Most certainly I tell you, there is no one who has left house, or wife, or brothers, or parents, or children, for the Kingdom of God's sake, who will not receive many times more in this time, and in the world to come, eternal life."
>
> *Luke 18:28-30*

But, aside from an additional reference in Revelation 14:4 to 144,000 virgins who would be welcomed into Jesus' kingdom before anyone else, that's pretty much all of it. Yet despite this paucity of Biblical discourse, the aim of celibate asexuality became a hallmark of spiritually committed Christian men and women over the intervening centuries. Why? Because of the rationale both Jesus and Paul offer us regarding a reprioritization of sexual desires: that those who remain free of distraction can devote themselves more fully to God and service to His kingdom. Jesus of course exemplified this, as did Paul. Paul further adds that he is concerned about there being little time before "the world in its present form" passes away – presumably an allusion to the second coming of Christ – so this added some urgency to his encouragement. Yet both Jesus and Paul make it clear that this teaching isn't for everyone, but only for those who can accept it and bear it without being continually overwhelmed by sexual urges. This avoidance of sexual entanglement is not characterized so much as a moral imperative, but as a spiritually profitable choice. Asexuality simply places *agape* above *eros* – unconditional spiritual love above erotic or romantic love – as a facilitator of committed intentions. Compassionate service is amplified, while all other types of relationship are attenuated.

Returning to another aspect of our hermeneutic, I'll offer some firsthand experiential insight into this topic. At age nineteen I chose to be celibate for one year. Through my reading of the New Testament at that time, prayer over my course of action, and discussion with Christian mentors, I decided to do more than just abstain from sex. I also decided to avoid sexually objectifying women; as Jesus said in Matthew 5:28 (WEB), "everyone who gazes at a woman to lust after her has committed adultery with her already in his heart." So this meant abstaining from sexual thoughts, sexual fantasies and, to my understanding at that time, any and all forms of sexual gratification.

Many people have experienced the positive benefits of fasting as part of their spiritual discipline. It is liberating to prioritize the nourishment of the mind, heart and soul by temporarily excluding nourishment to the physical body. Abstaining from sexual thoughts and gratifications can have a similar effect. Over the course of that year, my experience of a purifying, strengthening and clarifying impact on mind, heart, spirit and body increased exponentially. At first, it seemed as though both my flesh and imagination became more and more insistent that I indulge sexual needs and fantasies. After a few weeks, however, something miraculous occurred: the strength of those sexual urges faded, and I began to sense a connection to other people I had never felt before. Irrespective of gender, age, race and seemingly any other human variable, I felt a deepening, unconditional affection for others…for everyone in fact. My appreciation and celebration of everyone I met – even my sense of who was beautiful and attractive – changed completely. I began to sense the miracle of each person's being. And suddenly it all made sense. When I freed myself from what admittedly had been the primarily sexual focus of an adolescent male, I was able to love much more freely and equally. Without really being aware of it, all of my previous interactions had been unconsciously colored with the prioritization of self-serving intimacy and sexual gratification on some level. The only people I had thought were beautiful were the women I wanted to have sex with. But now I could enjoy others and give of myself without any thought to the consequences such interactions might have on my ability to garner affection, closeness or sex.

There was, however, one other, less fortunate consequence of my year-long celibacy. Because I had become so detached from my sexual desires, I gradually lost the ability to navigate sexual attraction at all. That is, after eleven months had passed, I abruptly found myself physically drawn to a young woman, but I had no idea how to manage my feelings. It was as if all the pent up desire of the past year was suddenly focused on someone, and I was completely off-balance. As a result, I allowed sexual desires to overtake all others and ardently pursued them. Soon the young woman and I were sexually involved, and many of my spiritual interests and disciplines – and most notably my devotion to serving others – were pushed aside in favor of romantic love.

This development seemed to illustrate for me the logic of the Apostle Paul's advice about marriage, and in fact that young woman and I did eventually get married. Now, some twenty-six years later, after a number of sexually rewarding relationships, I do not know if I could muster the discipline to remain so holistically celibate for an entire year. However, Paul suggests that for the purposes of prayer even short, mutually agreed upon periods of abstinence can be beneficial – and these, at least, are fairly easy to manage. But that year was my firsthand experience of celibacy, an experience from which I concluded that celibacy was in fact a spiritually profitable practice, but required both vigilance and, for many people like me, moderation. From this lesson, observations of many people I have counseled, and the New Testament writings on the topic, I have concluded that Christians would do best to be as celibate as possible in order to better serve God, but not so inflexibly that they become distracted or sabotaged by their own physical needs. That is, to practice whatever gradation of celibacy they are able in order to prioritize *agape* above *eros* in their daily lives. In recent history the world has become aware of the horrible consequences of rigidly imposed celibacy, as the tens of thousands of sexual abuses committed by Roman Catholic clergy came to light; if you have not seen Amy Berg's documentary about this issue, *Deliver Us from Evil,* I recommend it. Nevertheless, the benefits of voluntary sexual self-control and an asexual self-concept are numerous – however we can achieve them according to our own inclinations and capacities. If spiritually-minded folks can arrive at the most suitable gradation of personal celibacy in a pragmatic way, a broad continuum of mental, emotional and spiritual benefits readily come into view.

Looking at the larger picture, is there anything particularly progressive about an asexual identity? This is where things become interesting. Let's consider some of the consequences of Christians adhering to gradations of celibacy as a baseline expectation. Think of how different our planet would be if all the Christians in the world followed this teaching. Consider how history would have unfolded if this had been the norm since the first century. It probably would have resulted in lower populations in Christianized areas of the globe, with numerous beneficial consequences. For example, less competition for resources; less conflict, aggression and poverty as the result of competition; proportionally less pollution and denigration of the environment; slower reduction of natural habitats and resources; lower rates of disease, hunger, malnutrition and other human suffering; and so on. To fully appreciate the positive impact of reduced human populations and slowed population growth, please take a look at the information at www.populationconnection.org. Though it has not been a particularly popular approach, controlling human population has decidedly progressive implications for both society and planet Earth.

There are certainly those who would insist that anything seeming like suppression of sexual desires is extremely unhealthy. Others might say that a better approach is to sublimate sexual drives into mental, creative, expressive, mystical or other transformative energies. Regardless, a broad acceptance of celibacy is just as radical an idea today as it was in Jesus' time, and I would maintain that its potential impact readily aligns with many progressive principles. To shift the central dynamics of human relationships away from sexual satisfaction into a more platonic, mutually beneficial attitude of service could potentially transform the human species into a much more constructive force – for human society and the Earth as a whole. That is not to say that sexual attraction could not or should not retain an important place in human relationships – but what if that place was subordinate to compassionate, unconditional affection for everyone and everything? That is, what if human beings cared more about the greater good, the welfare and happiness of the whole, than their own individual gratification, reproduction, or sexual connection with a partner? What if Christians put the good of All above the good of themselves and their families? Isn't that what the New Testament exhorts them to do? Isn't that the heart of self-sacrifice in devotion to the Sacred? After all, according to Jesus, whatever we give up for the kingdom of God, we will receive many times over in this life and in the eternal hereafter – so, really, celibacy becomes more an issue of healthy and productive self-discipline than perpetual suppression or hardship. According to the New Testament, unless Christians wish to be one of the 144,000 virgins referenced in Revelation 14, sex remains an available option, but its importance changes.

Sexuality has undergone many evolutions during my lifetime, and on many different fronts here in the U.S. There was the "free love" movement and FDA approval of birth control pills in the sixties; feminist empowerment, The Joy of Sex, Cosmo and Penthouse in the seventies; the poppers fad, fears about HIV/AIDS, Madonna, and a watershed increase in unmarried teen birth rates in the eighties; webcam cybersex, Ecstasy, Viagra and "don't ask don't tell" in the nineties; an explosion of digitally animated pornography, a steady decline in overall abortions, and efforts to legalize same-sex marriage during the past decade; and a thousand other data points. All of these changes have had an impact on the accessibility of sex, social attitudes about sex, the safety of sex, and popular conceptions of acceptable sexuality and sexual identity. All we can say for certain is that sex has been a reliable constant in human culture, and that it likely won't fade away any time soon. So the balancing act in raising the issues of celibate practice or asexual identity is not to cast them in black-and-white, do-or-die proscriptions, but to introduce the subtle shades of desire and love that inform the most spiritually constructive evolutionary path.

And that is really the essence of the matter as I see it. So often sexual self-discipline is painted in the stark contrasts of Freudian imperatives vs. Puritanical oppression. But in my estimation the celibacy of the New Testament isn't about guilt, shame, suppression, or a moral indictment of sexuality. It's about promoting a specific flavor of motivation and orientation to ourselves and others. It's about committing to something bigger than ourselves, enlarging the realm of our affections, and celebrating that expansion of love above everything else. It is really no different than any other form of self-management for the greater good. To whatever degree each and every Christian can practice gradations of celibacy in this context, it seems to be a blessing to all generations present and future, to the Earth's systems and all its plants and creatures.

Of course, in what strikes me as a great irony, much of Christendom has traditionally focused on the importance of unhindered procreation instead of asexual identity or any gradation of celibacy at all. In the context of the New Testament, this focus has little basis, and is an unsupportable religious doctrine if we rely solely on that scripture. In fact, if we were to follow Paul's advice, we could easily assert that having children is not always a good idea even when Christians do get married – for just like remaining a virgin, or unmarried, or married, or whatever condition a Christian finds themselves in when first called to the faith, remaining childless would also seem prudent using the same reasoning. As Paul says in 1 Corinthians 7:17(NIV), "Nevertheless, each one should retain the place in life that the lord assigned to him, and to which God has called him." In this sense, individual reproductive rights certainly conform to the core considerations of Christian celibacy, and family planning actually facilitates this underlying intention. After all, there is only one place in all of the New Testament that encourages Christians to have children, and that is in 1 Timothy. Even if we can trust the sincerity and authenticity of this epistle (and, as we will explore, I have serious doubts about both), is it really wise for Christians to rely on just a couple of verses in one ancient letter to inform their life path and behaviors?

Based on the spirit of New Testament instruction and examples and my own experience, I believe Christians should attempt to remain celibate and childless in order to better serve the kingdom of God – to whatever degree they are able to do so. Getting married as quickly as possible, or having as many children as possible, are antithetical to *agape*. Each of these choices is a deliberate compromise that preserves the sanity and practicality of the Christian religion in secular society. As Paul says, these choices are "concessions," and not the main purpose to which Christians are called. Investing all of our hearts, minds and resources in our family does not amplify the love of Christ in the world in the same way that celibate, non-reproductive practices do – as long as those practices are pursued with the right intentions. So between the extremes of reflexive sexual gratification and ascetic self-denial is a constructive discipline that purifies the mind, heart and body in the same way regular fasting can. Indeed, it is not possible for most people to live without food, but, as Jesus reminded us, we do not live on bread alone. Our spiritual life is important, critical to our well-being and the well-being of humanity. In this context, to emphasize compassionate service above sex or romance is simply to prioritize what is loving and supportive for the greatest good possible.

Still, there is one last question coloring the edges of this discussion, and that is whether sexuality can in itself be spiritual. As a mystic, I believe that sexual energy (or, more accurately, vital energy that is expressed as sexual drive) can be harnessed to activate spiritual perception-cognition, and that this particular portal into mystical awareness is as viable as any other. I have experienced this mainly in the context of certain forms of Yoga and Taoist meditation, but I see no reason why any devoted Christian would not be able to experience the same redirection of their sexual-vital drive into spiritual awakening and connection with God. Indeed, however we become intimate with the Divine, that connection has correlations with the feelings of oneness experienced during genuine intimacy – sexual or otherwise. But is this view supported by New Testament scripture? Not particularly. Of course, the metaphor of a bridegroom is used to characterize the relationship between Jesus and his followers throughout the New Testament (Matthew 25, Mark 2:18-20, John 3:27-30, Revelation chapters 18 through 22), but there is nothing definitive in these verses about the consummation of the wedding night.

The Purpose of Money

There are few things as contentious in this life as our relationship with money, and no shortage in the U.S. of distorted sales pitches on how money integrates with spirituality and Christendom. However, the New Testament teachings regarding material wealth are fairly straightforward and difficult to convolute when taken as a whole. Here are some of the more direct and pertinent verses (ESV):

> "Do not lay up for yourselves treasures on earth, where moth and rust destroy and where thieves break in and steal, but lay up for yourselves treasures in heaven, where neither moth nor rust destroys and where thieves do not break in and steal. For where your treasure is, there your heart will be also."
>
> *Matthew 6:19-21*

And Jesus entered the temple and drove out all who sold and bought in the temple, and he overturned the tables of the money-changers and the seats of those who sold pigeons. He said to them, "It is written, 'My house shall be called a house of prayer,' but you make it a den of robbers."

Matthew 21:12-13

And as he was setting out on his journey, a man ran up and knelt before him and asked him, "Good Teacher, what must I do to inherit eternal life?" And Jesus said to him, "Why do you call me good? No one is good except God alone. You know the commandments: 'Do not murder, Do not commit adultery, Do not steal, Do not bear false witness, Do not defraud, Honor your father and mother.'" And he said to him, "Teacher, all these I have kept from my youth." And Jesus, looking at him, loved him, and said to him, "You lack one thing: go, sell all that you have and give to the poor, and you will have treasure in heaven; and come, follow me." Disheartened by the saying, he went away sorrowful, for he had great possessions. And Jesus looked around and said to his disciples, "How difficult it will be for those who have wealth to enter the kingdom of God!" And the disciples were amazed at his words. But Jesus said to them again, "Children, how difficult it is to enter the kingdom of God! It is easier for a camel to go through the eye of a needle than for a rich person to enter the kingdom of God."

Mark 10:17-25

And he sat down opposite the treasury and watched the people putting money into the offering box. Many rich people put in large sums. And a poor widow came and put in two small copper coins, which make a penny. And he called his disciples to him and said to them, "Truly, I say to you, this poor widow has put in more than all those who are contributing to the offering box. For they all contributed out of their abundance, but she out of her poverty has put in everything she had, all she had to live on."

Mark 12:41-44

And he lifted up his eyes on his disciples, and said: "Blessed are you who are poor, for yours is the kingdom of God. Blessed are you who are hungry now, for you shall be satisfied. Blessed are you who weep now, for you shall laugh. Blessed are you when people hate you and when they exclude you and revile you and spurn your name as evil, on account of the Son of Man! Rejoice in that day, and leap for joy, for behold, your reward is great in heaven; for so their fathers did to the prophets. But woe to you who are rich, for you have received your consolation. Woe to you who are full now, for you shall be hungry. Woe to you who laugh now, for you shall mourn and weep. Woe to you, when all people speak well of you, for so their fathers did to the false prophets."

Luke 6:20-26

Now the parable is this: The seed is the word of God. The ones along the path are those who have heard; then the devil comes and takes away the word from their hearts, so that they may not believe and be saved. And the ones on the rock are those who, when they hear the word, receive it with joy. But these have no root; they believe for a while, and in time of testing fall away. And as for what fell among the thorns, they are those who hear, but as they go on their way they are choked by the cares and riches and pleasures of life, and their fruit does not mature. As for that in the good soil, they are those who, hearing the word, hold it fast in an honest and good heart, and bear fruit with patience.

Luke 8:11-15

And he said to his disciples, "Therefore I tell you, do not be anxious about your life, what you will eat, nor about your body, what you will put on. For life is more than food, and the body more than clothing. Consider the ravens: they neither sow nor reap, they have neither storehouse nor barn, and yet God feeds them. Of how much more value are you than the birds! And which of you by being anxious can add a single hour to his span of life? If then you are not able to do as small a thing as that, why are you anxious about the rest? Consider the lilies, how they grow: they neither toil nor spin, yet I tell you, even Solomon in all his glory was not arrayed like one of these. But if God so clothes the grass, which is alive in the field today, and tomorrow is thrown into the oven, how much more will he clothe you, O you of little faith! And do not seek what you are to eat and what you are to drink, nor be worried. For all the nations of the world seek after these things, and your Father knows that you need them. Instead, seek his kingdom, and these things will be added to you. Fear not, little flock, for it is your Father's good pleasure to give you the kingdom. Sell your possessions, and give to the needy. Provide yourselves with moneybags that do not grow old, with a treasure in the heavens that does not fail, where no thief approaches and no moth destroys. For where your treasure is, there will your heart be also.

Luke 12:22-34

"And I tell you, make friends for yourselves by means of unrighteous wealth, so that when it fails they may receive you into the eternal dwellings. One who is faithful in a very little is also faithful in much, and one who is dishonest in a very little is also dishonest in much. If then you have not been faithful in the unrighteous wealth, who will entrust to you the true riches? And if you have not been faithful in that which is another's, who will give you that which is your own? No servant can serve two masters, for either he will hate the one and love the other, or he will be devoted to the one and despise the other. You cannot serve God and money." The Pharisees, who were lovers of money, heard all these things, and they ridiculed him. And he said to them, "You are those who justify yourselves before men, but God knows your hearts. For what is exalted among men is an abomination in the sight of God."

Luke 16:9-15

Before reading further, please take this opportunity to meditate, pray, and/or reflect upon all of these verses, discussing them with others and seeing how they apply to your own life. Try to maintain a neutral disposition throughout. What do they tell you about a Christ-like attitude towards material wealth, its use and its accumulation?

The principles we can assemble from these verses are not confusing. There are no exceptions, no subtle deviations, no nuanced interpretations that relieve us of the simple truth: worldly riches distract and divert human beings from the kingdom of God. How should Christians deal with wealth, then? Here some of the more specific conclusions this scripture offers:

1. Christians should not accumulate wealth, or concern themselves with material gain, or be worried about their material needs being met, but place their faith in God and do good works instead.

2. Among those good works, Christians should use whatever wealth they have to help those in need.

Are these same sentiments perpetuated later in the New Testament, after Jesus had left the Church in the hands of his apostles? Take a moment to apply our hermeneutic to these verses as well (ESV):

..ow the full number of those who believed were of one heart and soul, and no one said that any of the things that belonged to him was his own, but they had everything in common. And with great power the apostles were giving their testimony to the resurrection of the Lord Jesus, and great grace was upon them all. There was not a needy person among them, for as many as were owners of lands or houses sold them and brought the proceeds of what was sold and laid it at the apostles' feet, and it was distributed to each as any had need.

Acts 4:32-35

I coveted no one's silver or gold or apparel. You yourselves know that these hands ministered to my necessities and to those who were with me. In all things I have shown you that by working hard in this way we must help the weak and remember the words of the Lord Jesus, how he himself said, 'It is more blessed to give than to receive.'"

Acts 20:33-35

Now concerning the collection for the saints: as I directed the churches of Galatia, so you also are to do. On the first day of every week, each of you is to put something aside and store it up, as he may prosper, so that there will be no collecting when I come. And when I arrive, I will send those whom you accredit by letter to carry your gift to Jerusalem.

1 Corinthians 16:1-3

I rejoiced in the Lord greatly that now at length you have revived your concern for me. You were indeed concerned for me, but you had no opportunity. Not that I am speaking of being in need, for I have learned in whatever situation I am to be content. I know how to be brought low, and I know how to abound. In any and every circumstance, I have learned the secret of facing plenty and hunger, abundance and need. I can do all things through him who strengthens me.

Philippians 4:10-13

Now we command you, brothers, in the name of our Lord Jesus Christ, that you keep away from any brother who is walking in idleness and not in accord with the tradition that you received from us. For you yourselves know how you ought to imitate us, because we were not idle when we were with you, nor did we eat anyone's bread without paying for it, but with toil and labor we worked night and day, that we might not be a burden to any of you. It was not because we do not have that right, but to give you in ourselves an example to imitate. For even when we were with you, we would give you this command: If anyone is not willing to work, let him not eat. For we hear that some among you walk in idleness, not busy at work, but busybodies. Now such persons we command and encourage in the Lord Jesus Christ to do their work quietly and to earn their own living.

2 Thessalonians 3:6-12

If anyone teaches a different doctrine and does not agree with the sound words of our Lord Jesus Christ and the teaching that accords with godliness, he is puffed up with conceit and understands nothing. He has an unhealthy craving for controversy and for quarrels about words, which produce envy, dissension, slander, evil suspicions, and constant friction among people who are depraved in mind and deprived of the truth, imagining that godliness is a means of gain. Now there is great gain in godliness with contentment, for we brought nothing into the world, and we cannot take anything out of the world. But if we have food and clothing, with these we will be content. But those who desire to be rich fall into temptation, into a snare, into many senseless and harmful desires that plunge people into ruin and destruction. For the love of money is a root of all kinds of evils. It is through this craving that some have wandered away from the faith and pierced themselves with many pangs.

1 Timothy 6:3-10

Keep your life free from love of money, and be content with what you have, for he has said, "I will never leave you nor forsake you." So we can confidently say, "The Lord is my helper; I will not fear; what can man do to me?" Remember your leaders, those who spoke to you the word of God. Consider the outcome of their way of life, and imitate their faith. Jesus Christ is the same yesterday and today and forever.

Hebrews 13:5-8

Come now, you rich, weep and howl for the miseries that are coming upon you. Your riches have rotted and your garments are moth-eaten. Your gold and silver have corroded, and their corrosion will be evidence against you and will eat your flesh like fire. You have laid up treasure in the last days. Behold, the wages of the laborers who mowed your fields, which you kept back by fraud, are crying out against you, and the cries of the harvesters have reached the ears of the Lord of hosts. You have lived on the earth in luxury and in self-indulgence. You have fattened your hearts in a day of slaughter. You have condemned and murdered the righteous person. He does not resist you.

James 5:1-6

So I exhort the elders among you, as a fellow elder and a witness of the sufferings of Christ, as well as a partaker in the glory that is going to be revealed: shepherd the flock of God that is among you, exercising oversight, not under compulsion, but willingly, as God would have you; not for shameful gain, but eagerly; not domineering over those in your charge, but being examples to the flock.

1 Peter 5:1-3

Here we see an expansion of the original principles – variations on the same theme:

1. In the early Church, the needs of any and all believers were met by other believers who had the means to do so.

2. Christians were encouraged to work for their sustenance, but also to be content in all situations – even with a simple minimum of clothing and food.

3. The desire to become wealthy, to gain financially from the Church, or to in any way become enamored with money was considered repulsive by the apostles and a hindrance to spiritual practice and growth.

There are other monetary principles woven throughout the New Testament, some of which we have already covered. For example, the obligation to pay taxes to support governing authorities. There is also one story in Acts 5 where a married couple, Ananias and Sapphira, tried to withhold some of their wealth from service to the holy spirit, and were struck dead for it. I'm sure this has proved useful to many Church leaders asking for donations over the years. But the tenor of every verse, warning, or story relating to money in the New Testament is essentially the same: Christians should not allow themselves to become preoccupied with the pursuit of wealth, but instead give generously to everyone in need, be content with the most basic of needs being met, and devote themselves to doing good. The implication here is that it is simply not necessary to accrue wealth in order to do good.

When we compare this instruction to the pervasive habits found in modern Christendom, and especially the evolutions of the Church in the U.S., it is once again difficult to reconcile New Testament principles with the current state of conservative Christianity. On an individual level, the horrific distortion of these principles to fatten the purses of Christians via prosperity theology, televangelist fundraising, pyramid schemes and other capitalist takeovers of God's kingdom is both reprehensible and obvious in its self-delusion. On a collective level, Christian support of neoliberal economics, Libertarian ideals and other free market approaches to the world's pressing problems is either the most shameful of deceptions or the deepest and most harmful form of denial. How many warnings, explanations, examples and encouragements will it take to steer errant believers away from such false doctrines? The New Testament is full of them, but many modern-day Christians have clearly chosen faith in mammon over faith in God.

Interestingly, where we see both Jesus and Paul offering alternate paths for those who could not embrace a life without sex, no such exception is offered to those who could not live without their wealth. In Jesus' teachings, over and over again we see that it is relatively easy for adulterers, prostitutes, tax collectors and other "sinners" to enter the kingdom of God, but it is extremely difficult for someone attached to their wealth to enter the kingdom, almost as if such attachment interferes more profoundly with spiritual faith than any other condition. Loving money, desiring financial security, pursuing wealth, being stingy with what we have when others are in need...all of these appear to be at the top of the holy spirit's "highly objectionable" list. At one point, in Luke 16, a wealthy man is cast into the flames of hell, while the poor beggar who slept by his gate is swept up to heaven. Why? The story implies that being wealthy is itself a crime in the kingdom of God – at least if you have a poor beggar sleeping by your front door all the time. That is, to retain creature comforts in the presence of abject need is spiritually offensive, and there does not appear to be any exception to this rule anywhere in the New Testament.

The incongruity of these conclusions about wealth with many aspects of modern U.S. culture is readily apparent. But can these be described as progressive tendencies? When we read Jesus' advice to the wealthy, or what happens in Acts among the first believers who receive the holy spirit and divide up their belongings, or how Paul instructs the churches in Galatia and Corinth to support those in need, a startling turn of phrase bubbles to the surface in summarizing scriptural exhortations: "From each according to their ability, to each according to their need." And where did we get this phrase? From Karl Marx, of course, as he described how a communist society should function in his *Critique of the*

Gotha Program. Despite Marx's treatment of religion as a "sigh of the oppressed" and "illusory happiness" in writings such as his *Critique of Hegel's Philosophy of Right*, it appears that what he considered to be a progressive evolution of industrial and societal structures preceded him by a two-thousand-year-old religious document. For the primary thrust of New Testament teachings regarding wealth has distinctly socialist and indeed Marxist overtones, advocating common ownership over private property, cooperation over competition, and ensuring the welfare of those most in need above rewarding only those with cunning or merit.

How could things have gone so awry in America? How could "one nation under God" have gotten this so wrong? How could Christians in the U.S. have become so enamored of free enterprise, competitive capitalism, and highly commercialized religion that they ignore the clear guidance of scripture? And how could they so often have joined with conservatives in an angry opposition to socialist and Marxist ideals throughout U.S. history? I think that, at least in part, this once again demonstrates the principle of a dominant cultural meme – in this case a materialistic one – overtaking religious memes. The capitalist spirit of America is so strong that it has enslaved all other spirits to its domineering drive, and Christianity is just one more casualty of its aggressive market-based ideology.

There is one story in the New Testament that actually praises profit, and that is the "Parable of the Talents" in Matthew 25. Take a moment to read it in whatever translation is convenient to you, then consider what it means. The parable describes how a master about to set off on a long journey gave three of his servants some money. Two of the servants invested it and made more money, while one buried his portion in the ground out of fear of the master's wrath. When the master returned, he praised the two servants who had made a profit, and harshly rebuked the one who had buried his portion in the ground out of fear, taking away his money and casting him out "into the outer darkness."

Like all other parables about the kingdom of God, everything here is metaphorical and was never meant to be taken literally. Just like the Parable of the Ten Virgins didn't mean Christians should hoard lamp oil, or the Parable of the Sower didn't mean Christians should go around scattering actual seeds everywhere, or the Parable of the Mustard seed didn't mean that the kingdom of God exists solely to create shade for nesting birds, and so on. Jesus himself instructs his disciples that such parables should not be taken literally. As it says in Luke 8:9-10 (ESV): "And when his disciples asked him what this parable meant, he said, 'To you it has been given to know the secrets of the kingdom of God, but for others they are in parables, so that 'seeing they may not see, and hearing they may not understand.''" If we want to see and understand, we need to look beyond the literal.

At the end of the Parable of the Talents, Jesus says in Matthew 25:29 (ESV): "For to everyone who has will more be given, and he will have an abundance. But from the one who has not, even what he has will be taken away." So are the "talents" in this parable material resources, or are they spiritual insight and wisdom? Does the metaphor allude a Christian's responsibility regarding the wealth they accumulate, or rather what they should be doing with the good news of Jesus' message? Is someone who follows Christ supposed to make themselves rich so that they can give more money to God on Judgment Day, or are they supposed to store up good works of loving service, treasures in heaven, *spiritually profitable thoughts and deeds?* I think the answer is obvious, and amply reinforced by other scripture. However, many Christian conservatives seem to have hardened their hearts to the obvious, and so in some circles a literal interpretation of this parable has tended to outweigh the plethora of verses advising against the prioritization of mammon in the kingdom of God.

According to nearly all other New Testament teachings, following Christ is completely incompatible with amassing enormous amounts of wealth, and even more incompatible with the combative and often deceptive business practices so frequently required to do so in the U.S.. And yet huge swaths of Americans who self-identify as Christians routinely buy stock in unscrupulous corporations, indulge in flagrantly excessive consumerism, vote to support legislation that enlarges corporate dominance and destructive business practices, and elect politicians who proclaim loudly and unabashedly that true freedom in America is synonymous with unrestrained greed. In fact, if the approximately 80% of Americans who profess to be a Christian actually followed New Testament teachings regarding avarice, materialism and self-serving opportunism, America's competitive, consumerist, commercialistic system would either collapse entirely or evolve in a very different direction.

Of course, there are exceptions to this obsession with materialism among Christians. There are the Jesuit's vows of poverty, chastity and obedience. There is the striving for plainness, humility and separation from the world among the Amish. There is the eschewing of ostentation among Lutherans. In my own experience of different Christian communities, I have known many believers who tithed regularly, disciplined their hearts against greed and overconsumption, and devoted themselves to helping others with every means possible. Despite the worldly aspirations and misdeeds of many Christian conservatives, the more progressive principles of the New Testament regarding wealth are in fact subscribed to by countless believers – and I sincerely hope that such people are blessed in their humility and diligence. Nevertheless, we can clearly see how the enculturation of competitive, avaricious tribal tendencies has tended to trump more erudite spiritual memes in America. That the socialistic function ascribed to wealth in the New Testament cannot be reconciled with American capitalism is not surprising; what is surprising is that modern conservative Christians seem profoundly blind to their hypocrisy in this regard. Devotion to the power of free market capitalism and devotion to the God of Jesus Christ have always been – and likely always will be – utterly at odds with each other.

A Commission of Nonviolence in the Face of Evil

What was Jesus' position regarding anger, violence and aggression? And what does he impart about peaceful thoughts, intentions and conduct? How should Christians react to evil? Here are some relevant verses from the New International Version (NIV):

> "Blessed are the peacemakers, for they will be called sons of God."
>
> *Matthew 5:9*

> "You have heard that it was said to the people long ago, 'Do not murder, and anyone who murders will be subject to judgment.' But I tell you that anyone who is angry with his brother will be subject to judgment. Again, anyone who says to his brother, 'Raca,' is answerable to the Sanhedrin.

But anyone who says, 'You fool!' will be in danger of the fire of hell. Therefore, if you are offering your gift at the altar and there remember that your brother has something against you, leave your gift there in front of the altar. First go and be reconciled to your brother; then come and offer your gift."

Matthew 5:21-24

"You have heard that it was said, 'Eye for eye, and tooth for tooth.' But I tell you, do not resist an evil person. If someone strikes you on the right cheek, turn to him the other also. And if someone wants to sue you and take your tunic, let him have your cloak as well. If someone forces you to go one mile, go with him two miles. Give to the one who asks you, and do not turn away from the one who wants to borrow from you. You have heard that it was said, 'Love your neighbor and hate your enemy.' But I tell you: Love your enemies and pray for those who persecute you, that you may be sons of your Father in heaven. He causes his sun to rise on the evil and the good, and sends rain on the righteous and the unrighteous."

Matthew 5:38-45

"Whoever acknowledges me before men, I will also acknowledge him before my Father in heaven. But whoever disowns me before men, I will disown him before my Father in heaven. Do not suppose that I have come to bring peace to the earth. I did not come to bring peace, but a sword. For I have come to turn 'a man against his father, a daughter against her mother, a daughter-in-law against her mother-in-law – a man's enemies will be the members of his own household.' Anyone who loves his father or mother more than me is not worthy of me; anyone who loves his son or daughter more than me is not worthy of me; and anyone who does not take his cross and follow me is not worthy of me. Whoever finds his life will lose it, and whoever loses his life for my sake will find it."

Matthew 10:32-39

From that time on Jesus began to explain to his disciples that he must go to Jerusalem and suffer many things at the hands of the elders, chief priests and teachers of the law, and that he must be killed and on the third day be raised to life. Peter took him aside and began to rebuke him. "Never, lord!" he said. "This shall never happen to you!" Jesus turned and said to Peter, "Get behind me, Satan! You are a stumbling block to me; you do not have in mind the things of God, but the things of men." Then Jesus said to his disciples, "If anyone would come after me, he must deny himself and take up his cross and follow me. For whoever wants to save his life will lose it, but whoever loses his life for me will find it. What good will it be for a man if he gains the whole world, yet forfeits his soul?"

Matthew 16:21-26

At that time the disciples came to Jesus and asked, "Who is the greatest in the kingdom of heaven?" He called a little child and had him stand among them. And he said: "I tell you the truth, unless you change and become like little children, you will never enter the kingdom of heaven. Therefore, whoever humbles himself like this child is the greatest in the kingdom of heaven. And whoever welcomes a little child like this in my name welcomes me. But if anyone causes one of these little ones who believe in me to sin, it would be better for him to have a large millstone hung around his neck and to be drowned in the depths of the sea. Woe to the world because of the things that cause people to sin! Such things must come, but woe to the man through whom they come! If your hand or your foot causes you to sin, cut it off and throw it away. It is better for you to enter life maimed or crippled than to have two hands or two feet and be thrown into eternal fire. And if your eye causes you to sin, gouge it out and throw it away. It is better for you to enter life with one eye than to have two eyes and be thrown into the fire of hell."

Matthew 18:1-9

Jesus replied, "Friend, do what you came for." Then the men stepped forward, seized Jesus and arrested him. With that, one of Jesus' companions reached for his sword, drew it out and struck the servant of the high priest, cutting off his ear. "Put your sword back in its place," Jesus said to him, "for all who draw the sword will die by the sword. Do you think I cannot call on my Father, and he will at once put at my disposal more than twelve legions of angels? But how then would the Scriptures be fulfilled that say it must happen in this way?"

Matthew 26:50-54

Then Jesus asked them, "Which is lawful on the Sabbath: to do good or to do evil, to save life or to kill?" But they remained silent. He looked around at them in anger and, deeply distressed at their stubborn hearts, said to the man, "Stretch out your hand." He stretched it out, and his hand was completely restored. Then the Pharisees went out and began to plot with the Herodians how they might kill Jesus.

Mark 3:4-6

The next day as they were leaving Bethany, Jesus was hungry. Seeing in the distance a fig tree in leaf, he went to find out if it had any fruit. When he reached it, he found nothing but leaves, because it was not the season for figs. Then he said to the tree, "May no one ever eat fruit from you again." And his disciples heard him say it. On reaching Jerusalem, Jesus entered the temple area and began driving out those who were buying and selling there. He overturned the tables of the money changers and the benches of those selling doves, and would not allow anyone to carry merchandise through the temple courts. And as he taught them, he said, "Is it not written: 'My house will be called a house of prayer for all nations'? But you have made it 'a den of robbers.'" The chief priests and the teachers of the law heard this and began looking for a way to kill him, for they feared him, because the whole crowd was amazed at his teaching. When evening came, they went out of the city. In the morning, as they went along, they saw the fig tree withered from the roots. Peter remembered and said to Jesus, "Rabbi, look! The fig tree you cursed has withered!" "Have faith in God," Jesus answered. "I tell you the truth, if anyone says to this mountain, 'Go, throw yourself into the sea,' and does not doubt in his heart but believes that what he says will happen, it will be done for him. Therefore I tell you, whatever you ask for in prayer, believe that you have received it, and it will be yours. And when you stand praying, if you hold anything against anyone, forgive him, so that your Father in heaven may forgive you your sins."

Mark 11:12-25

Later Jesus appeared to the Eleven as they were eating; he rebuked them for their lack of faith and their stubborn refusal to believe those who had seen him after he had risen.

Mark 16:14

In the synagogue there was a man possessed by a demon, an evil spirit. He cried out at the top of his voice, "Ha! What do you want with us, Jesus of Nazareth? Have you come to destroy us? I know who you are—the Holy One of God!" "Be quiet!" Jesus said sternly. "Come out of him!" Then the demon threw the man down before them all and came out without injuring him. All the people were amazed and said to each other, "What is this teaching? With authority and power he gives orders to evil spirits and they come out!" And the news about him spread throughout the surrounding area. Jesus left the synagogue and went to the home of Simon. Now Simon's mother-in-law was suffering from a high fever, and they asked Jesus to help her. So he bent over her and rebuked the fever, and it left her. She got up at once and began to wait on them. When the sun was setting, the people brought to Jesus all who had various kinds of sickness, and laying his hands on each one, he healed them. Moreover, demons came out of many people, shouting, "You are the Son of God!" But he rebuked them and would not allow them to speak, because they knew he was the Christ.

Luke 4:33-41

"But I tell you who hear me: Love your enemies, do good to those who hate you, bless those who curse you, pray for those who mistreat you. If someone strikes you on one cheek, turn to him the other also. If someone takes your cloak, do not stop him from taking your tunic. Give to everyone who asks you, and if anyone takes what belongs to you, do not demand it back. Do to others as you would have them do to you."

Luke 6:27-30

One day Jesus said to his disciples, "Let's go over to the other side of the lake." So they got into a boat and set out. As they sailed, he fell asleep. A squall came down on the lake, so that the boat was being swamped, and they were in great danger. The disciples went and woke him, saying, "Master, Master, we're going to drown!" He got up and rebuked the wind and the raging waters; the storm subsided, and all was calm. "Where is your faith?" he asked his disciples. In fear and amazement they asked one another, "Who is this? He commands even the winds and the water, and they obey him."

Luke 8:22-25

As the time approached for him to be taken up to heaven, Jesus resolutely set out for Jerusalem. And he sent messengers on ahead, who went into a Samaritan village to get things ready for him; but the people there did not welcome him, because he was heading for Jerusalem. When the disciples James and John saw this, they asked, "lord, do you want us to call fire down from heaven to destroy them?" But Jesus turned and rebuked them, and they went to another village.

Luke 9:51-56

"I have come to bring fire on the earth, and how I wish it were already kindled! But I have a baptism to undergo, and how distressed I am until it is completed! Do you think I came to bring peace on earth? No, I tell you, but division. From now on there will be five in one family divided against each other, three against two and two against three. They will be divided, father against son and son against father, mother against daughter and daughter against mother, mother-in-law against daughter-in-law and daughter-in-law against mother-in-law."

Luke 12:49-53

Then Jesus asked them, "When I sent you without purse, bag or sandals, did you lack anything?" "Nothing," they answered. He said to them, "But now if you have a purse, take it, and also a bag; and if you don't

> have a sword, sell your cloak and buy one. It is written: 'And he was numbered with the transgressors'; and I tell you that this must be fulfilled in me. Yes, what is written about me is reaching its fulfillment." The disciples said, "See, lord, here are two swords." "That is enough," he replied.
>
> *Luke* 22:35-38

> When Jesus' followers saw what was going to happen, they said, "lord, should we strike with our swords?" And one of them struck the servant of the high priest, cutting off his right ear. But Jesus answered, "No more of this!" And he touched the man's ear and healed him. Then Jesus said to the chief priests, the officers of the temple guard, and the elders, who had come for him, "Am I leading a rebellion, that you have come with swords and clubs? Every day I was with you in the temple courts, and you did not lay a hand on me. But this is your hour—when darkness reigns."
>
> *Luke* 22:49-53

> "All this I have spoken while still with you. But the Counselor, the holy spirit, whom the Father will send in my name, will teach you all things and will remind you of everything I have said to you. Peace I leave with you; my peace I give you. I do not give to you as the world gives. Do not let your hearts be troubled and do not be afraid."
>
> *John* 14:25-27

> "As the Father has loved me, so have I loved you. Now remain in my love. If you obey my commands, you will remain in my love, just as I have obeyed my Father's commands and remain in his love. I have told you this so that my joy may be in you and that your joy may be complete. My command is this: Love each other as I have loved you. Greater love has no one than this, that he lay down his life for his friends. You are my friends if you do what I command. I no longer call you servants, because a servant does not know his master's business. Instead, I have called you friends, for everything that I learned from my Father I have made known to you. You did not choose me, but I chose you and appointed you to go and bear fruit—fruit that will last. Then the Father will give you whatever you ask in my name. This is my command: Love each other."
>
> *John* 15:9-16

It should also be noted that, in addition to these verses, Jesus routinely tells those he has healed or forgiven to "go in peace," as well as greeting his disciples with the phrase "peace be with you."

Before reading further, please take some time to meditate, pray or reflect upon all of these verses while delaying any fixed conclusions. Try to practice some of them as they apply to your situation. Discuss them with others. What do they tell us about a Christ-like attitude towards peacefulness and nonviolence versus anger, violence and aggression?

I think understanding Jesus' spectrum of responses is a nuanced study, but nevertheless fairly easy to summarize. First of all, according to New Testament accounts, Jesus doesn't appear to get angry very often. When does he become angry? Here are the examples we have:

1. When people's hearts were stubborn or arrogant in the presence of spiritual truths.
2. When demons possessed people or tried to expose Jesus' spiritual mission prematurely.
3. When people induced anyone, especially the innocent, to sin.
4. When his followers lacked faith.
5. When people prioritized family ties above their zeal for God.
6. When his followers intended harm to others.
7. When people who had an abundance of spiritual knowledge, material wealth or other good things refused to share with those in need.
8. When a fig tree didn't respond to his appetite.
9. When God's temple was defiled.

What was Jesus getting upset about in these instances? For the most part, what seemed to provoke him most were situations where human beings were somehow being prevented from nourishing themselves spiritually, emotionally or physically; that is, when some condition interfered with their growing and thriving in these areas. Whether the result of internal doubt or external deception, lukewarm commitment or outright rebellion, a lack of humility or stubborn arrogance, thoughtless neglect or deliberate harm – anything that disrupted personal nurturing and spiritual development incurred Jesus' wrath. Another way to describe these situations is to say that wherever love was absent, Jesus became stern and corrective. How did Jesus indicate that love was absent? By observing a lack of faith-in-action, a dearth of compassionate devotion to self and others, or an absence of generosity, kindness, worship, edification or service.

Yet, with the notable exception of the fig tree, even in the most extreme and flagrant violations of the law of love Jesus does not answer evil with evil. He does not kill, maim or destroy those whose actions deprive or harm others. Although Jesus can sometimes be fierce and harsh, he does so to wake people from their spiritual slumber, to stimulate change that results in the greatest good for everyone involved, and to eliminate barriers to individual and collective wholeness. Like a concerned parent who seeks to deliver his children from harmful choices and situations, Jesus raises his voice to get their attention, then acts swiftly and decisively to demonstrate a more enlightened way of being.

So most of Jesus' reactions fall neatly within a framework of fierce compassion that seeks to right wrongs without destroying people in the process. And these readily translate into instruction for those of the Christian faith as well. There may be times for Christians to sell their cloaks and buy swords, but those swords are never used to harm another person. There may be times to become angry, to rebuke someone who is arrogant and stubborn, to remind those who tempt others of the damning consequences of their actions…but Christians are not encouraged to become judge, jury and executioner of those who are thus accused. As we learned in the last chapter, that role is reserved first for governments, whom God has appointed for that very purpose, and then of course for God himself. So how should Christians respond to such wrongdoing? If they are to follow Christ's example, they should pointedly call attention to it, then let go. Ultimately, Christians must turn the other cheek, forgive, pray for evildoers, and move on. In this way they ground themselves in the bedrock of a love which transcends human vengeance, anger and justice, thereby purging their mind and heart of resentful or violent thoughts and intentions. So yes, Christ-like responses are intended to be illuminating and corrective, but without becoming rancorous, merciless or controlling.

But what about that fig tree? Does this incident contradict the nonviolent foundations of Jesus' message? On the surface it might seem that the fig tree was depriving someone of nourishment, and thus conforms to the general theme. But the fig tree didn't deliberately intend to deprive or harm anyone, did it? So why the destructive curse? Perhaps the story is a reminder that there is never a season where Christians shouldn't try to bear spiritual fruit in the form of loving, healing and nourishing thoughts and deeds. Or perhaps the fig tree is a metaphor for a future Church that, because it grew weary of doing good in the world, inadvertently denies access to spiritual nourishment and consequently withers and dies. Perhaps Jesus was indicating that the temple he was about to clear of thieves was depriving people in this way. Perhaps the story means that when someone in need asks for help, believers should respond even if the request seems unreasonable. Or perhaps, as 2 Timothy 4:2 suggests, Christians should be prepared to share Jesus' message at all times – in season and out of season. Some theologians have proposed that the fig tree is a metaphor for Israel, and that its lack of fruit represents Israel's rejection of the Messiah. Then again, perhaps this account documents the humanity of Jesus: maybe he was just irritable, or exhausted, or having a bad day…or really, really hungry.

I tend to think the primary meaning of this story flows in a different direction, and that Jesus was demonstrating the importance of careful attention whenever great power is involved. In this context the withering fig tree passage offers a promise and a warning that strong faith is potent enough to cast mountains into the sea, and can do great good or wreak grave havoc. Thus powerful faith must be accompanied by thoughtful consideration and love. To emphasize this balancing act, the story ends with a reminder to forgive: "when you stand praying, if you hold anything against anyone, forgive him." Throughout the New Testament, Christians are lavished with knowledge, with healing, with freedom, with miraculous abilities, all the while being reminded that those who receive these gifts should respond with restraint, forgiveness, obedience, faith and love, trusting that God will mete out all necessary judgments. If we can agree on this interpretation, then what Jesus was really saying was: "Hey, look out. Mind your heart. You are powerful beings, so be careful and disciplined in your reactions. Train your intentions toward compassionate thoughts and action, so that, in the strength of your faith, you can avoid doing harm."

We could also add some experiential wisdom to this assessment. What damage have any of us done to ourselves or others in a single moment of thoughtlessness? For me, all of my most destructive words and deeds have issued from this bitter soil. In every instance where I have chosen reactive resentment or retaliation over compassion and forgiveness, I have inflicted injuries on myself and often on those I care most deeply about. Righteous anger may indeed have a place in defending the weak, or exposing hypocrisy, or holding those in power to account – but even here, whenever it issues from selfishness, hatred or fear instead of love, it can only amplify and perpetuate conflict rather than invite resolution. This experience has been shared by many people I know. So in the fig tree incident, when Jesus reminded his followers to cultivate forgiveness when invoking the power of prayer, I think that, hungry or not, he may have been crafting an important lesson about the extreme consequences of a single impulsive act.

At the same time, it is equally clear that Jesus' mission and message would also inspire division and tension between people, and that anything and anyone interfering with that mission and message received a stern rebuke. Notice, however, that the height of Jesus' own aggression involved using a whip to drive out some petty thieves who were defiling God's temple. No one was killed or maimed. Yes, Jesus spoke truth to power, openly criticized those who questioned his spiritual authority, and was sometimes harshly direct and confrontational with his own disciples, but all of this was done out of love and concern for the well-being of others. These seem to be examples of a fierce compassion intended to infuse the most resistant darkness with Light, stimulating growth and evolution in inertial minds and hearts, without doing irreparable damage. It seems particularly noteworthy that even possessive demons were simply silenced or cast out rather than annihilated.

To summarize, then, here are the principles that emerge from Jesus' example and teaching regarding nonviolence:

1. Christians should be confident, forceful, direct and truthful in observations of wrongdoing in almost every situation – regardless of who has the most worldly power or influence in a given situation – and be especially assertive when the

clarification of spiritual principles, the destructive influence of evil spirits or disease, a demonstrated lack of faith in their fellow believers, obvious selfishness and greed, or the luring of innocents into temptation are involved.

2. Christians should be prepared for resistance to the gospel from others, even to the point of arming in defense against physical assault, and they should know that spiritual power is available that can cause substantial damage in the worldly realm. However, these fortifications and abilities should never be used to harm another human being – or even to injure an evil spirit. In fact, to condition their heart against potential missteps involving self-righteous aggression, Christians should practice loving forgiveness and compassion for everyone – even their enemies – at all times.

So…assertive, confident and sometimes forceful, though never violent to the point of injury, while being compassionate and loving at the same time. It almost sounds like a recipe for good parenting or caring communication between friends, doesn't it? And, perhaps most significantly, there is no justification for collective aggression or warfare anywhere. Not one passage or jot. But are these ideas supported later on in the New Testament as well? Can we find clarification of such principles in the lives and missives of the apostles? Take some time to apply our multidimensional hermeneutic to the following (NIV):

> Bless those who persecute you; bless and do not curse. Rejoice with those who rejoice; mourn with those who mourn. Live in harmony with one another. Do not be proud, but be willing to associate with people of low position. Do not be conceited. Do not repay anyone evil for evil. Be careful to do what is right in the eyes of everybody. If it is possible, as far as it depends on you, live at peace with everyone. Do not take revenge, my friends, but leave room for God's wrath, for it is written: "It is mine to avenge; I will repay," says the lord. On the contrary: "If your enemy is hungry, feed him; if he is thirsty, give him something to drink. In doing this, you will heap burning coals on his head." Do not be overcome by evil, but overcome evil with good.
>
> *Romans 12:14-20*
>
> Let no debt remain outstanding, except the continuing debt to love one another, for he who loves his fellowman has fulfilled the law. The

commandments, "Do not commit adultery," "Do not murder," "Do not steal," "Do not covet," and whatever other commandment there may be, are summed up in this one rule: "Love your neighbor as yourself." Love does no harm to its neighbor. Therefore love is the fulfillment of the law.

Romans 13:8-10

If I speak in the tongues of men and of angels, but have not love, I am only a resounding gong or a clanging cymbal. If I have the gift of prophecy and can fathom all mysteries and all knowledge, and if I have a faith that can move mountains, but have not love, I am nothing. If I give all I possess to the poor and surrender my body to the flames, but have not love, I gain nothing. Love is patient, love is kind. It does not envy, it does not boast, it is not proud. It is not rude, it is not self-seeking, it is not easily angered, it keeps no record of wrongs. Love does not delight in evil but rejoices with the truth. It always protects, always trusts, always hopes, always perseveres. Love never fails.

1 Corinthians 13:1-8

We put no stumbling block in anyone's path, so that our ministry will not be discredited. Rather, as servants of God we commend ourselves in every way: in great endurance; in troubles, hardships and distresses; in beatings, imprisonments and riots; in hard work, sleepless nights and hunger; in purity, understanding, patience and kindness; in the holy spirit and in sincere love; in truthful speech and in the power of God; with weapons of righteousness in the right hand and in the left; through glory and dishonor, bad report and good report; genuine, yet regarded as impostors; known, yet regarded as unknown; dying, and yet we live on; beaten, and yet not killed; sorrowful, yet always rejoicing; poor, yet making many rich; having nothing, and yet possessing everything.

2 Corinthians 6:3-10

I pray that out of his glorious riches he may strengthen you with power through his Spirit in your inner being, so that Christ may dwell in your hearts through faith. And I pray that you, being rooted and established in love, may have power, together with all the saints, to grasp how wide and long and high and deep is the love of Christ, and to know this love that surpasses knowledge—that you may be filled to the measure of all the fullness of God.

Ephesians 3:16-19

Therefore each of you must put off falsehood and speak truthfully to his neighbor, for we are all members of one body. "In your anger do not sin": Do not let the sun go down while you are still angry, and do not give the devil a foothold. He who has been stealing must steal no longer, but must work, doing something useful with his own hands, that he may have something to share with those in need. Do not let any unwholesome talk come out of your mouths, but only what is helpful for building others up according to their needs, that it may benefit those who listen. And do not grieve the holy spirit of God, with whom you were sealed for the day of redemption. Get rid of all bitterness, rage and anger, brawling and slander, along with every form of malice. Be kind and compassionate to one another, forgiving each other, just as in Christ God forgave you.

Ephesians 4:25-32

Finally, be strong in the lord and in his mighty power. Put on the full armor of God so that you can take your stand against the devil's schemes. For our struggle is not against flesh and blood, but against the rulers, against the authorities, against the powers of this dark world and against the spiritual forces of evil in the heavenly realms. Therefore put on the full armor of God, so that when the day of evil comes, you may be able to stand your ground, and after you have done everything, to stand. Stand firm then, with the belt of truth buckled around your waist, with the breastplate of righteousness in place, and with your feet fitted with the readiness that comes from the gospel of peace. In addition to all this, take up the shield of faith, with which you can extinguish all the flaming arrows of the evil one. Take the helmet of salvation and the sword of the Spirit, which is the word of God. And pray in the Spirit on all occasions with all kinds of prayers and requests. With this in mind, be alert and always keep on praying for all the saints.

Ephesians 6:10-18

Therefore, as God's chosen people, holy and dearly loved, clothe yourselves with compassion, kindness, humility, gentleness and patience. Bear with each other and forgive whatever grievances you may have against one another. Forgive as the lord forgave you. And over all these virtues put on love, which binds them all together in perfect unity. Let the peace of Christ rule in your hearts, since as members of one body you were called to peace. And be thankful. Let the word of Christ dwell in you richly as you teach and admonish one another with all wisdom, and as you sing psalms, hymns and spiritual songs with gratitude in your hearts to God. And whatever you do, whether in word or deed, do it all in the name of the lord Jesus, giving thanks to God the Father through him.

Colossians 3:12-17

For God did not give us a spirit of timidity, but a spirit of power, of love and of self-discipline.

2 Timothy 1:7

My dear brothers, take note of this: Everyone should be quick to listen, slow to speak and slow to become angry, for man's anger does not bring about the righteous life that God desires.

James 1:19-20

Who is wise and understanding among you? Let him show it by his good life, by deeds done in the humility that comes from wisdom. But if you harbor bitter envy and selfish ambition in your hearts, do not boast about it or deny the truth. Such "wisdom" does not come down from heaven but is earthly, unspiritual, of the devil. For where you have envy and selfish ambition, there you find disorder and every evil practice. But the wisdom that comes from heaven is first of all pure; then peace-loving, considerate, submissive, full of mercy and good fruit, impartial and sincere. Peacemakers who sow in peace raise a harvest of righteousness.

James 3:13-18

What causes fights and quarrels among you? Don't they come from your desires that battle within you? You want something but don't get it. You kill and covet, but you cannot have what you want. You quarrel and fight. You do not have, because you do not ask God. When you ask, you do not receive, because you ask with wrong motives, that you may spend what you get on your pleasures.

James 4:1-3

Brothers, do not slander one another. Anyone who speaks against his brother or judges him speaks against the law and judges it. When you judge the law, you are not keeping it, but sitting in judgment on it. There is only one Lawgiver and Judge, the one who is able to save and destroy. But you—who are you to judge your neighbor?

James 4:11-12

Finally, all of you, live in harmony with one another; be sympathetic, love as brothers, be compassionate and humble. Do not repay evil with evil or insult with insult, but with blessing, because to this you were called so that you may inherit a blessing. For, "Whoever would love life and see good days must keep his tongue from evil and his lips from deceitful speech. He must turn from evil and do good; he must seek peace and pursue it. For the eyes of the lord are on the righteous and his ears are attentive to their prayer, but the face of the lord is against those who do evil." Who is going to harm you if you are eager to do good? But even if

> you should suffer for what is right, you are blessed. "Do not fear what they fear; do not be frightened." But in your hearts set apart Christ as lord. Always be prepared to give an answer to everyone who asks you to give the reason for the hope that you have. But do this with gentleness and respect, keeping a clear conscience, so that those who speak maliciously against your good behavior in Christ may be ashamed of their slander.
>
> *1 Peter 3:8-16*

Here we see the same themes and principles of nonviolence we found in the gospels repeated. We never see discord praised, violence perpetrated, aggression rewarded, or righteous anger that is not mitigated by restraint, wisdom, forgiveness and kindness. Courage, strength, confidence, assertiveness…these things are plentiful, but the spiritual activism of the apostles never crosses the line into rebellion, insurrection, violence, murder or war against flesh and blood. Their battle strategy, defenses and weaponry are instead focused on the spiritual realm, on bringing Light into darkness and vanquishing the influence of inner demons. And that brings us to a clear conclusion: that the strength of Christian convictions are never expressed via force of arms, or by oppressively controlling others, or in a battle of wills, or through deceptive manipulation of their fellows. It is inconceivable that killing another human being in the name of God could ever be sanctioned by New Testament teachings, or that violence could ever be an answer to spiritual challenges.

So does this mean Christians are supposed to be pacifists? Certainly many pacifist principles resonate strongly with New Testament teachings. What justification could a Christian ever have to initiate murder? Why wouldn't Christians embrace nonviolent activism at a minimum, and submissive nonresistance as a legitimate ideal? How could violence or aggression ever be justified by a follower of Christ, even in the most extreme and clear-cut circumstances of imminent threat? In keeping with the principles outlined thus far, it seems reasonable for Christians to choose to arm themselves against evil and aggression (both metaphorically and literally), while at the same committing on the deepest moral and spiritual levels to never using those arms against any human being or even in the destruction of spiritual forces; in other words, to have the appearance of strength for deterrence, while at the same time embodying the far greater strength of nonviolent self-control. This strength is not merely a façade, but a transformation of intentions, thoughts, feelings and language...right down to the very core of a believer's being. And to what end? All of this is in service to the furtherance of good in the world, to the propagation of Love and Light and the exemplification and honoring of Jesus' own self-sacrificing love. It is, in effect, the amplification of good instead of reciprocating any sort of evil with more evil.

Are these progressive views? I think they are as progressive today as they were in Jesus' time. They represent the progressiveness of William Penn, Henry David Thoreau, Leo Tolstoy, Mohandas Gandhi, Simone Weil, Martin Luther King Jr., Nelson Mandela, Desmond Tutu and so many others who have advocated and advanced humanitarian causes without the use of force. And why do these writers and activists decry violence? Essentially, because violence begets violence – because "those who live by the sword die by the sword." And championing nonviolent resolutions to the world's contemporary problems is most certainly more progressive – that is, more supportive of positive change for everyone involved – than the traditionally hawkish values expressed by many conservative Christians in the U.S. In particular, the violent expansion of democracy that neoconservatives have championed during the last decade seems especially egregious.

Remember that Jewish resistance to Roman rule in Judea eventually led to open rebellion, and the expectation of the people at that time was a Messiah who would lead such a rebellion. Hyam Maccoby, in his book *Jesus and the Jewish Resistance*, offers some interesting insights into this historical context that invite thoughtful exploration. But Jesus' approach to change did not embrace an external revolution that cultivated hatred and violence, and he in fact spoke out repeatedly against such actions and intentions. Instead, his revolution was focused within, on radical love that forgave all things even as it rectified evil through kindness, generosity and healing. Instead of creating new wounds in society by destructively controlling or oppressing other people, the activism of the New Testament demonstrates the power of compassion through self-sacrifice in service to others...even those who persecute the bearers of spiritual Light.

From a New Testament perspective, Christian involvement in war and violent conflict simply does not make any sense. As James 4:2 (NIV) says so succinctly, such things result from "desires that battle within you;" the writer goes on: "You want something but don't get it. You kill and covet, but you cannot have what you want. You quarrel and fight." And how much clearer an explanation of the nature of war and violent conflict could there be? Whether a dispute over natural resources, a grasping after economic or political influence, an expression of military ego or any other such worldly concerns, individual and collective aggression is all too often a childish regression to an I/me/mine state of mind. And there really is no place for such destructive, combative reactions in the kingdom of God, is there? If Christians wish to emulate Christ's righteous indignation, it must be reserved for clearing greedy opportunists out of the Church itself, rebuking other Christians in love, speaking out against holier-than-thou religiosity in the Church, and bringing attention to the deceptions, temptations and injustices of modern society – while at the same time being fully ready and willing to forgive all of these things.

As the apostles offered in nearly every one of their epistles: may the grace, peace and love of Jesus Christ be ours in abundance. This is the promise of Christendom. As we will see in the chapter on antichrists and the apostate Church, war and destruction embody the antithesis of Christ-like spirituality. Historically, many Christian denominations and organizations have adopted a pacifist stance in the face of war. Leading the way were the Church of the Brethren, the Mennonites and the Quakers, who have traditionally held nonviolence – often to the point of acquiescent nonresistance – in highest regard. In 1914 in the United Kingdom, and then in 1915 in the U.S., the Fellowship of Reconciliation was formed as a multidenominational organization to support Christian pacifism. The original UK FoR principles, summarized in the 1914 "Basis" read as follows:

1. That love as revealed and interpreted in the life and death of Jesus Christ, involves more than we have yet seen, that is the only power by which evil can be overcome and the only sufficient basis of human society.

2. That, in order to establish a world-order based on Love, it is incumbent upon those who believe in this principle to accept it fully,

both for themselves and in relation to others and to take the risks involved in doing so in a world which does not yet accept it.

3. That therefore, as Christians, we are forbidden to wage war, and that our loyalty to our country, to humanity, to the Church Universal, and to Jesus Christ our lord and Master, calls us instead to a life-service for the enthronement of Love in personal, commercial and national life.

4. That the Power, Wisdom and Love of God stretch far beyond the limits of our present experience, and that He is ever waiting to break forth into human life in new and larger ways.

5. That since God manifests Himself in the world through men and women, we offer ourselves to His redemptive purpose to be used by Him in whatever way He may reveal to us.

In 1919, the International Fellowship of Reconciliation was formed as an umbrella organization for national branches, and its influence is still felt around the world today; you can find additional information at www.ifor.org. FoR and FORUSA also remain active, and more information on these organizations is available at www.for.org.uk and www.forusa.org respectively. There are of course many other Christian organizations and denominations dedicated to nonviolence, among them the Pax Christi of the Catholics, Seventh Day Adventists, Jehovah's Witnesses, some Churches of Christ, and others. It can be said with some confidence that advocating nonviolence as a superior spiritual choice to violent combat has been widely adopted among many believers throughout history. As the third century theologian Hippolytus of Rome wrote in *The Apostolic Tradition*: "A soldier of the civil authority must be taught not to kill men and to refuse to do so if he is commanded, and to refuse to take an oath. If he is unwilling to comply, he must be rejected for baptism. A military commander or civic magistrate must resign or be rejected. If a believer seeks to become a soldier, he must be rejected, for he has despised God."

There are of course some glaring historical counterexamples. Such as the religiously sanctioned military Crusades of the 12th and 13th centuries, which targeted Muslims and Jews in the Holy Land in hopes of regaining those territories for the Roman Catholic Church. Or the various Inquisitions – the imprisonment, torture and execution of alleged heretics – which originated during the same period and persisted well into the 16th century. At which point the Protestant Reformation took hold, leading to decades of conflict between different religious factions and the deaths of millions. And of course Christian language has been used by various leaders – most notably the Nazi's of 1930's Germany – to justify atrocious and murderous acts of hatred against Jews, Romani, homosexuals and other "undesirables" of a given time. Indeed such distortions of Christianity have at one time or other fueled fear, hatred and violence against any number of identifiable groups – the Gnostics of the 4th century; the Druids of 5th century Ireland; those (mainly women) accused of practicing witchcraft from the 15th through 17th centuries; and of course the Jewish people have been the focus of Christian antipathy fairly persistently over the past two millennia. You might consider Gerard Sloyan's essay, "Christian Persecution of Jews over the Centuries," for a snapshot of this unfortunate legacy; for a more in-depth exploration of anti-Semitism and its causes throughout the history of Christendom, Hyam Maccoby also offers many compelling insights in his writing.

It seems that today many Christians are returning to these ideas of justifiable violence. Otherwise, how could so many people who aspire to combat roles in the military – during times of active conflict initiated by the United States – identify as Christian? One 2005 report entitled "America's Military Population" from the Population Reference Bureau placed that number at around 68% of military personnel. A July 27th, 2005 report on National Public Radio asserted that while evangelical Christians make up only 14% of the U.S. general population, 40% of active military are evangelicals, and 60% of military chaplains are evangelicals. There are even evangelical groups like Military Ministry (www.militaryministry.org) that seek to proselytize new recruits and equip U.S. soldiers with justification for violence in the name of God. And why is it that so many conservative Christians in the U.S. have supported war? A 2003 Gallup Poll found approval among church-going Christians for the war in Iraq at 66%, with conservative evangelicals once again leading the way.

How is it possible that, along with enabling and magnifying the crimes of corporate opportunism, actively contributing to the overpopulation of the planet, stubbornly oppressing women, and flagrantly resisting other

New Testament teachings, vast numbers of modern Christians are also flocking to the battlefield? How could the zeal of Christian faith have become so misdirected? Part of the answer is, I think, described in careful detail the New Testament itself. However, before we examine that evidence, let's see if we can discern a few more progressive themes among Christian teachings.

Beneath the Surface: What Real Progress Looks Like

So far we have reviewed what could be described as pronounced and transparent progressive themes in the New Testament. For a Christian to somehow argue in favor of hawkish militarism can find no basis in this scripture, and flies in the face of everything Jesus and his apostles exemplified and preached. To continue to oppress women is to rely only on a handful verses that contradict a majority of scripture on the subject, and denigrates Jesus' liberating sentiments and actions towards women. To insist on marriage, large families and increases in human population ignores encouragement from Jesus and his apostles to place devotion to God above the desires of the flesh and attachments to family. To advocate that worldly wealth or political power should somehow become the objectives of Christian faith are so blatantly at odds with New Testament teachings that only the deepest and darkest sort of duplicity and denial could ever support them. Instead, we have concrete and reasonable scriptural evidence that the Christ-like path is empowering towards women, free of concern for worldly riches and power to the point of socialistic egalitarianism, consistently submissive to the existing rule of law, celibate to whatever degree possible, and advocating compassion and pacifism even while being courageous and outspoken in championing good.

The kingdom of God is not passive, but its activism is fixed on the reformation of the human heart from within, not on external conformance to tribal traditions and pressures, or maintaining institutions whose main priority is self-perpetuation at any cost. In interactions with non-believers, loving service, inclusion and understanding usurp sitting in judgment or trying to control others. The

New Testament perspectives we have touched upon so far were progressive in the first century and remain progressive today because, although we have made great strides in some arenas, humanity as a whole has yet to comprehensively embrace the personal, interpersonal and transpersonal ideals inspired by radical compassion; we have a long way to go to fully realize our potential.

So these are some obvious conclusions – but what about the more subtle and nuanced ones? For example, can we find support for Earth-centric environmentalism in the New Testament? What about same-sex marriage or other progressive-leaning civil liberties positions? What about promoting science and access to higher education? Is there any evidence that supports universal healthcare or other social safety nets? Should Christians advocate for organized labor and the reduction of corporate influence in society? That these represent a sociopolitically progressive perspective in the U.S. is readily verified by the political rhetoric of our times. For examples, check out the Democratic party platform as of this writing ("What We Stand For" at www.democrats.org), the Green Party's ideals (www.gp.org), or the language of many enduring progressive movements in the U.S. As far back as the platform of the 1912 Progressive Party led by Theodore Roosevelt, many if not all of these sentiments have been shared by self-described progressives.

Then, taking this examination one step further, are there traditionally progressive ideals that are not fully supported in the New Testament? Are there spiritual, political and cultural goals and practices found among modern Christians that, despite holding up the greatest good for everyone as the intended goal, can find little to no resonance with New Testament ideas? If so, what might this mean for modern Christian progressives? And, finally, what refuge can a conservative-minded Christian find in the New Testament, if any? Is there a way to support aspects of conservative ideology when guided by the internal logic and evidence of that scripture? And if there are conservative viewpoints to be found there, how might these moderate Christian progressivism? Then, taken altogether, how can all of this be synthesized into a "progressive Christianity" for modern times?

Environmentalism

We find compelling evidence regarding Jesus' attitude toward Nature in various descriptions of his praying in the New Testament. Although Jesus encourages people to pray privately in their room as a contrast to the frequent public praying of Judeans and pagans (Matthew 6:5-7), Jesus himself often sought relative solitude in Nature when he prayed. Using our established hermeneutic, consider the following(NASB):

> Immediately He made the disciples get into the boat and go ahead of Him to the other side, while He sent the crowds away. After He had sent the crowds away, He went up on the mountain by Himself to pray; and when it was evening, He was there alone. But the boat was already a long distance from the land, battered by the waves; for the wind was contrary.
>
> *Matthew 14:22-24*
>
> Then Jesus came with them to a place called Gethsemane, and said to His disciples, "Sit here while I go over there and pray." And He took with Him Peter and the two sons of Zebedee, and began to be grieved and distressed. Then He said to them, "My soul is deeply grieved, to the point of death; remain here and keep watch with Me." And He went a little beyond them, and fell on His face and prayed, saying, "My Father, if it is possible, let this cup pass from Me; yet not as I will, but as You will." And He came to the disciples and found them sleeping, and said to Peter, "So, you men could not keep watch with Me for one hour? "Keep watching and praying that you may not enter into temptation; the spirit is willing, but the flesh is weak." He went away again a second time and prayed, saying, "My Father, if this cannot pass away unless I drink it, Your will be done." Again He came and found them sleeping, for their eyes were heavy. And He left them again, and went away and prayed a third time, saying the same thing once more. Then He came to the disciples and said to them, "Are you still sleeping and resting? Behold, the hour is at hand and the Son of Man is being betrayed into the hands of sinners. "Get up, let us be going; behold, the one who betrays Me is at hand!"
>
> *Matthew 26:36-46*
>
> The apostles gathered together with Jesus; and they reported to Him all that they had done and taught. And He said to them, "Come away by yourselves to a secluded place and rest a while." (For there were many people coming and going, and they did not even have time to eat.) They went away in the boat to a secluded place by themselves. The people saw them going, and many recognized them and ran there together on

foot from all the cities, and got there ahead of them. When Jesus went ashore, He saw a large crowd, and He felt compassion for them because they were like sheep without a shepherd; and He began to teach them many things. When it was already quite late, His disciples came to Him and said, "This place is desolate and it is already quite late; send them away so that they may go into the surrounding countryside and villages and buy themselves something to eat."

Mark 6:30-36

But the news about Him was spreading even farther, and large crowds were gathering to hear Him and to be healed of their sicknesses. But Jesus Himself would often slip away to the wilderness and pray.

Luke 5:15-16

It was at this time that He went off to the mountain to pray, and He spent the whole night in prayer to God. And when day came, He called His disciples to Him and chose twelve of them, whom He also named as apostles: Simon, whom He also named Peter, and Andrew his brother; and James and John; and Philip and Bartholomew; and Matthew and Thomas; James the son of Alphaeus, and Simon who was called the Zealot; Judas the son of James, and Judas Iscariot, who became a traitor.

Luke 6:12-16

And He came out and proceeded as was His custom to the Mount of Olives; and the disciples also followed Him. When He arrived at the place, He said to them, "Pray that you may not enter into temptation." And He withdrew from them about a stone's throw, and He knelt down and began to pray, saying, "Father, if You are willing, remove this cup from Me; yet not My will, but Yours be done." Now an angel from heaven appeared to Him, strengthening Him. And being in agony He was praying very fervently; and His sweat became like drops of blood, falling down upon the ground.

Luke 22:39-44

There are other hints in evidence that Jesus spent much of his time praying out-of-doors. At the end of John 14, as the Passover feast comes to a close, Jesus says "come, let us leave," after which he and the disciples pray. We can easily conclude that this meant exiting the building where the Passover feast took place. And, in John 17, as Jesus lifts his eyes toward heaven and utters the longest prayer in the New Testament, we can be fairly certain that this was outside – especially since it coincides with similar references to his praying at Gethsemane at the Mount of Olives in Matthew, Mark and Luke.

Of course, Jesus had other experiences in Nature as well. For example (NASB):

> In those days Jesus came from Nazareth in Galilee and was baptized by John in the Jordan. Immediately coming up out of the water, He saw the heavens opening, and the Spirit like a dove descending upon Him; and a voice came out of the heavens: "You are My beloved Son, in You I am well-pleased." Immediately the Spirit impelled Him to go out into the wilderness. And He was in the wilderness forty days being tempted by Satan; and He was with the wild beasts, and the angels were ministering to Him.
>
> *Mark 1:9-13*

Also consider that many other momentous events occurred in the wilderness – most notably the word of God coming to John the Baptist (Luke 3:2), John the Baptist's own prophesies and teaching regarding Jesus' arrival (Matthew 3, Mark 1, John 1, Luke 3), and perhaps even Saul of Tarsus' conversion on the road to Damascus (Acts 9:1-9; 22:6-11). But what does any of this have to do with environmentalism? Well, quite simply, if Jesus preferred seeking solitude in the wilderness to pray, God preferred revealing his message to human beings when they were in the wilderness, and the prophets of God preferred to teach in the wilderness, then the reduction or destruction of that wilderness – even wild places easily accessible from areas inhabited by human beings – runs contrary to this desirable pattern. That is, an environmentalism that seeks first and foremost to preserve such wild spaces appears to be concordant with God's revelatory preferences, the habits of prophetic teaching, and Jesus' patterns of prayer.

There are other inferences we can make as well. For example, it would have been dangerous to baptize people in the Jordan river if it had been full of industrial pollutants (Matthew 3:6, Mark 1:5, Luke 4:1, etc.). And how could John the Baptist have eaten wild honey if bees were extinct (Matthew 3:4, Mark 1:6)? If there had been no uninhabited wilderness, where would Jesus have performed the miracle of the loaves and fish (Matthew 15:29-39; John 6:1-14, Luke 9:10-17, etc.)? Or where would Jesus and his disciples have gone to rest (Mark 6:31)? But perhaps most intriguing of all are the many references in Revelation to the role Nature will play in the final days before Jesus' triumphant return. Indeed, how could any of this prophecy be fulfilled if the Earth, its flora and fauna, its seas and rivers, all its wild and untamed places and indeed its elegant complexity and vital intelligence are destroyed by human habitation and exploitation? Consider the environmental implications of the following verses (ESV):

> And I looked, and behold, a pale horse! And its rider's name was Death, and Hades followed him. And they were given authority over a fourth of the earth, to kill with sword and with famine and with pestilence and by wild beasts of the earth.
>
> *Revelation 6:8*

> Then I saw another angel ascending from the rising of the sun, with the seal of the living God, and he called with a loud voice to the four angels who had been given power to harm earth and sea, saying, "Do not harm the earth or the sea or the trees, until we have sealed the servants of our God on their foreheads."
>
> *Revelation 7:2-3*

> The first angel blew his trumpet, and there followed hail and fire, mixed with blood, and these were thrown upon the earth. And a third of the earth was burned up, and a third of the trees were burned up, and all green grass was burned up.
>
> *Revelation 8:7*

> Then from the smoke came locusts on the earth, and they were given power like the power of scorpions of the earth. They were told not to harm the grass of the earth or any green plant or any tree, but only those people who do not have the seal of God on their foreheads.
>
> *Revelation 9:3*

> She gave birth to a male child, one who is to rule all the nations with a rod of iron, but her child was caught up to God and to his throne, and the woman fled into the wilderness, where she has a place prepared by God, in which she is to be nourished for 1,260 days.
>
> *Revelation 12:5-6*

> But the earth came to the help of the woman, and the earth opened its mouth and swallowed the river that the dragon had poured from his mouth.
>
> *Revelation 12:16*

> Then I saw an angel standing in the sun, and with a loud voice he called to all the birds that fly directly overhead, "Come, gather for the great supper of God…"
>
> *Revelation* 19:17

In other words, it is not an unreasonable assumption to believe protecting Nature's wildness, purity, diversity and potency resonates with the underlying sentiments in these New Testament accounts and prophecies. Of course, these sorts of conclusions rely less on clear and unambiguous directives in New Testament scripture, and more on discernment and sensitivity to more subtle currents flowing within the texts. For example, someone could argue that the term for "wilderness" in some of these references (ἔρημος) could viably be translated as "desert" or "desolate place" instead – and some translations choose to do so. However, the most constrained and specific definition would really be "uninhabited place," which could be a desert, grassland, wasteland, an abandoned town or any such lonely environment. But, for example, the critical mass of references to Jesus praying on mountainsides, amid olive groves, in gardens, etc. generally lends itself to the solitude of lush natural spaces as opposed to a desert specifically, so this is where I settled. Still, we need not quibble over such things if we expand our sight with non-analytical tools of interpretation.

Returning to our initial hermeneutic, my own experiential validation of the wilderness principle has persuaded me more than anything else. Nearly all of the most potent spiritual events of my life have occurred in Nature. That Jesus preferred praying and teaching his disciples in natural spaces just confirms for me what I knew long before I was exposed to Christianity: that for whatever reason our spirit is made more free and our soul somehow finds more intimacy with the Sacred in environments uncluttered by human habitation. But does this support the romantic ideal of somehow drawing closer to God in Nature? Does it encourage Nature Mysticism? Does it defend the holiness of a created world, or the infusion of that world with spirit in a panentheistic sense? Such conclusions are difficult to support with New Testament scripture alone, but I would say that, for me at least, the preservation of wild lands, reducing the impact of human beings on Nature, and the protection of plant and animal kingdoms is in fact a sacred duty. To draw your own conclusions, I recommend spending as much time praying or meditating in Nature as possible, and then comparing those experiences with prayer and meditation on a crowded city street at mid-day, inside of a noisy factory, as a passenger in rush-hour traffic, or even in your own private room while loved ones watch TV nearby or cook particularly pungent food.

Civil Liberties

There are a number of civil liberties themes to be found in the New Testament through a similar approach. If taken in concert with the sentiments already explored – and in particular the spiritual equality of women – it quickly becomes evident that a Christian has every justification to exemplify and promote egalitarian values and ideals. I believe the following verses lend themselves to a progressive perspective on this topic, and again would encourage you to mediate upon, pray about, discuss and indeed practice this scripture until you intuit your own conclusions on the matter.

The Inherent Goodness & Value of Every Individual

We have already touched upon many of the accounts where Jesus honors individuals for the rightness of their actions, their individual importance, and their inherent goodness. There was the woman at Simon's house who washed Jesus' feet with her tears, and whom Jesus forgave because "she loved much." There was the Italian Centurion whose humility and faith Jesus rewarded and praised by healing his servant. There was the Syrophoenician woman who begged Jesus for crumbs from the master's table, and was granted the healing of her daughter for her cleverness. And of course in all the beatitudes Jesus certainly seems to be saying "all of you are precious and important, no matter how the world has mistreated you." Later, in the Acts of the Apostles, there was the other Centurion, Cornelius, a Gentile whose prayers and generosity were heard and rewarded by God despite his lack of appropriate religious affiliation. And even the Apostle Paul acknowledged in Romans 2:15 that the law of God is written on the hearts of non-believers, as witnessed in the reactions of their conscience.

To add some additional substance to this Divine meal, here are a few more verses that I believe bolster the theme of individual value, goodness and capacity for wisdom (NASB):

> "You are the light of the world. A city set on a hill cannot be hidden; nor does anyone light a lamp and put it under a basket, but on the lampstand, and it gives light to all who are in the house. Let your light shine before men in such a way that they may see your good works, and glorify your Father who is in heaven."
>
> *Matthew 5:14-16*

> "Come to Me, all who are weary and heavy-laden, and I will give you rest. Take My yoke upon you and learn from Me, for I am gentle and humble in heart, and YOU WILL FIND REST FOR YOUR SOULS. For My yoke is easy and My burden is light."
>
> *Matthew 11:28-30*

> "Are not five sparrows sold for two cents? Yet not one of them is forgotten before God. Indeed, the very hairs of your head are all numbered. Do not fear; you are more valuable than many sparrows."
>
> *Luke 12:6-7*

> "For everyone who does evil hates the Light, and does not come to the Light for fear that his deeds will be exposed. But he who practices the truth comes to the Light, so that his deeds may be manifested as having been wrought in God."
>
> *John 3:20-21*

> Or do you not know that your body is a temple of the Holy Spirit who is in you, whom you have from God, and that you are not your own? For you have been bought with a price: therefore glorify God in your body.
>
> *1 Corinthians 6:19-20*

> Brethren, even if anyone is caught in any trespass, you who are spiritual, restore such a one in a spirit of gentleness; each one looking to yourself, so that you too will not be tempted. Bear one another's burdens, and thereby fulfill the law of Christ. For if anyone thinks he is something when he is nothing, he deceives himself. But each one must examine his own work, and then he will have reason for boasting in regard to himself alone, and not in regard to another. For each one will bear his own load.
>
> *Galatians 6:1-5*

> See how great a love the Father has bestowed on us, that we would be called children of God; and such we are.
>
> *1 John 3:1*

The Inappropriateness of Slavery

Slavery was common in first century Judea, and there are plentiful references to it in the New Testament – most of which are metaphorical. Slavery to our fears and sins, for example, as well as the spiritual slavery resulting from the Law of the Prophets. Of course, Christians are exhorted to set themselves free from such slavery through their faith in Christ. The first eight chapters of Paul's epistle to the Romans deals with this concept in great detail. There are also many verses where Jesus and the apostles encourage believers to become slaves to love and to righteousness in order to achieve good in the world. But unless we rework this metaphorical use of slavery rather creatively, it doesn't really speak to the cultural institution of slavery at the time or to the echoes of that institution which still persist in the modern world (and which we should never forget lingered in the United states until just over 145 years ago, spawning a bloody Civil War that raged for four years). The following are a few of the verses that more directly address this topic, revealing that, although Christians were encouraged to submit to their masters and not openly rebel, the preference and pattern of the epistles is nevertheless to encourage liberation from any and all conditions of worldly enslavement, and to disdain the slave trade itself (NIV):

> Each one should remain in the situation which he was in when God called him. Were you a slave when you were called? Don't let it trouble you—although if you can gain your freedom, do so. For he who was a slave when he was called by the Lord is the Lord's freedman; similarly, he who was a free man when he was called is Christ's slave. You were bought at a price; do not become slaves of men. Brothers, each man, as responsible to God, should remain in the situation God called him to.
>
> *1 Corinthians 7:20-24*

> We know that the law is good if one uses it properly. We also know that law is made not for the righteous but for lawbreakers and rebels, the ungodly and sinful, the unholy and irreligious; for those who kill their fathers or mothers, for murderers, for adulterers and perverts, for slave traders and liars and perjurers—and for whatever else is contrary to the

> sound doctrine that conforms to the glorious gospel of the blessed God, which he entrusted to me.
>
> *1 Timothy 1:8-11*

> Therefore, although in Christ I could be bold and order you to do what you ought to do, yet I appeal to you on the basis of love. I then, as Paul—an old man and now also a prisoner of Christ Jesus— I appeal to you for my son Onesimus, who became my son while I was in chains. Formerly he was useless to you, but now he has become useful both to you and to me. I am sending him—who is my very heart—back to you. I would have liked to keep him with me so that he could take your place in helping me while I am in chains for the gospel. But I did not want to do anything without your consent, so that any favor you do will be spontaneous and not forced. Perhaps the reason he was separated from you for a little while was that you might have him back for good—no longer as a slave, but better than a slave, as a dear brother. He is very dear to me but even dearer to you, both as a man and as a brother in the lord.
>
> *Philemon 1:8-15*

> Slaves, submit yourselves to your masters with all respect, not only to those who are good and considerate, but also to those who are harsh. For it is commendable if a man bears up under the pain of unjust suffering because he is conscious of God. But how is it to your credit if you receive a beating for doing wrong and endure it? But if you suffer for doing good and you endure it, this is commendable before God. To this you were called, because Christ suffered for you, leaving you an example, that you should follow in his steps. "He committed no sin, and no deceit was found in his mouth." When they hurled their insults at him, he did not retaliate; when he suffered, he made no threats. Instead, he entrusted himself to him who judges justly. He himself bore our sins in his body on the tree, so that we might die to sins and live for righteousness; by his wounds you have been healed.
>
> *1 Peter 2:18-24*

This isn't a lot to go on, and some it if seems contradictory at first glance. But within the larger context of the New Testament teachings about suffering, submission and the nature of service, these contrasting statements resolve into a clear directive. On the one hand, slaves should submit to their masters even when those masters are harsh – because that is the example of loving service that Jesus provided; to turn the other cheek, to trust in God, to heap loving kindness on those who persecute and revile. And yet if the opportunity to become free presents itself, a

Christian slave should take it. Why? Because becoming a slave to men denigrates the value of God's love and Christ's sacrifice, it belittles the honor and privilege of being a child of God. 1 Timothy even includes slave traders among the worst types of immoral offenders. All of this again contributes to the dominant theme of the New Testament that all people are valuable, precious to God, honored by Christ's life and death, and worthy of both profound respect and unconditional love.

So how could the institution of slavery have persisted for so many centuries in Christianized cultures? And how could the United States, so assertive of its own Christian heritage, have held onto the practice for so long, indeed creating the largest slave population in the world by the mid-eighteen hundreds? Was it because the language of the New Testament wasn't strong enough on this topic? When Paul said "do not become slaves of men" in 1 Corinthians, and encouraged those who were already slaves to become free if they could, was this simply discounted or dismissed by the southern states of the U.S. who sought secession? How could Paul's exaltation of Onesimus' freedom from slavery, or the condemnation of the slave trade in 1 Timothy, have been so entirely ignored?

The answer is complex, but in studying the history of the U.S. it becomes clear that there were strong economic motivations for southern agricultural states to perpetuate slavery, especially in competition with an industrializing North. There was also a cultural component, a way-of-life issue, in how the South viewed itself and its traditions. But once again we can observe that these cultural and economic factors trumped religious ideals. As culture inevitably conforms religion to itself, it stridently resists being fundamentally changed by new spiritual beliefs – unless those spiritual beliefs provide more efficient, attractive or successful ways of navigating the harsh realities of existence. This is as true for individuals as it is for entire nations. Why is this so? One reason is because all patterns of human thought and behavior evolve out of our fundamental drives to *exist, experience, adapt* and *affect*. So something that effectively facilitates these drives can inspire change, but only if it can prove its superior utility either rapidly, decisively or both. In the cultural tensions that led up to the Civil War, Christianity simply did not offer a viable alternative to slavery in the South, so any spiritual imperatives for freedom from slavery within the New Testament would understandably be deemed too inconvenient to put into practice.

The Sanctity of Marriage?

Given the recent public debate over this topic, it is particularly interesting that there is very little in the New Testament to support the view that marriage is somehow sanctified by God. In fact, as we have already explored in the *Gradations of Celibacy* section, marriage was considered a concession for those who might otherwise be enslaved by their sexual needs – a necessary compromise to accommodate the desires of the flesh. To renounce marriage in order to serve the kingdom of God was clearly the preferable state, but not mandatory; to again quote Jesus in Matthew 19:12, "For some are eunuchs because they were born that way; others were made that way by men; and others have renounced marriage because of the kingdom of heaven. The one who can accept this should accept it." What is most compelling about this statement, however, is that it is not only referring to people who haven't yet married, but also people who *are already married*. We know this because of Luke 18:29-30, where Jesus says "I tell you with certainty that no one has left their home **or wife** or brothers or parents or children – for the sake of the kingdom of God – who will not receive many times as much in this time and in the age to come, eternal life." Then, in Matthew 22:30, we also learn that "At the resurrection people will neither marry nor be given in marriage; they will be like the angels in heaven," a concept repeated in Mark 12:25 and Luke 20:35. Finally, according to 1 Corinthians 7:2, the death of a spouse also frees the surviving spouse from the marital bond, further minimizing the endurance and importance of what seems to have been viewed by Jesus and his apostles as a worldly compromise.

So where did the concept of the sanctity of marriage, so frequently bantered about by Christian conservatives today, come from? Most probably, it evolved out of the comparison of Christ's relationship to humanity and the Church to that of a bridegroom and bride. Jesus is referred to as a bridegroom repeatedly in this context, first by John the Baptist in John 3:29; then by Jesus himself, both directly (Matthew 9:15, Mark 2:19, Luke 5:34) and by implication in a parable (Matthew 25:1-13);

and finally by the Apostle Paul in Ephesisans 5:25-33. Here then are a few of those passages (ESV), which I would again encourage you to meditate upon, pray over, practice and discuss:

> "Then the kingdom of heaven will be like ten virgins who took their lamps and went to meet the bridegroom. Five of them were foolish, and five were wise. For when the foolish took their lamps, they took no oil with them, but the wise took flasks of oil with their lamps. As the bridegroom was delayed, they all became drowsy and slept. But at midnight there was a cry, 'Here is the bridegroom! Come out to meet him.' Then all those virgins rose and trimmed their lamps. And the foolish said to the wise, 'Give us some of your oil, for our lamps are going out.' But the wise answered, saying, 'Since there will not be enough for us and for you, go rather to the dealers and buy for yourselves.' And while they were going to buy, the bridegroom came, and those who were ready went in with him to the marriage feast, and the door was shut. Afterward the other virgins came also, saying, 'Lord, lord, open to us.' But he answered, 'Truly, I say to you, I do not know you.' Watch therefore, for you know neither the day nor the hour."
>
> *Matthew 25:1-13*

> And they said to him, "The disciples of John fast often and offer prayers, and so do the disciples of the Pharisees, but yours eat and drink." And Jesus said to them, "Can you make wedding guests fast while the bridegroom is with them? The days will come when the bridegroom is taken away from them, and then they will fast in those days."
>
> *Luke 5:33-35*

> Now a discussion arose between some of John's disciples and a Jew over purification. And they came to John and said to him, "Rabbi, he who was with you across the Jordan, to whom you bore witness—look, he is baptizing, and all are going to him." John answered, "A person cannot receive even one thing unless it is given him from heaven. You yourselves bear me witness, that I said, 'I am not the Christ, but I have been sent before him.' The one who has the bride is the bridegroom. The friend of the bridegroom, who stands and hears him, rejoices greatly at the bridegroom's voice. Therefore this joy of mine is now complete. He must increase, but I must decrease."
>
> *John 3:25-29*

> Husbands, love your wives, as Christ loved the church and gave himself up for her, that he might sanctify her, having cleansed her by the washing of water with the word, so that he might present the church to

> himself in splendor, without spot or wrinkle or any such thing, that she might be holy and without blemish. In the same way husbands should love their wives as their own bodies. He who loves his wife loves himself. For no one ever hated his own flesh, but nourishes and cherishes it, just as Christ does the church, because we are members of his body. "Therefore a man shall leave his father and mother and hold fast to his wife, and the two shall become one flesh." This mystery is profound, and I am saying that it refers to Christ and the church. However, let each one of you love his wife as himself, and let the wife see that she respects her husband.
>
> *Ephesisans 5:25-33*

We see here that the Apostle Paul really does believe that the mystery of marriage is profound, but he emphasizes that he is referring to the marriage between Christ and the Church – not to the marriage of two human beings. Like the previous use of the bridegroom metaphor, it is the sanctity of Christ's commitment to and union with humanity that is wonderful, powerful and Divine. And thus the example of commitment and union can be called upon to inspire the quality of human interactions – in this case between a husband and wife. So it is not the marriage of two human beings that is holy, but their willingness to emulate the example of Christ that is holy.

Are there any other verses that assist us here? 1 Corinthians 7 might also inform Christian ideas about marriage. Consider verses 1-16 (ESV):

> Now concerning the matters about which you wrote: "It is good for a man not to have sexual relations with a woman." But because of the temptation to sexual immorality, each man should have his own wife and each woman her own husband. The husband should give to his wife her conjugal rights, and likewise the wife to her husband. For the wife does not have authority over her own body, but the husband does. Likewise the husband does not have authority over his own body, but the wife does. Do not deprive one another, except perhaps by agreement for a limited time, that you may devote yourselves to prayer; but then come together again, so that Satan may not tempt you because of your lack of self-control. Now as a concession, not a command, I say this. I wish that all were as I myself am. But each has his own gift from God, one of one kind and one of another. To the unmarried and the widows I say that it is good for them to remain single as I am. But if they cannot exercise self-control, they should marry. For it is better to marry than to burn with passion. To the married I give this

> charge (not I, but the Lord): the wife should not separate from her husband (but if she does, she should remain unmarried or else be reconciled to her husband), and the husband should not divorce his wife. To the rest I say (I, not the Lord) that if any brother has a wife who is an unbeliever, and she consents to live with him, he should not divorce her. If any woman has a husband who is an unbeliever, and he consents to live with her, she should not divorce him. For the unbelieving husband is made holy because of his wife, and the unbelieving wife is made holy because of her husband. Otherwise your children would be unclean, but as it is, they are holy. But if the unbelieving partner separates, let it be so. In such cases the brother or sister is not enslaved. God has called you to peace. For how do you know, wife, whether you will save your husband? Or how do you know, husband, whether you will save your wife?

Here we see some clear instruction from Paul that married people should have sex and not deprive each other except for periods of prayer, that married people shouldn't divorce unless they are willing to remain single, and that unmarried people should remain single if they can. Then Paul offers his personal opinions about the union of believer and non-believer, and how the believing spouse can sanctify the non-believing spouse – that is, make them holy. And here we have the only direct reference in the New Testament to the "sanctity" of marriage – not as an institution established by God for believers, but as a possible method of spiritual propagation from believer to non-believer. What Paul actually intended by this statement is difficult to nail down, especially since he then reminds his readers that they can't know if their faith will save their unbelieving spouse. We can infer, however, that someone acting in Christ-like devotion and humility toward their spouse is indeed sanctifying that relationship – in the same way such behavior would sanctify any relationship. Regardless of the precise meaning, however, Paul's subjective musings remain those of a celibate man who wished everyone could be celibate like him. For Paul, marriage between mortals has pragmatic utility and provides an opportunity for spiritual growth, but it is not holy in and of itself.

The principles we can glean, taking all of these passages together, are straightforward:

1. The metaphor of Christ's marriage to the Church represents the sanctity not of the human institution of marriage, but of Jesus'

commitment and sacrifice. As bridegroom, Jesus has a singular position of honor and intimacy with respect to his bride, and it is his sacrifice that makes the Church holy in that relationship.

2. The opportunity and indeed preference in Christendom is to be free from marriage in order to better serve the kingdom of God. This is true for those who haven't yet married, as well as those who are already married.

3. Marriage among Christians is a worldly concession for believers who struggle to manage their sexual desires. Even so, anyone who chooses to maintain a marital relationship should emulate Christ's relationship to the Church in their devotion and self-sacrifice. In this way, they can "sanctify" that relationship and indeed their spouse through imitating Christ.

4. Marriage between mortals does not endure beyond death, and in fact there will be no more marriage after Jesus' final return – just as members of the angelic host do not marry. And why don't angels marry? Because marriage is an earthly, mortal, human institution.

Historically, we know that marriage over the centuries has most often been a financial arrangement between families, a socially stabilizing factor in secular society, a way to broker power and influence among those who wield it, and a formal acknowledgement by the State of certain rights, responsibilities and privileges for married individuals and their children. In first century Judea, we have already touched on how marriage was a way to enforce the enslavement of women to the husband's household in Jewish and Roman society. Marriage has always been and for the most part continues to be a secular institution everywhere around the globe. Why then has it become such a flashpoint between conservative Christians and secular society in the U.S.? Why would a Christian ever want to forbid marriage between any two people? Other than encouraging brothers and sisters in the faith not to marry in order to better serve the kingdom of God, why would believers have any opinion on this at all?

In California, where I have lived for the past decade, the tumult around Proposition 8, the "Marriage Protection Act," has exposed the flawed understanding of some Christians regarding this issue. Marriage must be between a man and a woman, the amendment says. By admission of ProtectMarriage.com, the largest single source of both financial and volunteer backing for the initiative came from Mormons in Utah. Other Christian groups supported Prop 8 as well, including the Eastern Orthodox Church, the Roman Catholic Church, and Focus on the Family. Influential evangelical figures such as Rick Warren, Miles McPherson, Jim Garlow and others rallied Christians to get behind the measure. We saw a similar sampling of Christianity behind the federal "Defense of Marriage Act" (DOMA) in 1996, the 2006 "Sanctity of Marriage Amendment" in Alabama, and of course the many ballot measures of the 2004 elections that sought to prevent same sex marriage. At this point, the California initiative seems destined to be overturned in the courts because it gives some citizens one set of rights, and other citizens another set of rights; this sort of inequality has been consistently abolished in deference to the U.S. Constitution in past court rulings. Yet for Christian conservatives in the U.S., defining marriage to be between one man and one woman has been a political rallying cry.

Yet if this prejudice isn't based in the teachings or examples of Christ and his apostles, on what is it grounded? In Western culture, we didn't see suggestions of a romantic – in contrast to pragmatic – ideal of marriage until very recently. It wasn't until the late eighteenth and nineteenth centuries that writers reworked what had been the provenance of courtly love – a passionate devotion found *outside of marriage* and celebrated by troubadours since the 1200s – and incorporated it into a marriage that came about by choice rather than in response to familial or societal obligations. It was writers like Alexander Pushkin, Jane Austen, Heinrich von Kleist and Jean Paul who reinvented marriage as a "romantic happy ending" to their poetry and stories; prior to the popularity of their work, marriage was viewed largely as a duty and necessity. Thomas Klinkert and Weertje Willms' essay "Romantic Gender and Sexuality" in the 2008 collection *Romantic Prose Fiction* carefully outlines this innovation. Yet today, U.S. culture is mired in the romantic ideal that marriage is the natural conclusion of love between two people, as well as an assumption that this has always been the case throughout history. But this simply isn't true.

Against this backdrop, it seems almost silly that some conservatives believe they are championing or protecting "Christian values" by defining marriage as one thing or another. Their definition isn't Biblically or spiritually based, it is merely a confused muddle of romantic ideals and cultural prejudices that have fueled a judgmental reflex – the reflex to impose certain values on non-believers and other Christians with whom they disagree. And this is precisely the sort of mistaken zeal over which Jesus and his apostles chastised the devoutly religious many times in the New Testament. On one hand marriage is clearly under the purview of secular society and the State, not the Church, and on the other the whole idea of marriage being something spiritual – or even connected to feelings of love – is a relatively recent invention. In the U.S., it is certainly the powers of the secular State vested in religious officials that allows them to perform marriage ceremonies at all, not the power or authority of any particular religion. And whenever the Church has intervened in the secular institution of marriage in the past, it has generally led to disastrous and divisive consequences, just as similar interference promises to do today.

Governmental Social Safety Nets

U.S. history has often been shaped by the coexistence of contradictory impulses. Our system of glorious National Parks can be viewed as a result of the preservationist idealism of folks like John Muir and George Catlin in concert with the more exploitative interests of the Northern Pacific Railway Company and other free enterprise. Americans have always been quick to fiercely defend their free speech and a free press, even while persecuting and jailing those who voice particularly unpleasant or unpopular opinions as happened during the McCarthy era. U.S. consumers consistently insist on the highest quality products, delivered to them the most rapidly, with the best customer service, but only if all of this is available at the lowest possible price with free shipping and free product support.

In the same vein, the fierce individualism and persistent self-absorption of Americans has often coexisted with a fundamental generosity of spirit and desire for the greater good. For example, on the one hand, most Americans appreciate the benefits of social security, Medicare and government programs for the poor, but on the other hand we really resent having to pay any taxes for these entitlements. We tend to give a lot to charities, but we have also ensured that, via the National Do Not Call Registry, charities cannot hire telemarketing firms to contact us via the phone to solicit donations. In recent years, these sorts of contradictory impulses have manifested in a cry from conservative ideologues to invest in the social services of non-governmental community organizations – what President George H.W. Bush called "a thousand points of light" – while reducing reliance on government-based social welfare programs. The goal seems mainly to have been reducing any tax burden on the wealthy, regardless of the impact on those who are sick, children, the poor, the homeless, the unemployed, etc.

The Christian responsibility in such matters is fairly transparent, and we have covered many of the core principles already. However, how services are delivered to widows, orphans and anyone else in need is not as relevant as the priority of that care. How the sick are healed is less important than the healing itself. The mechanism of relieving suffering in the world is by far less critical than ensuring relief is available to everyone. In Mark 9, how did John and the other disciples respond when they saw someone who wasn't a disciple casting demons out in Jesus' name? "We tried to stop him because he wasn't following us," said John. And what was Jesus response? "Don't stop him…for someone who isn't against us is for us." Apparently, John was uncomfortable with someone doing good in Jesus' name who wasn't properly sanctioned or authorized to do so. In the same way, many modern Christians seem to struggle with allowing secular institutions and government to take the lead in doing good work, but this really makes little sense. Mighty works are mighty works, and Divine Light shines through them all.

However, I will say that in my experience one element that increases the spiritual and interpersonal value of such service is the level of personal involvement. If I am helping people myself, this is a more valuable service to all – including my own spirit – than if I donate to someone else's efforts. So whether I am supporting an NGO, a faith-based organization or a governmental program is a far less significant factor than whether I am personally engaged in charitable contact with those in need. Yet even this principle does not preclude my supporting other efforts; why would it? Resisting the support of government programs that help those in need because I prefer more direct personal involvement would just be hiding selfish miserliness or stubborn rectitude behind what appear to be more lofty sentiments.

Remember that the New Testament's instruction and examples encourage Christians to give to those who ask of them, to go the extra mile, to pay taxes, to care for the poor and the sick, to be a good Samaritan, and to do what is right for others even if it contradicts some dogmatic principle of religious law. So to say "I don't want to support a nationalized healthcare system because I believe free market approaches are more efficient" is simply not a Biblically based response to a perpetual human need. I also have to say that such insistence is also not supported by any data, in the U.S. or anywhere else, as profit-based medicine consistently increases the cost of care without proportionally improving health outcomes; in other words, you don't get as much bang for your buck in free market medical systems as you do in socialized or highly regulated ones. In addition, free-market healthcare systems necessarily exclude the elderly, the disabled, the poor, the chronically ill, and anyone else who is simply not profitable enough to be covered – a dearth of market-based coverage for these groups was, after all, why Medicare and Medicaid came into being.

Among the myriad studies that support these healthcare realities, perhaps the most accessible are the consecutive annual "Mirror, Mirror" reports available at www.commonwealthfund.org. These show how U.S. profit-based healthcare consistently underperforms other, more regulated and governmentally coordinated systems around the world in terms of health outcomes, system efficiency, accessibility, quality of care and several other detailed metrics. However, regardless of capitalistic principles or ideological preferences, the Christian's responsibility is to support meeting these needs rather than obstructing their support in any way. In the *Didache*, an instructive text credited to the Twelve Apostles and circulated among Christian congregations in the second century, it says: "Let your money sweat in your hands until you know whom to give it to." If we are highly motivated to give in support of others, we won't refuse to give because service delivery isn't as efficient or as targeted as we would like it to be – or because some particular ideology we favor isn't adequately represented.

Now, this doesn't mean that the New Testament forbids Christians from being discerning in their giving or placing conditions on their efforts…does it? For example, when the Apostle Paul indicated that those who refuse to work shouldn't be fed (2 Thessalonians 3:10), it might at first seem reasonable to translate this instruction into support for welfare reform that helps people transition off of welfare into viable jobs – especially if those transition efforts are effective, and if they stem from a desire to heal and help and not an impulse to persecute or judge others. Even though Paul was undoubtedly restricting his admonishment to those within the Church, as long as loving intentions are foremost, such precedents would certainly appear to help guide interaction between believers and non-believers in the spirit of service. Wouldn't they? Well…not exactly. Let us not forget that even though Jesus sometimes hesitated in demonstrating his generous powers – such as when asked to turn water into wine, or to remove a demon from the Syrophoenician's daughter – he ultimately followed through without issuing any demands or conditions. In fact, the only times Jesus refused to respond to a request for a miracle was when the religious elite were testing him, soliciting a sign to further their nefarious designs rather than to meet a real need. And even then, Jesus nevertheless promised them the sign of Jonah. So Jesus gave unceasingly to those who asked, just as he preached others should do, and he did so unconditionally.

But still, isn't a Christian allowed to be discerning in their giving? Well, there are some guidelines for this to be found in the New Testament. I think this line of questioning guides us – often against what may seem prudent instincts – to a New Testament principle I call *the greatest and most immediate good.* Consider the parable of the good Samaritan (WEB):

> Behold, a certain lawyer stood up and tested him, saying, "Teacher, what shall I do to inherit eternal life?" He said to him, "What is written in the law? How do you read it?" He answered, "You shall love the Lord your God with all your heart, with all your soul, with all your strength, and with all your mind; and your neighbor as yourself." He said to him, "You have answered correctly. Do this, and you will live." But he, desiring to justify himself, asked Jesus, "Who is my neighbor?" Jesus answered, "A certain man was going down from Jerusalem to Jericho,

> and he fell among robbers, who both stripped him and beat him, and departed, leaving him half dead. By chance a certain priest was going down that way. When he saw him, he passed by on the other side. In the same way a Levite also, when he came to the place, and saw him, passed by on the other side. But a certain Samaritan, as he traveled, came to where he was. When he saw him, he was moved with compassion, came to him, and bound up his wounds, pouring on oil and wine. He set him on his own animal, and brought him to an inn, and took care of him. On the next day, when he departed, he took out two denarii, and gave them to the host, and said to him, 'Take care of him. Whatever you spend beyond that, I will repay you when I return.' Now which of these three do you think seemed to be a neighbor to him who fell among the robbers?" He said, "He who showed mercy on him." Then Jesus said to him, "Go and do likewise."
>
> *Luke 10:25-37*

Paralleling some common conservative Christian arguments I have encountered, a modern-day priest or Levite in this parable might react to the robbed man this way: "If that guy is smart, took advantage of opportunities in his life, invested wisely and made morally sound decisions, he would have excellent private insurance that will take care of his medical needs, as well as replace any of his material losses. Therefore he should already be taken care of and I need not do anything." Or perhaps, "I'm concerned that this stranger will sue me if I help him, so he'll just have to pull himself up by his own bootstraps. Since he took the risk of walking along this road alone, he'll just have to suffer the consequences." Or maybe, "Hey, wait a minute, I have a business to run. If my business is successful, what I provide my community – jobs, improvements, long-term investments, etc. – will eventually benefit everyone, including this guy! So I just can't stop to help him…I need to continue building my business." But instead of these rationalizations to avoid giving assistance or getting involved, those who seek to imitate Christ would have mercy, and love, and generosity, and willingness to suffer inconvenience and personal sacrifice while taking immediate responsibility for the well-being of a stranger. And however that good Samaritan ministered to the stranger's needs, they wouldn't ask for anything in return, or interrogate the victim to determine why such bad luck befell them, or expect them to change their ways to avoid getting mugged again. The Christ-like would instead demonstrate affectionate caring for someone in need without preconditions, and let God and the recipient's conscience take care of the rest.

This theme is repeated throughout the New Testament so frequently that additional references can be found in many of the verses already included earlier in this book. Over and over again, the love of Christ equates self-sacrificing, unconditional service inspired by compassion. Jesus and his apostles do encourage believers to have discernment in such actions, but that discernment is mainly directed inward to the state of the heart and intentions of the mind. The questions a Christian should ask in any situation that demands wisdom, compassion and generosity of spirit are things like: "Am I doing this for the right reasons? Do I desire what is best for this person? Am I emulating Christ? Is my love sufficient? Am I withholding anything out of selfishness or greed? Am I doing this to gain attention or approval, or because I feel compassion for this person?" And so on. The estimation of free market efficiencies, or how overreaching governmental authority may be, or whether someone has been abusing the system, etc. simply do not factor into this equation.

When a Christian is asked to support government programs that feed and cloth the poor, heal the sick, house widows and orphans, or rehabilitate prisoners, their responsibility is therefore not to protect corporate interests, or advocate neoliberal economic principles, or decry the wastefulness of governmental programs, or in any way justify rebellion against governing authorities – which would just be emulating the priest and the Levite passing on by without compassion. No, the Christian obligation is to support all such efforts in the same spirit that Christ and his followers demonstrated in the New Testament. We could also cite the fact that early Christians modeled socialist ideals within the Church – distributing wealth equally among all members – as justification to support social safety nets however they are created and maintained. But, once again, I think the means of service delivery is, for the most part, far less relevant than the compassionate intent behind providing help. Surely Christians can and should refine the effectiveness of their giving, but never at the expense of those in need.

Sadly, the current sentiment among many Christian conservatives in the U.S. is one of taking away social safety nets without providing anything to replace them, leading some political pundits to dub Republicans "The

Party of No." Yet decades of tax cuts for the wealthy have not provided better living for the poor or the sick, so why perpetuate them? Not everyone can home-school, pay for the best private education or move somewhere with a good charter school, so why insist on these options to the detriment of a publicly funded system? To eliminate welfare, repeal healthcare reforms, dismantle public education, cut funding to prison programs, or otherwise undermine government services to children, the poor, sick, orphaned, widowed and jailed is really a direct slap in the face of Christ. Christ would, of course, offer his other cheek to be reddened, but Christian conservatives should blush a deeper crimson with the shame of these hypocritical affronts to both common sense and the law of love.

Capitalist Enterprise vs. Organized Labor & Consumer Protection

Large corporations and labor unions of course did not exist in first century Judea as they do today. However, I think it is possible – and useful – to project the spirit of New Testament teachings into the U.S. corporate arena. For example, Christians are encouraged to avoid becoming slaves and to free themselves if they can. But working for large corporations that, in pursuit of a better bottom line, disregard workers' health and well-being, avoid providing a living wage whenever possible, and seek to circumvent any established rule of law (regulatory restrictions, etc.) that might impact profits, can certainly be viewed as a form of slavery. Indeed the term "wage slave" was coined in response to the oppressive relationship between industry and workers in the 1800s, a relationship which continues into the modern era.

Before the advent of labor organizations in the United States, many workers were subject to horrific working conditions. Child labor, twelve-hour work days, hazardous work environments and extremely low pay were common. Truck systems, sharecropping and debt bondage were methods frequently used to ensure that workers could enlarge the profits of their masters while remaining unable to free themselves from a particular enterprise. In response to these conditions, laborers united to bargain collectively for safer work environments, shorter workdays and work weeks, wages that could support a family and indeed provide more financial freedom, and the ability for workers to have more say regarding the conditions, opportunities and benefits of employment. For detailed data about the evolution of labor in U.S. history, try the *Encyclopedia of U.S. Labor and Working-Class History, Volume 1*, edited by Eric Arnesen. For a broader overview of organized labor's response to exploitation well into modern times, see Nelson Lichtenstein's *State of the Union: A Century of American Labor*.

We can compliment this anti-slavery argument with observations about corporate capitalism's focus on consumerism and wealth. The priorities of capitalist enterprise have endured for centuries: to continually maximize profits and reduce overhead; to expand business opportunities while undermining competitors; to get the most productivity out of workers while paying them as little as possible; to aggressively pilfer natural resources without regard to the natural environment or indigenous communities; and to creatively and often deceptively seduce people into consuming one brand of goods or services over another, often to excess. For the type of corporate capitalism found in the U.S. in particular, we can add to that list a callous disregard for the health and well-being of everyone and everything involved in the process. From the egregious and illegal practices of tobacco, pharmaceutical, petrochemical, banking, insurance, agriculture, fast food and many other industries, we have ample proof of that. In short, U.S. corporate capitalism encourages a desire for ever-increasing material wealth while facilitating a self-serving greed in both producers and consumers – spawning reckless attitudes and behaviors that are harmful to both. Clearly this set of values and priorities is precisely what Jesus and his apostles warned against, and are emblematic of the destructive self-absorption from which following Christ is intended to deliver humanity. To buy into corporate advertising, become obedient workers and consumers, or otherwise subscribe to the efficacy of the U.S. business model are certainly ways of conforming to this world, but they are not ways to live by the spirit.

And then there is the issue of corporate personhood: the idea that corporations have the same liberties and protections that human beings do. It can be argued that this concept, in concert with an unprecedented concentration of wealth and power within corporations, has created one of the most unstoppable forces in human history, a force capable of both great good and great evil. Whether we believe that the balance of corporate actions generates more positive or negative consequences in the world is an interesting and important debate, but it skirts the real danger. The real danger is vesting such an unimaginably huge amount of influence in any institution or association of institutions that promote similar values and interests. Consider for a moment what it means that corporations control a majority of the world's monetary wealth, that they either already possess or seek to possess access to a majority of the world's natural resources, that they employ directly or indirectly much of the world's population, that they effectively shape public opinion by delivering a staggering amount of multimedia information, that they have unprecedented access to and influence over world governments and election processes. And although they may sometimes be in competition with each other for consumer dollars, they are increasingly conglomerated into transnational entities that all share the same primary interest: that of captivating global populations in obedient consumerism and protecting corporate power. Doesn't this sound like a recipe for absolute power corrupting absolutely?

Now, lest you think this particular progressive view isn't clearly supported by the New Testament, I would encourage you to read chapters 13 and 17 of Revelation with an eye for how the beasts described there share many characteristics with corporate power. (In fact, you might consider taking a moment to do that right now before reading further here.) Although I think it stretches credibility to assert with any confidence that we know what specific events the visions of Revelation represent, I tend to view them as metaphors or archetypes representing qualities and characteristics of intention and action, meant to encourage discernment regarding spiritual currents in the world. That is, they help us identify important road signs in the evolution of the kingdom of God. But whether we read Revelation as an archetypical warning for all generations or a prophecy for a specific age – whether as figurative imagery or literal events – the text itself promises to bless those who read it and take it to heart (Revelation 1:3).

In this light, it is my belief that the continuing rise of corporations as beings with the same protections and privileges as people has placed them in the running for embodying the strongest opposition to everything the kingdom of God represents, indeed allowing them to become the most destructive force on Earth. For it seems to me that we are rapidly approaching the point where no one will be permitted to buy or sell without corporate sanction (Revelation 13:17); where worldly authority everywhere on the planet will exist primarily in, by and for corporations (Revelation 13:4; 17:13&17); where anyone who resists the expansion of corporate interests will be killed (Revelation 13:15); where the legal status of corporate personhood has breathed life into the corporate image, which has in turn routinely been expanded and protected by the lethal force of the world's armies (Revelation 13:15); and where all the peoples of the Earth proclaim, "What else compares to corporate capitalism, and who can fight against it?" (Revelation 13:4). And, when we look at how pervasively modern conservative Christendom – especially in the U.S. – adores and defers to corporate capitalism, devotedly advocating and enriching its power and interests at every opportunity, it confirms to me that corporations have already successfully made war on the saints and conquered them (Revelations 13:7). In terms of fulfilling the archetype of a destructive, all-powerful, self-serving beast, corporate capitalism fits the bill quite nicely.

But let's move the conversation back into the realm of personal choices. According to the spirit of Christ, should a Christian side with collective bargaining efforts that ensure a safer work environment and a more equitable distribution of wealth, or with corporate leadership that seeks to protect the profits of shareholders and management? Should Christian wage slaves become free if possible, or encourage further enslavement? Should Christian consumers rely on the rule of law to protect the innocent and punish evildoers, or weaken that rule until it can no longer contain corporate power? Should Christian business owners subscribe to different ethical standards than their non-Christian competitors, or operate with the same worldly orientation? Should Christians eschew the idolatry of mammon and the harmful deception of corporate personhood, or embrace these things unquestioningly?

Among those who support corporate capitalism, there is an argument that corporations amassing such wealth and power are benefitting human populations with jobs, goods, services and increasing affluence, thus creating a rising tide that inclusively lifts everyone's boat. This is indeed the potential for great good that comes with prolific wealth creation and far-reaching influence. And yet even where these tangible benefits can be measured, for each one generated by corporate wealth production, there are a plethora of indirect costs – what economists call *externalities* – that undermine these benefits. There is the depletion of natural resources; the injurious pollution of soil, air and water; increased stress, illnesses, injury, birth defects and premature death among workers and consumers; and, perhaps most damaging of all, the creation of lifelong dependencies on goods and services for which the perceived nourishment and value is really a fabricated illusion. And as wealth increases, consumption increases, so that all these externalities spiral out of control. So once again a choice can be described as being between what genuinely benefits everyone in the most equitable way (a progressive value), and what enriches a few stakeholders at the expense of everyone and everything else (a conservative value).

To illustrate this destructive relationship, consider that the greatest consumers on Earth – those of us who live in the U.S. – also have the largest carbon footprint on Earth. By this metric, to consume is to destroy, and the primary raison d'être for corporations is to foster ever-accelerating consumption. For an entertaining exploration of the pitfalls of corporate capitalism, you might consider watching *The Corporation,* a documentary by Joel Bakan, Mark Achbar and Jennifer Abbott, and peruse related resources at www.thecorporation.com. Or you might read Noam Chomsky's *Profit Over People: Neoliberalism & Global Order*, or Greg Palast's *The Best Democracy Money Can Buy*. Or you could watch Robert Kenner's *Food, Inc.*, Robert Greenwald's *Wal-Mart: The High Cost of Low Price,* Josh Fox's *GasLand,* or other such revealing documentaries for additional perspectives. And of course I always try to promote E.F. Schumacher's *Small is Beautiful,* which offers inspiring solutions as it identifies the problems of corporate capitalism. My book *True Love* provides additional thoughts, resources and solutions as well.

Yet whether we cast this question as a civil liberties issue, a materialism issue, a rule-of-law issue, a sustainability issue, or an end times predicament evoking the beasts of Revelation, the spirit of the New Testament's instruction is clear: a Christian's responsibility is to serve God and not mammon, to promote the inherent value of all human beings above their enslavement, and to advocate a cooperative spirit of loving service for the common good above aggressive competitiveness and self-serving greed. Where the established rule of law restricts corporations, regulating free enterprise to the point of reducing jobs and hindering profits, a Christian's duty is to submit to those governing authorities in acknowledgment that Divine will is working through this governance – once again for the common good. In the starkest of terms, corporate capitalism as it exists today is responsible for some of the greatest evils perpetrated on humankind, so why would someone following Christ wish to empower, endorse or defend it? In the spirit of promoting the well-being of workers, consumers, children, the environment, and indeed the kingdom of God, how could any Christian support the agendas of big business over the preservation and well-being of everyone and everything else?

~

To be intellectually honest, we could of course offer up an entirely different, perhaps even contradictory set of themes than those covered so far in this book. By using other combinations of verses we might be able to support a more conservative perspective on civil liberties, social safety nets, environmentalism, capitalism and so forth. But that is where the other tools in our hermeneutical toolkit come in. When we apply scriptural principles in disciplined practice, when we begin to intuit the underlying imperatives of the New Testament through meditation and prayer, when we let go of cultural programming and bare our hearts to the reality of spirit, then the Light shines out from our center to illuminate the truth. If the compassion of Christ is our guide, we can't help but discern that encouraging civil liberties, helping the poor, healing the sick, protecting the rights of workers, escaping corporate enslavement, protecting the environment and honoring everyone's desire to marry are natural extensions of New Testament teachings. For Christians, this applies first and foremost to decisions and interactions within the Church, and then to humble service to the world – that is, submitting unconditionally through interpersonal relationships and civil society to the needs of those outside of the Church and becoming all things to all people.

Liberation Theology & Social Justice

One interesting question in this context is whether all of the progressive themes we find in the New Testament effectively add up to some of the more progressive movements in recent Christian history. To begin, let's take a look at the *liberation theology* that took root in Latin America in the 1960s and 1970s. After doing a bit of research on the topic, I have to say that any well-rounded treatment of liberation theology probably deserves its own book, especially since the movement has evolved in many different directions within many different cultures over the past several decades. However, by sampling books like Robert McAfee Brown's *Liberation Theology: An Introductory Guide*, and Paul Sigmund's *Liberation Theology at the Crossroads*, we can assemble a few key features this influential movement has advocated from its beginnings. For example:

- Liberation theology maintains that those who are poor and oppressed are important to God and deserve to be prioritized within the Christian faith. This prioritization is expressed first and foremost by interpreting scripture from the perspective of those suffering from poverty and injustice. It is also expressed in the concerted and committed action of Christian believers on behalf of the poor and oppressed.

- The nature of this action – this *orthopraxis* – is multifaceted, but demands an element of sociopolitical activism that intends to reform cultures, economic systems and governments that have perpetuated oppression, exploitation, suffering and poverty. This activism has often been cast in terms of grassroots revolutions that empower the common person. The theological support for that activism seems primarily to be derived from the actualization of an egalitarian kingdom of God on Earth.

- The ultimate goal of liberation theology's orthopraxis is the attenuation of suffering, injustice and poverty – that is, overcoming evil with good. This has often expressed itself as opposition to capitalism and the promotion of Marxist concepts and ideals, which in turn has invited criticism from pro-capitalist and anti-socialist evangelical Christians.

In many ways, liberation theology addressed head-on the tensions between social conformance, the conservation of tradition and the progressive teachings of the New Testament. Where scriptural interpretation and convictions of faith are so often filtered through cultural and institutional bias, liberation theology boldly asserted a prejudice in favor of the poor and oppressed and refuted favoring the wealthy social elite. In this sense, it certainly conformed to the New Testament ideals we have discussed so far. In its emphasis on personal action on behalf of others – that is, a commitment serving those most in need – it also finds strong support in New Testament attitudes, examples and instruction. And of course, as we have seen, many socialist and even Marxist sentiments align quite nicely with New Testament principles.

On the other hand, in promoting certain forms of revolutionary activism as a primary mode of Christian service, liberation theology has contradicted some of the conclusions we have explored regarding the apolitical nature of Christ's example and teachings and the patterns of the early Church. Where the New Testament describes humble and self-sacrificing service to the poor, suffering and oppressed – within the social organization of the Church and within existing civic structures, systems and governments – liberation theology endorsed a more confrontational, subversive and often agitative form of advocacy that served those same beleaguered communities by actively reforming existing civic structures, systems and governments. Although the ends may be the same, the means have been quite different.

In the *The Secular City*, a book often touted as planting the seeds for liberation theology, Harvey Cox argued that the Church could and should work in harmony with secular society – that neither is an effective force for good in isolation. And, in a powerful fulfillment of this premise, liberation theology became part of all manner of human rights movements around the globe in the following decades. From the liberation of African peoples from their European colonizers, to the Black Power and feminist eras in the U.S., to guerilla movements in Central America, to the freeing of Eastern Europe from Soviet rule, this ideology has found resonance among ardent revolutionaries. But the question remains: have these social, political, and economic liberations resulted in improvements for the poor and oppressed? In some cases yes, in others no. In Alexa Smith's article, "Latin American Christians Reshape Liberation Theology," the consequences of liberation theology in Latin America are described as a transition "from poverty to misery," where socialist proposals did not alleviate the oppressions of capitalism. In particular, when we observe the legacy of many of these movements, it is difficult to conclude that the results of such liberation have been consistent or effective expressions of a "secularized" kingdom of God.

For example, with the notable example of East Germany, can we really say that former Easter Block countries are better off today than they were under the Soviets? In particular, many of the governmental systems that served the poor have been dismantled, with nothing to replace them, while capitalist enterprise has enriched only a select few. And although there have been new and important legal protections for women in the U.S. over the decades, the feminist movement did not alleviate the ongoing suffering and abuse of the poorest American women. The Black Power movement likewise did not successfully transform the majority of poor African American communities in the U.S. And, very unfortunately, most of the African nations freed from colonial rule have experienced some of the worst violence and poverty imaginable since their liberation.

So does liberation theology really honor the spirit of Christ's teachings, or subtly misrepresent them? We've already discussed many of the key features of Christ-like activism in that section earlier in the book, and I think liberation theology provides an excellent opportunity for contrast and comparison. In one sense, it seems as though such progressive activism is a natural extension of following holy spirit, a logical expansion of compassionate affection from the interpersonal realm to communal, societal, national and global arenas of action. We also learn from the New Testament that fierce compassion does sometimes require speaking truth to power, clearing the temple with a whip, laying down our life for our friends, arming oneself in defense of the gospel and so forth. And yet there is also the call to peace, patience, gentleness and self-control; the insistence that Christians should subject themselves to governing authorities; the instructions to live quietly, work hard and be above reproach in the community; the exhortation to trust in the power of prayer and the constancy of Divine love; the warning that human anger cannot achieve the righteousness of God; an insistence that we must forgive those who sin against us, love our enemies and bless those who persecute us; and so on. As these contrasting orientations to faith-in-action lead to very different approaches, which path is really the most spiritual in nature or most profitable for the kingdom of God?

I recall watching Roland Joffé's film *The Mission* years ago, where the two main characters – portrayed by Jeremy Irons and Robert De Niro – seemed to represent these contrasting manifestations of Christian faith. It's a compelling story, beautifully filmed and acted, adding artistic dimension to this debate; rather than spoiling the ending, I'll recommend it as one way to explore this topic. Another avenue is to view each unique expression of faith-in-action throughout Church history as part of the memetic evolution of Christianity itself; that is, appreciating different modes of activism as stages or cycles any religious meme passes through during its cultural lifetime. I touch on this idea in my book *True Love*. In my own journey of faith, the most definitive answer to the question of how I can best serve others in love has always been found in prayerful meditation, and is usually highly specific to a given situation and the phase of my spiritual journey. About the only generalization I can make about those insights is that the state of my heart always comes into sharpest focus, as if this itself is a primary component of the answer. Do my thoughts reflect caring and kindness, or rationalizing and intellectualization? Do my intentions flow out of love for others, or the indignations of ego? Do my actions demonstrate an immediate, concrete, felt compassion for other human beings, or the shortest path to what I want? So these are some of the means to navigate the distances and differences between various forms of faith-in-action.

With this said, we don't really find much support for the agitant or revolutionary elements of liberation theology in the pages of the New Testament. The chief concern of those scriptural teachings remains the guidance and transformation of an intimate spiritual interiority. Jesus and his apostles do promote liberation, but it is a spiritual liberation, a revolutionary orientation of intentions, which only incidentally frees believers from material or situational concerns. The objective description of poverty and oppression is that they are real suffering that any kind-hearted person would seek to alleviate, and the New Testament encourages this relief as one component of faith-in-action, expressed mainly through interpersonal generosity and compassion. But such action is secondary to the main work, which is the liberation of the mind, heart and body from willfulness, selfishness, worldliness and materialism; this internal transformation must occur before its external manifestations have any meaning or import – other than helping train these intentions. The subjective experience of poverty and oppression result from rejecting a spiritual life, and a spiritual life in turn alleviates the subjective experience of suffering. This is the true emancipation to be found in Christianity and the durable power of the kingdom of God. All other expressions of liberation are ripples in the pond, flowing outward from this center.

For more information regarding liberation theology, you might consider visiting www.liberationtheology.org.

The Social Justice Imperative

We can see that the ideals of social justice – that is, a philosophy that emphasizes human dignity, human rights, equality and economic egalitarianism – is inherent to New Testament teachings. It is also clear that some sort of activism that enables social justice both within the Church and as an expression of faith-in-action towards society is woven into the fabric of New Testament Christianity. However, as we have already touched upon in examining both conservative and progressive responses to many social justice issues, the more controversial question is what specific form that activism should take.

I think to some degree the modern availability of so many avenues of constructive action has clouded this issue. For example, we can click a "Give Here" button on the website of some social justice organization or other. We can vote for an initiative or sign and petition that we believe helps further social justice concerns. We can help a candidate campaign for public office, or join in a march or rally to stimulate collective conscience, or speak truth to power through letter-writing campaigns, or participate in labor strikes, or leverage our consumer status to boycott some unscrupulous company. And throughout all of these actions, despite the fact that we may often be far removed from both the suffering of the individuals involved and the equitable outcomes that might occur as the result of our efforts, we can still experience a sense of accomplishment in doing what we think is right. And, because of the astounding innovations of the past century, we may believe that all of these are unique mechanisms and avenues of engagement, and so could never be fully addressed by a two-thousand-year-old document.

But I don't think this is the case. Like many modern conveniences, these new mechanisms for social justice really just create layers of abstraction around the primary issue. The essence of appropriate action does not revolve around our demonstrated level of commitment to a cause, or how much money we give, or how eloquently and vociferously we can argue our position, or how creative or innovative our proposals are. No, the heart of this question has more to do with the intimacy and authenticity of our involvement with those who are suffering, and the depth of our personal sacrifice on their behalf – in spiritual, emotional and interpersonal terms. In this context, it matters less how I vote, or what charities I support, or how politically sophisticated my arguments have become, and much more how I conduct myself in each and every interaction.

Jesus healed people with his own hands, touching their bodies and hearts in face-to-face intimacy. He also washed his disciple's feet himself, instructing them to serve each other in the same way. And when Jesus confronted the cultural power brokers of his day, he made sure to do so in their presence, often speaking his truth in their homes or in environments where they held positional authority. Likewise, the good Samaritan bound the wounds of the robbed man himself, put the victim on his own animal, and spent the entire night personally ministering to the man's well-being before he left. Paul, when he used his Roman citizenship to appeal to the authority of Rome, subjected himself to chains and prison in order to spread the gospel himself. James encourages believers to "visit orphans and widows in their suffering" to demonstrate the sincerity of their faith. And so on.

I have some experience of this sort of faith-in-action that informs my understanding as well. When I did some street preaching in those first years after committing to the Christian faith, I quickly learned that what mattered most in those interactions was not what I had to say, but what was on the hearts and minds of the people with whom I shared the good news. Likewise, when I opened my home to the homeless and people with mental, emotional and substance abuse challenges, the most charitable act I performed was listening to their troubles, feeling the breadth of their sorrows, touching their lives with an openness and warmth of heart, and allowing them to teach me about my own humanity. And when I accompanied a minister friend on his rounds to visit widows in the community, it was powerfully evident that although the fires of their joy were stoked with our attentiveness and genuine caring, it was equally important to allow them the opportunity to serve us in return, to allow them to feel useful and important. From these experiences, I do not believe it is possible to serve the world without doing so on an intimate level of mutual exchange.

Life-changing acts of service may sometimes be collective – as was the redistribution of wealth within the first century Church – but first and foremost such acts are personal. The communication is personal. The healing is personal. The giving is personal. And the consequences are personal. Within all of the confusing choices of the modern world, the primary context and qualities of Christian service are really quite simple: Have I seen their face? Did I touch their heart? Did I allow them to see and touch my most authentic personality? Have I given of my innermost self to their most innermost self? Has some sort of exchange occurred on the most intimate level of spirit? Did I love them with all of my being, allowing my life to comingle with theirs on some level? Did I humble myself before them, honoring them for their greatness in the kingdom of God? Did I give them an opportunity to serve me, and did I receive the gift of their presence with gratitude? Was my joy grounded in all of these things?

Whether other modes of faith-in-action – other levels of giving and serving – are more or less effective than such personal interactions (in terms of measurable social justice outcomes or other quantitative metrics) is outside the scope of my point. What I am trying to get at here is the *spiritual efficacy* of interactions that express Christian faith – that is, the quality of outcomes in an intersubjective sense. In all of the most poignant and powerful New Testament accounts, one person's compassionate action on behalf of another is what created a lasting echo throughout the halls of time. When Jesus exhorted his disciples to love one another, his example defined that love first and foremost as intensely personal participation; a felt reality of grace in-the-moment. In contrast, the formalizing or institutionalizing of loving service distances believers from the most meaningful and transformative action for everyone involved. The impersonal may seem easier and efficient in materialistic terms, but the personal is paramount in the realm of spirit.

In its most concrete definition, what does this personal approach really mean? What does it look like? Perhaps it means, for example, that instead of organizing lectures about inclusivity, or initiating interfaith dialogues and intercultural exchanges, or creating a "welcoming environment" for diversity in our institutions, we personally befriend as many people from as many different walks of life as possible, regularly inviting them into our homes and into our lives. Or perhaps it means that instead of just sending money to our favorite charity, we make more room in our lives to help those in need one-on-one. Or perhaps it means that instead of rallying vociferously around some cause or candidate, we reach out personally to those with alternate perspectives, befriend and heap blessings on people who dispute our values or ideas, and break bread with anyone whose perspective we don't yet understand so we can get to know them better. Or perhaps it means that instead of voting for political half-measures to protect the environment or reduce our carbon footprint, we change how we consume, stop increasing human population, or move to a developing country – that is, we stop contributing to the U.S.'s disproportionate appetite for the Earth's resources. Whatever we choose to do, it will demand that we make substantive, radical, personal sacrifices to heal ourselves and the world.

Evidence of Modern Christian Progressivism

With all this support for a progressive orientation in the New Testament, are there any indications that progressivism has taken root in modern Christendom? Absolutely. There are a number of Christian movements, organizations and resources that promote many of the progressive New Testament viewpoints already described. These are quite diverse, and don't necessarily agree with each other (or this book) on all points, but they all share a distinctly progressive approach to modern Christianity. Among them are the following:

- *The Center for Progressive Christianity (TCPC)* advocates critical inquiry, opposition to dogmatic approaches to truth, the loving treatment of all human beings, and many other progressive values. One of the introductory paragraphs on their website reads: "We promote an understanding of Christian practice and teaching that leads to a greater concern for the way people treat each other than for the way people express their beliefs, the acceptance of all people, and a respect for other religious traditions." TCPC develops eight specific points that define progressive Christianity. See www.tcpc.org for more information.

- *Crossleft* describes itself as "strategy clearing-house and central hub for grassroots activism among progressive Christians." See www.crossleft.org for more information.

- *The Christian Left Welcomes You* advocates social justice and networking and mutual support among progressive Christians. It also offers an extensive "Christian Left" booklist. See more at www.thechristianleft.org.

- *Crosswalk America* created twelve "Phoenix Affirmations" that seek to define a more progressive direction for Christianity. The first paragraph of this document begins "The public face of Christianity in America today bears little connection to the historic faith of our ancestors…" and goes on to remedy this by pledging completely to "the way of Love." You can find all of the affirmations at www.phoenixucc.org/docs/affirmations.pdf. There is also a book available by Eric Elnes, *The Phoenix Affirmations: A New Vision for the Future of Christianity*, which explores these ideas.

- The evangelical "Emerging Church" (or "Emergent Church") movement is cast in a progressive light as well, with its emphasis on postmodern self-examination, left-leaning politics and inclusivity. A February, 2007 Christianity Today article by Scot McKnight entitled "Five Streams of the Emerging Church" touches on some of the key elements of this movement. As of this writing, this article is available at: http://www.christianitytoday.com/ct/2007/february/11.35.html. Christianity Today also has a resource section on the movement at: http://www.christianitytoday.com/ct/special/emergent.html.

- *The Religious Society of Friends* certainly embodies many of the progressive attitudes and ideals discussed so far. Here is a fairly concise overview of Quaker beliefs and practices: www.religioustolerance.org/quaker2.htm. You can find more in-depth information about the Quakers at www.quaker.org and www.quakerinfo.org.

- Scotty McLennan's book *Jesus Was a Liberal: Reclaiming Christianity for All* makes a case for one flavor of progressive Christianity by drawing on his experiences in pastoral ministry, the historical promotion of social justice by Christians, and a reasoned responses to atheism.

- The book *What Does a Progressive Christian Believe?* by Delwin Brown charts a course for progressive-minded Christians that presents considered justifications for progressive activism in modern times. At the same time, he also explores some of the problems he perceives in traditional liberal theology.

- *Jesus: A Revolutionary Biography* by John Dominic Crossan is an eloquent exploration of Jesus' life and teachings that touches on many progressive ideas, aligning with traditional liberal theology (Crossan is co-founder of the Jesus Seminar) for yet another take on what progressive Christianity looks like.

- And for yet another flavor, *Jesus Wants to Save Christians: A Manifesto for the Church in Exile* by Rob Bell and Don Golden describes the U.S. as an empire similar to those of ancient Egypt and Babylon, and the role of the modern Church as one of liberating people from those empirical influences rather than conforming to them.

Other resources include www.progressivechristiansuniting.org, www.instituteforprogressivechristianity.org, and additional resources can be found at www.progressivechristianity.net.

My own efforts to find a progressive-minded spiritual community have had mixed results. In my experience, each denomination or congregation has its own strengths and weaknesses. While one promotes honest intellectual discourse, another has a more genuine focus on service; while one is inclusive and even pluralistic, another is more invested in promoting social justice; while one is welcoming and supportive, another has more authentically deepened the art of worship. And so on. The metaphor of many members (denominations) of one body (Church) comes to mind, each with its own function. So as with any relationship, it often comes down to a question of what is most spiritually nourishing for us personally, and where doors of the loving service towards the world open most readily.

Is There Any NT Refuge for Christian Conservatives?

In all the topics we have discussed so far, we have focused the New Testament's progressive leanings. But is there any scripture that bolsters a distinctly conservative viewpoint? Is there any refuge to be found for Christians who are socially, economically, religiously or governmentally conservative in their attitudes and values? Actually, if we look carefully and gather the most sparse of evidences, in fact there are. And if I am to be intellectually honest in this exploration, I need to offer at least some of the conservative perspectives to be found.

Male Homosexuality

There are two passages in the New Testament that utilize the term "αρσενοκοίτης," which means *male homosexual* (ESV):

> Or do you not know that the unrighteous will not inherit the kingdom of God? Do not be deceived: neither the sexually immoral, nor idolaters, nor adulterers, nor men who practice homosexuality, nor thieves, nor the greedy, nor drunkards, nor revilers, nor swindlers will inherit the kingdom of God.
>
> *1 Corinthians 6:9-10*

> Now we know that the law is good, if one uses it lawfully, understanding this, that the law is not laid down for the just but for the lawless and disobedient, for the ungodly and sinners, for the unholy and profane, for those who strike their fathers and mothers, for murderers, the sexually immoral, men who practice homosexuality, enslavers, liars, perjurers,

> and whatever else is contrary to sound doctrine, in accordance with the gospel of the glory of the blessed God with which I have been entrusted.
>
> *1 Timothy 1:8-10*

We should also include what appears to be a reference to male homosexuality (and possibly, by implication, female homosexuality) in Romans 1:18-27 (ESV):

> For the wrath of God is revealed from heaven against all ungodliness and unrighteousness of men, who by their unrighteousness suppress the truth. For what can be known about God is plain to them, because God has shown it to them. For his invisible attributes, namely, his eternal power and divine nature, have been clearly perceived, ever since the creation of the world, in the things that have been made. So they are without excuse. For although they knew God, they did not honor him as God or give thanks to him, but they became futile in their thinking, and their foolish hearts were darkened. Claiming to be wise, they became fools, and exchanged the glory of the immortal God for images resembling mortal man and birds and animals and creeping things. Therefore God gave them up in the lusts of their hearts to impurity, to the dishonoring of their bodies among themselves, because they exchanged the truth about God for a lie and worshiped and served the creature rather than the Creator, who is blessed forever! Amen. For this reason God gave them up to dishonorable passions. For their women exchanged natural relations for those that are contrary to nature; and the men likewise gave up natural relations with women and were consumed with passion for one another, men committing shameless acts with men and receiving in themselves the due penalty for their error.

Beyond these verses, we don't find much more on homosexuality – male or female – in the New Testament. There are other passages, such as Jude 1:7, where some translations render phrases like "having gone after strange flesh" (ἀπελθοῦσαι ὀπίσω σαρκὸς ἑτέρας) as "engaged in homosexual activities," but this is an error – based either on a string of faulty assumptions, a poor understanding of the Greek, or both. Of course Jesus is certainly never quoted as raising the issue at all, and female homosexuality is never clearly and specifically discussed anywhere in the New Testament. Be that as it may, the language in 1 Corinthians, 1 Timothy and Romans is both transparent and negative regarding sexual relations between men – such propensities are characterized as dishonorable, unrighteous, unnatural, impure and so forth.

And yet, to understand the context of such judgments, it should be noted that the following additional behaviors are grouped along with male homosexuality: lying, adultery, various kinds of theft, greed, alcoholism, sexual immorality, idolatry, parental abuse, murder, profanity, and enslaving (slave trading). Most modern cultures – Christianized or not – would tend to agree that these other traits or behaviors are at a minimum unattractive, and indeed immoral or even illegal in certain circumstances. Yet if we are to believe conservative Christian resources that address homosexuality – the Moody Bible Institute's "Coming to Grips with Homosexuality" pamphlet; the www.freetobeme.com website; CNLGLFG Outreach materials; "The Facts on Homosexuality" by John Ankerberg & John Weldon; Focus on the Family's "prevention and treatment of homosexuality" strategies and "Love Won Out" campaign, etc. – homosexuality is to be cast in strong, black-and-white rhetoric, then placed in an entirely different class than everything else enumerated in these verses. It has in fact been systematically elevated to a hot topic of theological debate. As Stanley Hauerwas writes in his contribution to *Theology and Sexuality: Classic and Contemporary Readings*, "Of course now no one, at least no one who teaches Christian ethics, is allowed to be indifferent about the status of homosexuality...No matter where you are or with what subject you are engaged you can count on someone saying something like this: 'That is all well and good but what does what you have said have to do with homosexuality?'"

In the political landscape of the U.S., we have recently witnessed a slew of aggravated rants from Christian conservatives regarding gay marriage somehow threatening the marital tradition, or the dangers of teaching children about homosexuality, or the assault on religious freedoms that homosexuality somehow constitutes, or a host of other irrational, unsupportable homophobic propaganda. Documentaries like Reed Cowan's *8: The Mormon Proposition* examine some of the more strident efforts to characterize homosexuality as a destroyer of civil society. Listening to the prejudiced and hurtful language of Jimmy Swaggart, Rod Parsley, James Dobson and other mouthpieces of conservative Christianity regarding homosexuality is shocking and sad. Yet, with all of this excitement over being gay, there does not appear to be the same intensity or duration of focus on adultery, lying, greed, theft, etc. in rightwing Christendom's public theological and political discourse. So why do these anti-homosexual attitudes have such a prominent place among conservative Christians? Why would anyone invest so much effort in constructing a pointed sociopolitical agenda around two or three New Testament references?

One reason is the *speck vs. log* phenomenon. As Luke quotes of Jesus in Luke 6:41-42 (ISV): "And why worry about a speck in your friend's eye when you have a log in your own? How can you think of saying, 'Friend, let me help you get rid of that speck in your eye,' when you can't see past the log in your own eye? Hypocrite! First get rid of the log in your own eye; then you will see well enough to deal with the speck in your friend's eye." This account is repeated in Matthew 7. I am of course referring to the reality that the other behaviors cited in 1 Timothy, 1 Corinthians and Romans – lying, adultery, theft, greed, idolatry, alcoholism, sexual immorality, etc. – are as common among Christian conservatives as anyone else, and yet within current conservative marketing and outreach there is far less ethical debate or concern over these issues than over homosexuality. We can in fact see in news reports and websites such as www.crewsmostcorrupt.org and www.republicanoffenders.com that conservatives are not immune to straying from a straight-and-narrow moral high ground; they are as human, quirky and fallible as anyone else. However – and I think this is the crux of the matter – unlike an un-closeted gay relationship, many of the other propensities referenced in these passages are either more easily concealed or more frequently tolerated. If we are to believe conservative advocates of the death penalty or aggressive military action, even murder is more allowable than homosexuality in their eyes. Thus it is easier to ignore, trivialize or deny behaviors that are common yet hidden, or that have in effect been normalized or tolerated in mainstream conservative Christianity, as opposed to behaviors that are more exposed, still perceived as being "different," and therefore more vulnerable to ridicule. Thus the most vociferous conservative Christians are able to grasp at the straws of homosexuality to deflect attention from the surfeit of moral failures within their congregations.

The targeting of homosexuality among Christian conservatives has also become a useful rallying cry in public dialogue; it is more self-empowering to dwell on the log in someone else's eye than the speck in our own when trying to galvanize and unite a religious community or a political party. In November 4, 2004, James Dao wrote an article for the New York Times entitled "Same-Sex Marriage Issue Key to Some G.O.P. Races." In this and other assessments of the 2004 elections, the importance of opposition to same-sex marriage in energizing a socially conservative Republican base was repeatedly raised. For example, Dao quotes Robert T. Bennett, chairman of the Ohio Republican Party, as saying opposition to same-sex marriage "helped most in what we refer to as the Bible Belt area of southeastern and southwestern Ohio, where we had the largest percentage increase in support for the president." Amendments banning same-sex marriage appeared on the ballots of eleven states during the 2004 elections, drawing increased numbers of Republicans to the poles.

Of course, most of the contemporary debate has centered around Christian concern over secular laws and institutions, which is once again at odds with the types of activism endorsed by the New Testament. Even if homosexuality were somehow provably antagonistic to Christian spirituality, this verdict would not extend to anyone or anything outside of the Church. As the Apostle Paul wrote in 1 Corinthians 5:12-13 (ESV), "For what have I to do with judging outsiders? Is it not those inside the church whom you are to judge? God judges those outside." Interfering with secular institutions just isn't promoted by New Testament scripture and in fact contradicts it. Thus conservative Christendom's obsession with "outsider" homosexuality seems to be further confirmation that this is really about removing the speck while ignoring the log.

From my own experience and observations, I do not believe homosexual relationships – or many of the other expressions of kind and loving human sexuality that exist in the world – are barriers to holiness. I agree with Marilyn McCord Adams where, in her own contribution to *Theology and Sexuality: Classic and Contemporary Readings,* she frames the more critical questions about Christian relationships, such as: "Would we aid or obstruct one another's spiritual progress? Would (this sort of) bodily intimacy help or thwart our ability to love God and one another? Would it be compatible with our joint and individual responsibilities to others? Would cohabitation make us better or worse channels of charity and benevolence towards God's world?" Echoing the Apostle Paul's advice on heterosexual unions, a Christian's interest should really be in how their own sexuality can best serve the kingdom of God, regardless of sexual identity or inclinations.

So my conscience cannot affirm the negative references in the New Testament as a baseline for evaluating homosexuality. But is there any way to refute them? The passage in Romans presents a characterization of wanton abandonment to sexual lust in the context of idolatry, and as such is really speaking to a broader issue – the consequences of willfully rejecting the Divine. However, Paul does use language here that casts homosexual acts in an unfavorable light, and we can only speculate how he came to these conclusions. Are they the result of his own homophobic prejudices? His training as a Pharisee? The prevailing views of his surrounding culture? Or are they sentiments inspired by holy spirit and convictions of Paul's conscience? We can't know from the text alone, but I tend to lean towards one of the former options rather than the latter. And I believe the same applies to 1 Corinthians and 1 Timothy, though I have also encountered scholarly opinions that the Greek term referenced in those verses may refer non-consensual acts or the exploitation of young male prostitutes. Whatever the case, I suggest any refutation be grounded in our guiding hermeneutic; that is, synthesized out of a marriage of reason, intuitive insight, communal dialogue and experiential wisdom.

Of course, these are just my observations and opinions, but anyone who has witnessed the devoted and enduring love that gay and lesbian couples can share would be hard pressed to dismiss those relationships as less spiritually profitable than heterosexual relationships. I also tend to side with researchers like Alfred Kinsey, who describe sexual desires and preferences as a broad continuum, with no two people sharing identical proclivities, and all people sharing some combination of competing inclinations – passive, assertive, homosexual, bisexual, heterosexual, transgender, etc. In other words, there is rarely if ever a 100% heterosexual or 100% homosexual person. And if we extend Paul's logic in 1 Corinthians 7 to such endless varieties of sexual identity and expression, a publically accepted relationship – and indeed marriage – should really have been afforded gays, lesbians, bisexual and transgender people from the very beginning of Christianity. In a Christ-like attitude that subordinates sexual desires in service to the greater good, nearly all forms of sexuality effectively become equivalent. In this spirit, I wish that I could somehow show that the New Testament embraces homosexuality, for I think this would be healing for many people. But any such effort would be a creative reworking of scripture to suit my progressive sensibilities; that is, yet another example of religion conforming to a particular worldview and cultural experience. Instead, all I can do is appeal to the law of love, to a more mature knowledge and wisdom than the Apostle Paul's, and to the promptings of holy spirit in the present.

Be that as it may, if conservative Christians choose to view homosexuality as religiously objectionable, they do have New Testament scripture to support their position. Perhaps this is another reason why anti-gay rhetoric and activism has become so pronounced in rightwing religion over the past thirty years; it is one of very few scriptural havens left to them – perhaps the only one. At the same time, there is nothing in the New Testament to justify any sort of elevation, singling out or emphasis of homosexuality as particularly dangerous or threatening to Christian faith or civil society. Such exaggerated concerns and inordinate fear are distractions from the real work in the kingdom of God, whether it be self-sacrificial service to others, living a quiet life above reproach in the eyes of non-believers, becoming all things to all people, or perfecting inclusive and unconditional love. For we know that the law of love overrides judgmental reasoning. In Christ, no one should ever feel condemned for loving someone of the same sex, or for feeling sexual attraction toward the same sex. This certainly applies to all relationships within the Church, and doubly so to those outside of the Church. Whether believer or non-believer, varieties of sexual feelings should never become a barrier to someone's experiencing the love of God – as manifested in the grace of Jesus Christ, the sacrificial service of the Christian community towards each other and towards outsiders, the kindness of a friend, or any other evidences of supreme compassion. Whoever is moved to cast metaphorical stones at homosexuals should therefore first examine their own lives for any needs, desires, tendencies or prejudices that might interfere with their own spiritual progress, and always avoid presuming that they know for certain what constitutes a spiritual barrier for anyone else.

Women, Abortion and Birth Control

Some of the other, more hotly contested issues in modern Christendom are not addressed in the New Testament at all. For example, although the Church Fathers advocated against abortion, there is no discussion of this in the New Testament. There is also nothing about the use of birth control – though I have already argued that encouraging gradations of celibacy certainly would have the same effect on human populations. It should be noted in this context that several methods of both abortion and birth control were widely available throughout first century Mediterranean cultures. I would point anyone interested in researching this toward the utilization of Queen Anne's Lace (Wild Carrot), Silphium, pessaries, and lactation amenorrhea in the ancient world.

Along the same lines, there is nothing in the New Testament to support prohibiting sex education for teenagers, and nothing to discourage masturbation or non-procreative sex – except perhaps that same general encouragement already alluded to: that is, for the spiritually-minded to pursue a lifestyle that prioritizes *agape* above sexual gratification. Regarding teaching safe sex practices, there are of course other considerations as well, such as the prevention of disease afforded by certain methods of contraception. Even the traditionally conservative Vatican has recently recognized the importance of condoms to prevent the spread of HIV/AIDS, describing it as a first step to taking moral responsibility for one's actions (see David Gibson's November 27, 2010 article in *The New York Times* entitled "The Catholic Church, Condoms and Lesser Evils"). But it is the absence of clear and unambiguous New Testament instruction on all of these topics that reinforces the disconnect between values advocated so emphatically by conservatives and the spiritual obligations of the Christian religion.

As we have already covered, practicing oppressive, belittling or hateful attitudes towards women can to some degree be justified by the Pastoral Epistles (1 & 2 Timothy and Titus) and one or two additional verses attributed to the Apostle Paul, but such prejudices are strongly overridden by the radical actions of Jesus, the contrary evidences in Acts, and the contrasting encouragements of Paul regarding several honored, privileged and influential sisters in Christ. Beyond these few judgmental smatterings regarding homosexuals and women, however, there simply isn't much in the New Testament that supports either current conservative viewpoints or longstanding conservative traditions in the vast majority of frequently debated issues. It still seems that despite these slimly supportable scriptural refuges, many of the values held by the "Christian Right" are inventions of a regressive and fearful secular culture, a culture that relies on oppressive and controlling attitudes and traditions to maintain its sense of safety and order. A majority of the time, these conservative values suppress the law of love and the power of the spirit, and diametrically oppose Christ's teaching and example.

A Progressive Trajectory: In the World, But Not a Worldly Structure

Some of the finer points of spiritually aligned progressive ideology are probably more a matter of conscience and discernment than clearly delineated New Testament teaching. As such, however, we can still assemble what constitutes a progressive trajectory of Christian values that enfolds many of these issues. Here is what I would propose as the overarching principle in all such discussions: that Christ intended his spiritual kingdom to express progressive values in nearly every dimension of life, but advocated against that kingdom manifesting as worldly structures and authority. His community of souls would not constitute a political party, governmental power or economic force, or even seek to influence the non-Christian world through anything but loving, humble service and an example of submission to the existing rule of law – and most of this was to be executed on an interpersonal level. What Jesus consistently criticized in the religious elite of his day was their attempt to codify spiritual principles into legalistic and judgmental constraints; what he promoted instead was a devotion to love and its expression in compassionate personal interactions. New Testament Christians are consistently portrayed as a community of believers who operate within secular society, not above it, and who, aside from sharing the gospel itself, never impose their spiritual or moral convictions on anyone else.

I think we see the failure of Christianity again and again across the centuries whenever it attempts to depart from these first principles. Whenever the Church wields worldly authority, becomes intolerant and inflexible, or departs from the law of love, it loses its way. For the kingdom of God to remain spiritually focused, it cannot become a worldly institution or moral enforcer – at least not until a time when the Bible predicts Jesus will dramatically return to make it so. And I think this can be applied uniformly across many different disciplines. For example, ongoing education and edification were clearly venerated in the early Church, but the establishment of a "Christian" university was never encouraged in the New Testament. Why not? After all, there were established schools of other philosophies and religions at that time. Roman, Greek and Jewish societies all encouraged education of the cultural elite, so why is there no evidence that Christian education was institutionalized in the first century? Could this be a deliberate effort to avoid rigid formalization, and instead rely on the guidance of holy spirit and the law of love?

In the same way, although the early Church embodied socialistic labor and economic principles, the formalization of those principles in a code of commercial conduct was never promoted by Christ or his apostles. Why not? Perhaps for the same reason: to place trust in God above concerns about mammon and formal institutions. An interesting historical note is that the Quakers attempted to conform capitalism to Christian ideals in the 1800s with the formation of companies that, according Deborah Cadbury's book *Chocolate Wars*, focused on "wealth creation for the benefit of the workers, the local community, and society at large." But again, Jesus and his followers never went into detail about such things, instead encouraging believers to embody progressive spiritual values while operating within existing secular economic systems and constraints.

In other arenas, scientific inquiry as we understand it today of course did not exist in the first century, but we do see logic, observations of the natural world, rhetorical and dialectical arguments – and other techniques that modern science still relies upon – within New Testament accounts and missives. Once again, however, we never hear Jesus or his apostles mandating that Christians use a scientific approach to every question, but instead they encourage believers to trust in holy spirit and mature their spiritual understanding through multiple input streams of edification. So while there is no reason why a Christian could not utilize science to serve the kingdom of God – and certainly no reason for the

Church to suppress or oppose scientific inquiry – there is also no reason to "Christianize" the sciences; that is, to inflexibly filter, conform or confine all data through a Christian worldview. This is just another form of legalism, and encourages the formalizing, systemizing, and codifying of how believers should interact with their environment. Legalism is natural enough tendency in human beings, but Jesus dedicated his life to liberating people from its constricting consequences.

Likewise, although Jesus aggressively sought to obliterate the oppressive stigma of first century womanhood – even to the point of dismissing any "spiritually unclean" associations with a woman's menstrual cycle, marital history or sexual misconduct – he never established a religious order equivalent to the Vestal virgins or a list of laws regarding female equality. Here again, there is no inflexible code of conduct imposed upon Christendom or formalization of such a code into an institution; the emphasis always remains on the spirit of the law, rather than the letter of the law. In a similar vein, Jesus relied on freedom of speech, on the availability of wilderness, on the rule of law and a number of other essential conditions to further the gospel, but he never advocated the creation of Christian institutions to maintain or police those conditions. Nor did he insist that his followers act collectively as an economic or political force to champion any cause other than the expansion of the kingdom of heaven, the amplification of empathy and compassion in the world, and serving the basic needs of other human beings. As we understand it, even the first century Church itself was a loose, cooperative association of congregations rather than a hierarchical, precisely structured, centrally administered organization.

What I think we are getting at here is really at the heart of the New Testament experience: that the kingdom of God was founded on personal expressions of spirituality that were never intended to be institutionalized, codified or formalized in any way. To live by the law of love was to supplant such artifices with a more refined intention that transcended religious doctrine, the cultural practices and institutions of a given society, the structure and politics of government, the advantages and influence of wealth, tribal or familial groupthink, and sometimes even logical reasoning. As Christians consciously seek to harmonize their individual will with the Divine, insight into fruitful actions synchronizes with that intent in dynamic and spontaneous ways. This is essential to a living faith because no doctrine can ever be so complete that it prescribes appropriate responses for every situation. This is a defining aspect of Christ's liberating message, but has often been neglected by those who wish to preserve tradition.

Here are some additional verses that I feel enhance this important idea from the English Standard Version (ESV). Once again, I would encourage you to reflect upon, meditate over, pray about, discuss, and where possible put these passages into practice to arrive at your own conclusions:

> Now as they went on their way, Jesus entered a village. And a woman named Martha welcomed him into her house. And she had a sister called Mary, who sat at the Lord's feet and listened to his teaching. But Martha was distracted with much serving. And she went up to him and said, "Lord, do you not care that my sister has left me to serve alone? Tell her then to help me." But the Lord answered her, "Martha, Martha, you are anxious and troubled about many things, but one thing is necessary. Mary has chosen the good portion, which will not be taken away from her."
>
> *Luke 10:38-42*

> "Now his older son was in the field, and as he came and drew near to the house, he heard music and dancing. And he called one of the servants and asked what these things meant. And he said to him, 'Your brother has come, and your father has killed the fattened calf, because he has received him back safe and sound.' But he was angry and refused to go in. His father came out and entreated him, but he answered his father, 'Look, these many years I have served you, and I never disobeyed your command, yet you never gave me a young goat, that I might celebrate with my friends. But when this son of yours came, who has devoured your property with prostitutes, you killed the fattened calf for him!' And he said to him, 'Son, you are always with me, and all that is mine is yours. It was fitting to celebrate and be glad, for this your brother was dead, and is alive; he was lost, and is found.'"
>
> *Luke 15:25-32*

> "The wind blows where it wishes, and you hear its sound, but you do not know where it comes from or where it goes. So it is with everyone who is born of the Spirit."
>
> *John 3:8*

"I have given them your word, and the world has hated them because they are not of the world, just as I am not of the world. I do not ask that you take them out of the world, but that you keep them from the evil one. They are not of the world, just as I am not of the world. Sanctify them in the truth; your word is truth. As you sent me into the world, so I have sent them into the world. And for their sake I consecrate myself, that they also may be sanctified in truth. I do not ask for these only, but also for those who will believe in me through their word, that they may all be one, just as you, Father, are in me, and I in you, that they also may be in us, so that the world may believe that you have sent me."

John 17:14-21

But now we are released from the law, having died to that which held us captive, so that we serve in the new way of the Spirit and not in the old way of the written code.

Romans 7:6

Do not be conformed to this world, but be transformed by the renewal of your mind, that by testing you may discern what is the will of God, what is good and acceptable and perfect.

Romans 12:2

One person esteems one day as better than another, while another esteems all days alike. Each one should be fully convinced in his own mind. The one who observes the day, observes it in honor of the Lord. The one who eats, eats in honor of the Lord, since he gives thanks to God, while the one who abstains, abstains in honor of the Lord and gives thanks to God. For none of us lives to himself, and none of us dies to himself.

Romans 14:5-7

If one of the unbelievers invites you to dinner and you are disposed to go, eat whatever is set before you without raising any question on the ground of conscience. But if someone says to you, "This has been offered in sacrifice," then do not eat it, for the sake of the one who informed you, and for the sake of conscience—I do not mean your conscience, but his. For why should my liberty be determined by someone else's conscience? If I take part in the meal with thankfulness, why am I denounced because of something I thank God for? So whether you eat or drink or whatever you do, do it all for the glory of God.

1 Corinthians 10:27-31

Now the Lord is the Spirit, and where the Spirit of the Lord is, there is freedom. And we all, with unveiled face, beholding the glory of the

> Lord, are being transformed into the same image from one degree of glory to another. For this comes from the Lord who is the Spirit.
>
> *2 Corinthians 3:17-18*

> I mean that the heir, as long as he is a child, is no different from a slave, though he is the owner of everything, but he is under guardians and managers until the date set by his father. In the same way we also, when we were children, were enslaved to the elementary principles of the world. But when the fullness of time had come, God sent forth his Son, born of woman, born under the law, to redeem those who were under the law, so that we might receive adoption as sons. And because you are sons, God has sent the Spirit of his Son into our hearts, crying, "Abba! Father!" So you are no longer a slave, but a son, and if a son, then an heir through God.
>
> *Galatians 4:1-7*

> And so, from the day we heard, we have not ceased to pray for you, asking that you may be filled with the knowledge of his will in all spiritual wisdom and understanding, so as to walk in a manner worthy of the Lord, fully pleasing to him, bearing fruit in every good work and increasing in the knowledge of God. May you be strengthened with all power, according to his glorious might, for all endurance and patience with joy, giving thanks to the Father, who has qualified you to share in the inheritance of the saints in light. He has delivered us from the domain of darkness and transferred us to the kingdom of his beloved Son, in whom we have redemption, the forgiveness of sins.
>
> *Colossians 1:9-13*

> But solid food is for the mature, for those who have their powers of discernment trained by constant practice to distinguish good from evil.
>
> *Hebrews 5:14*

> Draw near to God, and he will draw near to you.
>
> *James 4:8*

In our discussion of the kingdom of God in the beginning of the book, we saw how the idea of a spiritually transcendent kingdom was reinforced many times in scripture. To be part of that kingdom is to exemplify progressive values and exhort fellow believers to live by them. But this does not mean that Christians conform to such ideals out of fear, or enforce rigid proscriptions and prescriptions upon themselves or others. Instead, they pursue these ideals out of love, and exemplify them for others in the hope that when spiritual Light is demonstrated in this way, it will lovingly inspire others to follow Christ. Thus the focus of a devout Christian is the expansion of a spiritual kingdom through reformed intentions, with concern for worldly kingdoms restricted to obeying the rule of law, paying taxes, praying for enemies and leaders, and living a life of service that is above reproach in the eyes of non-believers. And this is how a progressive trajectory is fully realized: by the devotion and compassion that Christians express in their relationship with God, with each other and with everyone they meet. That is, by becoming a living testimony to the power of faith, hope and love that truly progressive values represent, they propagate an unseen kingdom into the seen world.

HYPOCRISY FORETOLD: ANTICHRISTS & THE APOSTATE CHURCH

To reiterate what we have encountered so far, with a little conscientious attention to the New Testament texts, we see that there are very few conservative values represented there. There is no prioritization of free markets in the gospels or epistles. There is no bitter rallying against paying taxes. There is no justification for lifting an assault weapons ban or defending Second Amendment rights. There is no promotion of the death penalty. There is no hateful persecution of gays and lesbians. There is no imposition of Christian values and practices on non-believers. There is no insistence on nationalistic pride or the critical importance of a nuclear family. There is no war mongering, encouragement to do violence, or compulsion to spread democracy. There is no opposition to scientific inquiry. There is no destructive denigration of the Earth in service to human priorities and needs. There is no advocacy of hateful, deceptive and belittling speech against political leaders or anyone with opposing views. There is no encouragement to accumulate worldly wealth or subscribe to competitive capitalism. There is no sabotaging of labor unions that protect the rights of workers, and no mandate to enlarge corporate influence. None of these conservative practices are supported by the internal logic and evidences of the New Testament, especially when that scripture is embraced as a whole. Not one. In fact, most of these values are repeatedly described as worldly and sinful at worst, or incomplete and immature at best, while the rest oppose the spirit of New Testament teachings by their very nature. Even where we can ferret creative counterexamples out of a few selected verses, any attempt to represent such attitudes as Christ-like would tremble and crumble in the presence of the healing, humbling, harmonizing and unifying power of the supreme compassion Jesus demonstrated to the world.

To observe so much conservative Christian activism throughout history and in modern times that countermands New Testament teachings leads us to an obvious question: do these scriptural guidelines and promises really make a difference in people's lives? Does Christianity really reform personal, community and societal attitudes and behaviors, or is it always subjugated to political, economic and cultural forces? Can believers really be born anew in the promised power of the holy spirit, bearing the fruits of mature spiritual insight and love, or will they continue to be influenced by the fear, ignorance, prejudice and greed that has so often plagued humankind? Is the kingdom of God real, or a comforting fantasy that distracts people from confronting their own demons and dealing with their own inadequacies? Are the revolutionary ideas and examples of Jesus Christ destined to be vanquished by the stubborn willfulness of self-righteous religiosity and empty legalism, or is there a way out?

I recall one discussion I had with some non-Christian friends a couple of years after my own conversion to the faith. I was attempting to point out that their hostility to Christianity seemed to generalize a few unfortunate facts about the history of the Christian Church into a wholesale condemnation of millions of people...including me. It was indeed a common prejudice that I experienced whenever I divulged my beliefs during those years in Seattle, Washington, and it was personally quite painful to be so summarily judged. In reply, my friends pointed out that the Church seemed to encourage ignorance rather than enlightenment, and they called upon Darwinian evolution as an example. I bristled, of course, insisting as I had been taught in my church that Darwin had offered a theory, that there were plenty of holes in that theory to allow a reasonable person to question it, and that creationism was also a viable though contrasting possibility to consider. But after an hour or so of discussion, it became clear that it was my own thinking that was full of holes, and indeed astonishing ignorance about Darwin and science in general, and for the first time in my Christian journey, I recognized the fallacy of at least some of what my own religious community had been holding up as truth. Not only was evolution supported by a tremendous amount of evidence, but I found myself wondering why the Church of Christ was so invested in rejecting it – and indeed why any Christian would think that evolution and creation were somehow mutually exclusive. I was bewildered.

The more I learned about evolution, the more I saw that Darwin and a created universe could easily and peacefully coexist. There was no reason to set science and Christianity in opposition to each other. What was so scary about a Deity that was infinitely creative in the mechanisms of creation? As I thought and prayed about it, it became clear that it wasn't really Darwin's ideas about common ancestry and selective adaptation that so threatened my Christian community, it was his practice of challenging fundamental assumptions about the nature of Nature, casting doubt on an inflexibly literal interpretation of the Old Testament, and offering new directions for scientific inquiry – these were what really seemed to rattle anyone set in their ideas and ways. That is, it was Darwin's progressivism – his advocacy of new assumptions that achieved a more complete and useful understanding of life – which challenged a conservative ideology that resisted new ideas and change of any kind. This was the real tension: progressivism verses conservatism, not science verses God. But because of the dominance of conservative views within a highly vociferous evangelical Christendom, my non-Christian friends had come to perceive Christianity itself to be a source of resistance to scientific thought. Unfortunately, to my chagrin and dismay, their observation about Christian institutions enforcing ignorance on unsuspecting believers was, at least from my experiences at that time, grievously accurate.

That was the beginning of my questioning my affiliation with the Church of Christ and evangelical Christianity in general. From that point I began a much more rigorous examination of own spiritual education. The more I studied and reflected on various issues, the more betrayed I felt, and that sense of betrayal continued to be magnified as I realized that many of my elders and ministers were deliberately avoiding some of the more challenging questions about Christian belief. Why insist on a literal interpretation of the Bible that only amplified its inconsistencies? Was a person allowed to be an intellectual and a critical thinker, and still believe in Christ? If Darwin's theory of evolution was true, why did that have to negate the creative genius of God? What if

God had also created life on other planets? Why unquestioningly accept a scriptural canon that was assembled so long ago? Did the New Testament really represent what Christ intended Christianity to look like? Why weren't the Nag Hamaddi texts useful to a Christian's edification? Why were there so few miraculous evidences of the holy spirit – so few indisputable "spiritual gifts" – in the Church today? Was nationalistic pride really a Christian value? And so on.

But these questions were distractions, most of these same elders and ministers would say. All that mattered was the word of God and the saving grace of Jesus Christ. Stop invoking these divisive doubts – you are causing your brothers and sisters to stumble, you are leading the innocent into sin, Satan is whispering in your ear, etc. In other words, many of the religious leaders of my community tended to emphasize the milk of the New Testament message, sidestepping more substantive issues and treating complex or nuanced explorations of Christian faith with grave mistrust. At the time, they seemed more concerned with increasing our congregation's numbers than being intellectually honest or adventurous. When I pointed this out, many of the believers still willing to discuss such things with me contended that the milk remained more important in terms of winning converts to Christ, and that perhaps I was just enlarging my ego with such heady discourse. It was a difficult time.

These evasive patterns did not apply to everyone I knew, and I am grateful to those few Christians who were able to openly explore the more controversial issues of faith with me. I also continued to observe evidences of authentic loving kindness – what I considered to be the first and foremost evidence of holy spirit – in the lives of my brothers and sisters, which helped maintain my devotion to that community. There were even some folks in the COC ministerial discipleship program who wholeheartedly agreed with many of my observations, but were nervous about jeopardizing their position and ongoing education – they didn't want to rock the boat. Even one of the elders in my congregation seemed supportive, at least in private. But as my relationship with the more influential leaders became increasingly strained, the fears expressed by our ministers-in-training began to be justified. Relying on hearsay rather than firsthand observation, some of the elders began to challenge the sincerity of my faith. I was accused of indulging in excesses like watching too many secular movies and drinking wine more often than I should. A fantasy role-playing game I created for Christians was viewed with fear and suspicion, and a junior minister was asked to investigate it and report back to the elders. My leadership position in Bible studies (what we called "fellowship groups") was challenged, and my access to study materials was revoked. Some of my Christian friends were questioned about my lifestyle and attitudes. Eventually, my church relationships began to be undermined with pernicious threads of malicious gossip. Without publically casting me out of the congregation, the accusations and implications of those fearful leaders subtly but effectively ostracized and isolated me from a formerly welcoming spiritual community.

This personal experience of a judgmental, close-minded, frightened and controlling response in my own denomination's leadership – to no greater threat than a curious mind, a seeking heart and some difficult questions – eventually led to my exiting that fellowship altogether. And when similar things happened to some of the other members of that congregation, they also chose to leave. I think gradations of this same dynamic have probably alienated countless millions of people from their spiritual communities and the message of Christ. For me, the progression from feeling misled to being treated with hostility was the first glimpse that something was horribly amiss in the body of Christ. That nonbelievers like my Darwinist friends would feel alienated, scorned or persecuted by Christian believers raged against everything Jesus taught and exemplified. But even more, how could believers who had embraced such a tremendous gift of grace ever choose to deliberately alienate other believers? How was it possible for kindness to ebb, for unity to dissolve, for love to fail? What had happened to our humility and forgiveness? Where was that precious sense of sacrificial service to fellow Christians, and the joyful willingness to engage every aspect of the world in the most accepting and tolerant of ways? How could I end up feeling so isolated and alone amid my spiritual brothers and sisters?

As I began to conclude that there was something fundamentally broken or misplaced within the Church, I tried to understand it. As I continued to study the New Testament, I realized that these developments should not have been so surprising to me. To understand why, I'll offer the following verses for your consideration (NASB):

> "At that time many will fall away and will betray one another and hate one another. Many false prophets will arise and will mislead many. Because lawlessness is increased, most people's love will grow cold. But the one who endures to the end, he will be saved. This gospel of the kingdom shall be preached in the whole world as a testimony to all the nations, and then the end will come. Therefore when you see the ABOMINATION OF DESOLATION which was spoken of through Daniel the prophet, standing in the holy place (let the reader understand), then those who are in Judea must flee to the mountains. Whoever is on the housetop must not go down to get the things out that are in his house. Whoever is in the field must not turn back to get his cloak. But woe to those who are pregnant and to those who are nursing babies in those days! But pray that your flight will not be in the winter, or on a Sabbath. For then there will be a great tribulation, such as has not occurred since the beginning of the world until now, nor ever will. Unless those days had been cut short, no life would have been saved; but for the sake of the elect those days will be cut short. Then if anyone says to you, 'Behold, here is the Christ,' or 'There He is,' do not believe him. For false Christs and false prophets will arise and will show great signs and wonders, so as to mislead, if possible, even the elect. Behold, I have told you in advance."
>
> *Matthew 24:10-25*

> "Be on guard for yourselves and for all the flock, among which the Holy Spirit has made you overseers, to shepherd the church of God which He purchased with His own blood. I know that after my departure savage wolves will come in among you, not sparing the flock; and from among your own selves men will arise, speaking perverse things, to draw away the disciples after them. Therefore be on the alert, remembering that night and day for a period of three years I did not cease to admonish each one with tears."
>
> *Acts 20:28-31*

> Now we request you, brethren, with regard to the coming of our Lord Jesus Christ and our gathering together to Him, that you not be quickly shaken from your composure or be disturbed either by a spirit or a message or a letter as if from us, to the effect that the day of the Lord has come. Let no one in any way deceive you, for it will not come unless the apostasy comes first, and the man of lawlessness is revealed, the son of destruction, who opposes and exalts himself above every so-

called god or object of worship, so that he takes his seat in the temple of God, displaying himself as being God. Do you not remember that while I was still with you, I was telling you these things? And you know what restrains him now, so that in his time he will be revealed. For the mystery of lawlessness is already at work; only he who now restrains will do so until he is taken out of the way. Then that lawless one will be revealed whom the Lord will slay with the breath of His mouth and bring to an end by the appearance of His coming; that is, the one whose coming is in accord with the activity of Satan, with all power and signs and false wonders, and with all the deception of wickedness for those who perish, because they did not receive the love of the truth so as to be saved. For this reason God will send upon them a deluding influence so that they will believe what is false, in order that they all may be judged who did not believe the truth, but took pleasure in wickedness.

2 Thessalonians 2:1-12

But the Spirit explicitly says that in later times some will fall away from the faith, paying attention to deceitful spirits and doctrines of demons, by means of the hypocrisy of liars seared in their own conscience as with a branding iron, men who forbid marriage and advocate abstaining from foods which God has created to be gratefully shared in by those who believe and know the truth. For everything created by God is good, and nothing is to be rejected if it is received with gratitude; for it is sanctified by means of the word of God and prayer.

1 Timothy 4:1-5

Children, it is the last hour; and just as you heard that antichrist is coming, even now many antichrists have appeared; from this we know that it is the last hour. They went out from us, but they were not really of us; for if they had been of us, they would have remained with us; but they went out, so that it would be shown that they all are not of us. But you have an anointing from the Holy One, and you all know. I have not written to you because you do not know the truth, but because you do know it, and because no lie is of the truth. Who is the liar but the one who denies that Jesus is the Christ? This is the antichrist, the one who denies the Father and the Son. Whoever denies the Son does not have the Father; the one who confesses the Son has the Father also.

1 John 2:18-23

Beloved, do not believe every spirit, but test the spirits to see whether they are from God, because many false prophets have gone out into the world. By this you know the Spirit of God: every spirit that confesses that Jesus Christ has come in the flesh is from God; and every spirit that does not confess Jesus is not from God; this is the spirit of the antichrist, of which you have heard that it is coming, and now it is already in the world. You are from God, little children, and have overcome them; because greater is He who is in you than he who is in the world. They are from the world; therefore they speak as from the world, and the world listens to them. We are from God; he who knows God listens to us; he who is not from God does not listen to us. By this we know the spirit of truth and the spirit of error.

1 John 4:1-6

But false prophets also arose among the people, just as there will also be false teachers among you, who will secretly introduce destructive heresies, even denying the Master who bought them, bringing swift destruction upon themselves. Many will follow their sensuality, and because of them the way of the truth will be maligned; and in their greed they will exploit you with false words; their judgment from long ago is not idle, and their destruction is not asleep.

2 Peter 2:1-3

These are springs without water and mists driven by a storm, for whom the black darkness has been reserved. For speaking out arrogant words of vanity they entice by fleshly desires, by sensuality, those who barely escape from the ones who live in error, promising them freedom while they themselves are slaves of corruption; for by what a man is overcome, by this he is enslaved. For if, after they have escaped the defilements of the world by the knowledge of the Lord and Savior Jesus Christ, they are again entangled in them and are overcome, the last state has become worse for them than the first. For it would be better for them not to have known the way of righteousness, than having known it, to turn away from the holy commandment handed on to them. It has happened to them according to the true proverb, "A DOG RETURNS TO ITS OWN VOMIT," and, "A sow, after washing, returns to wallowing in the mire."

2 Peter 2:17-22

Before reading further, please take some time to meditate, pray, reflect upon and discuss all of these verses while maintaining a neutral disposition. Do the principles in these excerpts apply to situations in your own life in any way? How do they inform our understanding of why so many attitudes and actions of Christians have contradicted New Testament teachings over the centuries and into present times?

New Testament verses that describe the falling away of Christians and corruption of the Church in the end times define what is called the apostasy (αποστασία), that is, a pervasive abandonment of authentic faith within Christendom. In most instances, the interpretation of these verses has conveniently leant itself to the condemnation of the perceived adversaries of a particular denomination. The first Protestant reformers saw the Roman Catholic Church as apostate. Mormons view the entire history of the Church as apostate, with Joseph Smith's primary role as one of restoring the Church; as Barry Bickmore, in his *Restoring the Early Church, Joseph Smith and Early Christianity*, writes: "The simple fact is that had there been no 'apostasy,' or 'falling away,' from Christ's original Church, there would have been no need for God to restore the Church through Joseph Smith." Some Roman Catholics (Sedavacantists) believe an apostasy began after the Second Vatican Council. Evangelical dispensationalists hold the apostate Church to be a continually unfolding event, perpetually revealing itself well into the future until the second coming of Christ – yet even here Christian scholars disagree about the phases, signs and timing of this event.

Coinciding with the apostasy is the appearance of a series of antichrists who share certain characteristics. First and foremost, although they were once Christians themselves, they have fallen away from their beliefs and propagate false doctrine. They are men of lawlessness, sons of destruction, exalting themselves above everything else that is worshiped, setting themselves up as God. People will believe in them because of a deluding influence, and because of the false wonders they perform. These antichrists will distort the truth and deliberately lead people away from the faith, denying that Jesus is the Christ and or that he came from God. In these times, Christian will turn against Christian, and they will no longer love each other.

At this point I don't wish to focus on the many conclusions others have drawn regarding antichrists throughout history. Rather than vilifying specific individuals, I tend to view the "antichrist" concept as an archetype for attitudes and behaviors that are destructive to the kingdom of God; so anyone in the Church can become an antichrist. Nevertheless, there are clear indications here as to why so many people who profess to be Christian selectively disregard New Testament teachings and promote attitudes and actions that directly oppose scriptural principles and values. To destroy government programs that serve the poor, protect the environment or improve the health and well-being of an entire nation certainly seems in keeping with the proclivities of antichrists. To set oneself up in judgment of nonbelievers and aggressively seek to restrict their rights and liberties also seems akin to setting oneself up as God. And what better example of a *son of destruction* is there than someone who promotes needless war and the murder of countless innocents, fabricating dangers that do not exist, as occurred when the U.S. invaded Iraq? Aren't *men of lawlessness* people who rebel against government authority, such as those who refuse to pay taxes, or who seek to eliminate government laws and regulations that hold evildoers accountable, or insist on owning guns in order to take the law into there own hands, or generate gossip and lies about elected leaders and political opponents in order to gain an advantage? All of these seem to be evidence of antichrists at work.

Returning to Jesus' words in Matthew 24 (NASB): "At that time many will fall away and will betray one another and hate one another. Many false prophets will arise and will mislead many. Because lawlessness is increased, most people's love will grow cold. But the one who endures to the end, he will be saved." It certainly seems as if Christians were expected to abandon each other and the core elements of their faith as a predictable matter of course in the end times. And all of this would be evidenced by the loss of love, the chilling of the human heart to the will of God, a degrading of the unity and harmony of the Church, and abandoning the needs of the world in favor of its destruction. And what better explanation for my own experience was there than betrayal, discord and love grown cold? It wasn't that my elders and ministers had blatantly fallen away from the faith – in fact, that was a better description of what was gestating in me as a result of their intolerance. No, it was more a recognition that fear-based reasoning is what destroys religious communities – through suspicion, accusation, the imposition of self-protective controls and an attitude of moral and spiritual superiority. To lord over people without loving them is the heart of destruction within any group, and although belief in Jesus as Christ may not have been completely cast aside, faith in Christ's teachings and example most certainly had.

Of course it was only a selective, authoritative few in my church who seem to have deserted a Christ-like attitude and understanding – and in fact I believe it is rarely a majority of the members of a given faith community who do so – but it was enough to reap a harvest of division, bitterness and turmoil for me as well as others I knew, just as the New Testament predicted. From those experiences and further research into the history of the Church, I began to piece together that the mistrust of change, the egoistic righteousness, the aversion to difficult questions, the intolerance of ambiguity, the insistence on tribal conformance – and a host of other reflexes that tend to be congruent with conservative proclivities – were really at the heart of the most acute failures in the kingdom of God. And when I recognized that these characteristics also happened to correlate with prophesied indicators of an apostate Church and the end times, I concluded that my own religious experience had actually been somewhat predictable. So how could I be upset about something that was prophesied to occur? Then again, perhaps this was just a creative rationalization after-the-fact on my part, invented to help me forgive and heal. Looking back, it still helps me make sense of it all.

These prophecies are important for other reasons as well. According to these same New Testament references, the end times began in the first century – from Jesus, Paul and John, we hear that the "last hour" had already arrived in their time. And if it is truly the case that the apostasy was itself initiated with establishment of the kingdom of God, it certainly explains some of the rampant hypocrisy of Christians over the centuries. To be fair, the hypocrisy of the Church is no greater than what we find in any other human institution. But because Christianity professes and exalts a set of elevated standards, higher self-imposed expectations that should in fact be facilitated by the indwelling of the holy spirit, this hypocrisy seems all the more discordant. For if the fruits of the Spirit – joy, peace, patience, gentleness, self-control, etc. – are not abundantly evident in the Church, then where is the power of Christ? Where is the transcendent reality of the kingdom of God in the here-and-now?

And so we come full circle to the initial swarm of troubling questions regarding the transformative impact of religion. Here is how I would answer them: Remember that, according to the New Testament, before the promised gift of the holy spirit, the human heart already contained the law of God; the capacity for the kingdom of heaven already resided within everyone; people already had the willingness and ability to draw near to the Divine and be embraced as righteous; their prayers could be heard and their conscience could guide them into the Light. That is, human beings still had choices before them that would result in loving and spiritually profitable deeds – deeds that effectively brought them closer to the sacred – as well as choices that would lead them into a dark pit of their own making, separating them from all that is loving, holy and good. Jesus effectively paved a way for his followers to approach the Light with confidence, and to become more aware of the import and consequences of their actions on Earth and in heaven, but his teaching did not alleviate any of the choices, attributes or natural propensities that humanity has always possessed.

Therefore, the decisions to consciously take up residence in the kingdom of God, believe in Jesus' message, and receive the holy spirit do not alleviate the constant stream of challenges and choices before believers. To believe in Christ is not to abdicate responsibility for bearing the fruits of the spirit, but to consciously and actively pursue them. To become a Christian is to gain additional responsibility for self-awareness and self-discipline, and to reinforce a spiritual perspective regarding every thought and action; in short, a Christian has the opportunity to evolve spiritually, but only by choosing to do so on a daily basis. If a Christian instead externalizes their efforts, relying on conformance to expectations of a religious institution or community, or if they assume that a physical baptism will somehow imbue all subsequent actions with holiness, or if they in any way attempt to relinquish careful self-awareness and inner devotion in favor of outward expressions of obedience born more of fear than love, then they have already lost the good fight. For a person to believe in Christ's message is to raise the threshold of their spiritual accountability, first and foremost to their own conscience, then to the Divine authority that inspired Jesus to devote his life to others, and only coincidentally to fellow believers or anyone else. We could even say that the only real and effective baptism is therefore a constantly renewed commitment within, and the only effective expression of devotion is the acquiescent, patient, tolerant and continuously grateful state of the heart. This intimate acknowledgement of personal responsibility and interior diligence is what differentiates a belief of convenience or conformance from truly transformative faith.

So it should not surprise anyone that a parallel between conservative-leaning Christian communities and a seemingly increased propensity for pride, hypocrisy, worldliness, war mongering, deception, false teaching, sexism, judgmentalism, lording it over others and otherwise non-Christ-like behavior is so evident. For the more anyone cleaves to institutional traditions, the codification of spiritual laws and the other external trappings of religion, the more likely they will lose touch with the essence of Christ's power; for love cannot be institutionalized, codified, contained or rigidified in any way. Love is organic, adaptive, evolving, revolutionizing and *progressive*. Love cares infinitely more about the well-being of humans than the appearance of moral rectitude or adherence to established tradition. Love cares about the most immediate and greatest good more than the efficiencies or ideologies reflected in the systems providing that good. Once again, as Jesus insisted when he healed on the Sabbath, "Which is lawful on the Sabbath: to do good or to do evil, to save life or to kill?" In a modern context, the intent of this admonition is clear. Which is the best way to love others and serve God: to act from sincere compassion in the moment, or cleave to tradition with legalistic rigidity? When conservative Christians reinvent the judgmental legalism of the Pharisees and Sadducees, they disconnect from the loving kindness of God and the guiding light of empathy; they disconnect from all that is Divine within themselves.

The revolutionary power of Christian belief can therefore only be found in a heart that cultivates overflowing love for All that Is. When the growth of that love is absent, then every other truth that Jesus preached is absent. It is simply impossible for Christians to act like Christians when their hearts are full of fear, hate, rebellion, willfulness, bitterness and prejudice. Eliminating hypocrisy and indeed apostasy requires the eradication of these manifestations of chaos and darkness within. And the only Light that can drive them out, the only liberation from perpetual failure, is the flavor and depth of love that Jesus exemplified, and which every believer is encouraged to embrace. The opportunity to do good or evil still remains before every person, the temptations still distract, the impulses to derail individual and collective spiritual progress or taint the Divine emanations of *agape* are still resident within, but the kingdom of God is also there, waiting for those who believe to make the most healthy, constructive and radical sacrifices for the greatest good. This is why the Church has been both riddled with antichrists and pregnant with promise from its beginnings, why darkness and Light have always been present. Thankfully, a Christ-like person is compelled to make spiritually profitable choices not because they are afraid of the dark or even because they love what is right, but because they love people more. It is this supreme compassion that constitutes the highest form of righteousness, and it both prevents destructive opportunists from finding a permanent home within Christianity, and casts apostasies and antichrists out whenever they take root.

Why Sustaining Transformative Change is So Difficult

On the one hand, we read in James that a belief without actions expressing and validating belief is useless (James 1:22-27; 2:14-26); Jesus himself echoed these sentiments when he warned that believers don't demonstrate their faith by declaring worshipful words or intentions, but by actually following through with action (Matthew 7:21; Luke 6:39-49; John 15:1-14; etc.). Yet, on the other hand, Paul warns that even actions expressing tremendous faith are pointless if they are not infused with love (1 Corinthians 13:1-13); and this, too, is something Jesus emphasized (Luke 7:36-48; Mark 12:28-34; John 13:34-35, etc.). This is one reason why devout religion is so often impotent in the face of personal and cultural desires and habits: without appreciation of this dichotomy and a careful and constant effort at balance, most people will naturally tend to gravitate toward one extreme or the other. The momentum and potency of human will is such that even in our most well-intentioned and skillful efforts, we remain in motion between these two opposing conditions – either right actions that lack loving intentions, or loving intentions that lack skillful follow-through. This juxtaposition reminds me of Joni Mitchell's *Slouching Towards Bethlehem*, where she sings: "The best lack conviction, given some time to think, and the worst are full of passion without mercy." Individually and collectively, we live in a perpetual state of flux that disrupts self-actualization and the transformative manifestations of the Divine.

There are other reasons why faith traditions cannot reliably transform individuals – and then society as a whole, as a natural consequence of individual transformation – or sustain that change over time. Earlier, in our discussion of slavery, we touched on the facilitation of fundamental drives (to *exist, experience, adapt* and *affect*), and the requisite advantage any new patterns of thought and behavior must offer for sustainable change to occur. Expanding on this, in my theory of Integral Lifework, the success of any transformative effort is determined by how completely it nourishes all dimensions of our being in a balanced and holistic way – not just the spiritual, but the emotional, physical, interpersonal, intellectual, sexual, purposeful and other essential components of self. If some part of us still clings to a previous mode of being, it is probably because we believe on some level that we won't be adequately nourished otherwise. This is precisely why "old habits die hard;" those old habits are the safe place we return to whenever we are unsure that new habits will meet our most critical needs. Sometimes, through sheer conviction and determination, we can summon the discipline necessary to stay the course with some new practice until we see its benefits in our lives. But this is a fairly rare occurrence, and is usually precipitated by our observation that someone else – someone we admire and respect – has demonstrated attractive advantages when utilizing a new mode of being. Even then, however, if our practice is not complimented with equally disciplined nourishment in all our other facets of self, then our efforts at transformation will eventually come crashing down around us. We will revert to what nourished us more holistically or conveniently in the past – old habits will reassert themselves because they appear to meet our highest priority needs more easily or reassuringly.

And of course we cannot discount the power of materialism's influence on individual and societal development either. If survival or flourishing in a given family, community or nation is persistently defined and achieved mainly through material wealth and power, a perverse kind of natural selection occurs over time. As greed, selfishness, competitiveness, slyness, thievery, deceit, egoism and arrogance are persistently rewarded above other human attributes, these reinforced traits begin to dominate personal and collective self-concept. When the ruthless businessperson is esteemed more highly than the compassionate civil servant, and monetary gain at the expense of others becomes the greatest measure of success, then human beings will train themselves into these roles and patterns even if it is not healthy or sustainable. What is most highly valued becomes the norm, even if it is destructive, and that is precisely what the U.S. brand of commercialized consumption has accomplished. In America, we have come to define ourselves by what we consume, what we own, how our urges can be gratified most quickly, how our possessions and accomplishments compare to others, who we can dominate, and how everything can be commoditized for sale – including religion. And since empathy, wisdom, compassion and generosity are not required to be materially successful in American society, these attributes have been devalued, if not entirely dismissed. It should be no surprise, then, that commercialization and commoditization have corrupted access to the realm of spirit, systematically exterminating authentic spiritual nourishment.

Finally, there appear to be all sorts of structural, environmental and even genetic components in our efforts to evolve, either restraining or inspiring individuals and society with regards to transformative change as a matter of basic physiological function. With each passing year we learn more about physiological conditions that influence cognitive and behavioral processes. For example, a chemical deficiency that results in a compulsive-obsessive thoughts and behaviors; nutrients critical to brain and nervous system growth that cannot be found in highly processed foods; industrial pollutants that accelerate or instigate disorders like autism; technological exposure that leads to ADHD; a genetic predisposition to being fearful and close-minded verses open-minded and adventurous. And so on. Without appropriate physiological, environmental and genetic support, growth and transformation can become unsustainable for individuals. And if these barriers are widespread, society as a whole may suffer a regressive drift.

So perhaps the New Testament predictions of apostasy and antichrists describe the natural consequences of an avaricious materialism that has always been present in human society. Or perhaps they are a recognition of the enduring principle that human beings require balanced nourishment, but can quite easily revert to old patterns that are perceived to be the more nourishing or advantageous for survival (even when they aren't). Or perhaps the presence of apostasies and antichrists evidences the natural barriers to progressive evolution that have always been present in our environment and in our genes. Perhaps they merely reflect what was occurring throughout the early Church, with unfortunate echoes into modernity. Or maybe these conditions indicate some inexplicable spiritual necessity in the kingdom of God: that an enriching synthesis that can only be achieved when there is tension between the desires of the flesh and the longings of the spirit, between gritty effort and acquiescent tranquility, between conservative influences and progressive ones. Perhaps all of these ideas contribute to the truth.

Whatever the case, such barriers to spiritual evolution remind Christians of the necessities of diligent self-examination, of carefully pursuing a balancing act between excessive zeal and ineffective inaction, of how spiritual principles must ultimately facilitate more effective thriving through individual and collective nourishment, and of how the constant lure of materialistic modes of thought and behavior will eventually undermine spirit if they are not moderated. For anyone, hypocrisy, hatred, fear and destruction are really only possible when we allow ourselves to become distracted from the kernel of Divine love within. The Christian's chief responsibility then – indeed the heart of Jesus' message – is to constantly remember the existence and source of that Light, along with its enduring and immutable power. Apostasies and antichrists may persist, but the opportunity to revive and renew a compassionate faith endure as well.

So there is a way out of this conundrum, and that is to persistently seek a way out. Like ancient branches that continue to reach towards the sun, transformative change is possible, and there is as much to celebrate as there is to courageously bear. If someone chooses to do both out of a conviction of faith, a loyalty to conscience and a fervency of love, they can navigate a maze of distractions, achieve the required balance, and overcome all obstacles. This is how a mustard seed becomes a tree, and how temples of a living God express an immortal purpose. This is how each personal choice a Christian makes helps heal and transform the body of Christ even as that body struggles to remain whole.

BEYOND THE NEW TESTAMENT

With all the evidence we have explored thus far, there is ample justification for claiming that the New Testament expresses many progressives values and attitudes. But what about a progressive spirituality? What about the possible evolution of Christianity beyond the baseline established in the New Testament itself? Whatever the reasons Christians might consider seeking additional wisdom, the New Testament actually encourages believers to look beyond its pages. Please take some time to reflect on, meditate about, pray over, discuss, and if possible evaluate through practice the following verses (ESV):

> But this is what was uttered through the prophet Joel: "'And in the last days it shall be, God declares, that I will pour out my Spirit on all flesh, and your sons and your daughters shall prophesy, and your young men shall see visions, and your old men shall dream dreams; even on my male servants and female servants in those days I will pour out my Spirit, and they shall prophesy.'"
>
> *Acts 2:16-18*

> And Paul said, "John baptized with the baptism of repentance, telling the people to believe in the one who was to come after him, that is, Jesus." On hearing this, they were baptized in the name of the Lord Jesus. And when Paul had laid his hands on them, the Holy Spirit came on them, and they began speaking in tongues and prophesying. There were about twelve men in all.
>
> *Acts 19:4-7*

> When we had finished the voyage from Tyre, we arrived at Ptolemais, and we greeted the brothers and stayed with them for one day. On the next day we departed and came to Caesarea, and we entered the house of Philip the evangelist, who was one of the seven, and stayed with him.

He had four unmarried daughters, who prophesied. While we were staying for many days, a prophet named Agabus came down from Judea. And coming to us, he took Paul's belt and bound his own feet and hands and said, "Thus says the Holy Spirit, 'This is how the Jews at Jerusalem will bind the man who owns this belt and deliver him into the hands of the Gentiles.'" When we heard this, we and the people there urged him not to go up to Jerusalem. Then Paul answered, "What are you doing, weeping and breaking my heart? For I am ready not only to be imprisoned but even to die in Jerusalem for the name of the Lord Jesus." And since he would not be persuaded, we ceased and said, "Let the will of the Lord be done."

Acts 21:7-14

Having gifts that differ according to the grace given to us, let us use them: if prophecy, in proportion to our faith; if service, in our serving; the one who teaches, in his teaching; the one who exhorts, in his exhortation; the one who contributes, in generosity; the one who leads, with zeal; the one who does acts of mercy, with cheerfulness.

Romans 12:6-8

Love never ends. As for prophecies, they will pass away; as for tongues, they will cease; as for knowledge, it will pass away. For we know in part and we prophesy in part, but when the perfect comes, the partial will pass away.

1 Corinthians 13:8-10

Pursue love, and earnestly desire the spiritual gifts, especially that you may prophesy. For one who speaks in a tongue speaks not to men but to God; for no one understands him, but he utters mysteries in the Spirit. On the other hand, the one who prophesies speaks to people for their upbuilding and encouragement and consolation. The one who speaks in a tongue builds up himself, but the one who prophesies builds up the church. Now I want you all to speak in tongues, but even more to prophesy. The one who prophesies is greater than the one who speaks in tongues, unless someone interprets, so that the church may be built up.

1 Corinthians 14:1-5

And he gave the apostles, the prophets, the evangelists, the shepherds and teachers, to equip the saints for the work of ministry, for building up the body of Christ, until we all attain to the unity of the faith and of the knowledge of the Son of God, to mature manhood, to the measure of the stature of the fullness of Christ, so that we may no longer be children, tossed to and fro by the waves and carried about by every wind of doctrine, by human cunning, by craftiness in deceitful schemes.

Ephesians 4:11-17

The word for "prophesy" here is προφητεία, which means both Divine revelation and the gifted faculty for sharing Divine teaching. Over and over again in the New Testament we see that Christians were granted the gift of prophecy for the Church's "strength, encouragement and comfort," and that these gifts descended on apostles and ordinary Church members – men and women, young and old alike. There is nothing to indicate that prophecy did not continue well into the first century, and plentiful evidence to conclude that other writings considered prophetic existed at that time that were never canonized. Although some Biblical scholars speculate that 1 Corinthians 13 presages the decline of prophecy and other spiritual gifts as a sign of spiritual maturity, we certainly have an abundance of references in the New Testament to the reliance on the prophetic utterances of ordinary Christians in those first century congregations. Even so, has Christendom attained "the unity of the faith and mature knowledge of the Son of God" as described in Ephesians 4 at any point in the past 2,000 years? Has the perfect and mature knowledge of the Divine already manifested itself among believers? As we have explored extensively in the preceding chapters, there is still plentiful imperfection and spiritual immaturity within the Church – still ample opportunity to become complete, perfect and fully realized (διὰ τέλειος). And without any clear statement to narrow or nullify the permanence and importance of prophecy, there is justification for expecting such prophetic works to exist outside of the New Testament, and indeed for holy spirit continuing to guide believers "into all truth" today.

A confirmation of this assessment arrives with the inclusion of Jude in the New Testament. Although this may be the Jude referred to in Matthew 13:55, that is, the brother of Jesus, or possibly "Judas son of James" described as an apostle in Luke 6:16, we have no indication from the writer of this epistle that either of these is the case. There is in fact no clear evidence that this writer has an esteemed position or pedigree. So is this an example of a believer who is prophesying in the holy spirit for the edification of the Church? Regardless of his status, it seems so. And, as if to answer the very question of what kinds of prophetic teachings might be appropriate for Christian edification, Jude reminds his readers of Old Testament accounts from Genesis, Exodus, Deuteronomy, Hosea, Daniel and Ezekiel in broad, sweeping strokes, relating their relevance to what was happening in the early Church at that time.

What does he do then? Beginning in verse 14, Jude cites a prophesy from Enoch regarding God's judgment (ESV):

> It was also about these that Enoch, the seventh from Adam, prophesied, saying, "Behold, the Lord comes with ten thousands of his holy ones, to execute judgment on all and to convict all the ungodly of all their deeds of ungodliness that they have committed in such an ungodly way, and of all the harsh things that ungodly sinners have spoken against him." These are grumblers, malcontents, following their own sinful desires; they are loud-mouthed boasters, showing favoritism to gain advantage.
>
> *Jude 1:14-16*

Clearly, Jude believes that Enoch prophesied. And yet Enoch's scripture is not a part of the Old Testament or New Testament canon; the Book of Enoch has been considered apocryphal for centuries by most Jewish and Christian religious groups. And yet the epistle of Jude was canonized in the New Testament, offering an inherent contradiction: how could the Book of Enoch not be inspired by the holy spirit, but the epistle of Jude, which references Enoch, be considered holy scripture? What does this contradiction mean? I think it establishes a principle that revolutionizes what is sanctioned by canonized scripture itself as a source for spiritual edification: it declares unambiguously that prophesy is not limited to what was formally accepted and canonized in later centuries. Just as the earlier New Testament verses regarding prophesy convey, the energies of holy spirit cannot be bound in a book or constrained to a narrow slice of scriptural authorship.

So, to better understand how to approach what is available to Christians for spiritual edification – canonized or not – let's begin with the Old Testament and expand out from there.

The New Testament's View of the Old Testament

How did the New Testament treat the Old Testament? First we can say that the Old Testament was quoted frequently by both Jesus and his apostles to support various concepts and, apparently, reinforce the authority of what was being relayed. Almost all modern versions of the New Testament include footnotes for each of these references, so this pattern is easy to confirm – there are something like two hundred quotes or paraphrases of the Septuagint among New Testament texts. In many of the instances where Jesus quotes scripture, he claims that the Old Testament is in fact prophesying his arrival and the events of his life (Matt 11:1-18; Luke 4:16-20; John 17:12), and furthermore that, as he says in John 10:35, "the scripture cannot be broken;" that is, its truths remain true. In the same way, the gospel writers often claim the events in Jesus' life occurred "so that the scripture would be fulfilled" (Matthew 1:18-23, 8:14-17; 21:1-5, 27:3-10; John 12:37-41, 19:18-37; etc.). The epistles likewise use references from the Old Testament to explain Christ's actions, validate his Divinity, and clarify important ideas.

There is also direct discussion about using the Old Testament in Christian practice, for example, in Romans 15:4 it says (NIV): "For everything that was written in the past was written to teach us, so that through endurance and the encouragement of the Scriptures we might have hope." In 2 Timothy 3:14-17 it says (NIV): "But as for you, continue in what you have learned and have become convinced of, because you know those from whom you learned it, and how from infancy you have known the holy scriptures, which are able to make you wise for salvation through faith in Christ Jesus. All scripture is God-breathed and is useful for teaching, rebuking, correcting and training in righteousness, so that the man of God may be thoroughly equipped for every good work." We find similar encouragements in 2 Peter 1:20 and elsewhere. Thus we can see that what today we call the Old Testament played a prominent roll in evangelism, worship and personal edification in the early Church.

And yet we know from Jesus' many pronouncements on the topic that the Old Testament's covenant was also moderated and fulfilled by the new covenant of *agape*. Therefore, folks shouldn't try to "put new wine into old wineskins," (Matthew 9:17, Mark 2:22, Luke 5:37), that is, Christians shouldn't try to conform the freedom they have in Christ to the Law of the Prophets. And of course Paul devotes most of Romans to this topic as well, which he summarizes concisely in Romans 13:8-10: "Don't owe anything to anyone except to love one another, for those who love each other fulfill the law. The commandments 'You shall not commit adultery,' 'You shall not murder,' 'You shall not steal,' 'You shall not covet' and any other commandments are summed up in these words: 'You shall love your neighbor as yourself.' Love perpetrates no evil on its neighbor, therefore love is the fulfillment of the law." When Christians forget this and invoke Old Testament scripture as justification for some inflexible doctrine or other, they are destroying the gracious gift of freedom that Christ provided them.

There is another important caveat in the frequent use of Old Testament verses by Jesus and his apostles, and that can be found in Luke 24:44-45 (NIV): "He said to them, 'This is what I told you while I was still with you: Everything must be fulfilled that is written about me in the Law of Moses, the Prophets and the Psalms.' Then he opened their minds so they could understand the Scriptures." That it was necessary for Jesus to open the minds of disciples that had been with him from the beginning in order for them to "understand the scriptures" presents an interesting dilemma for the modern reader: is it possible to comprehend the Old Testament completely without such assistance? In fact, is it possible to accurately interpret the New Testament or other Christian writings without similar intervention? I tend to think that this is part of how holy spirit will guide believers into all truth, and that is indeed why inner inquiry and invocation are an integral part of any recommended hermeneutic; we must create sacred space within ourselves for the Divine to expand and illuminate our understanding.

Returning to that hermeneutic, we should also remember that actively applying scripture to our thoughts and actions also helps us gain a fuller comprehension of it. Through disciplined practice, we can better appreciate the value inherent to various teachings. I remember a year or so into my own Christian journey, I decided to meditate on one Old Testament proverb each day for a month, filtering all of my thoughts and actions through my meditation for the day, trying to practice the essence of each proverb from moment-to-moment. By the end of that month, my insight into Proverbs had improved a hundredfold, despite having extensively studied the text both on my own and in study groups previously. So as we incorporate scripture into our analytical, intuitive, communal and experiential processing engines, we discover new horizons of edification.

However, what encourages the most intimate and sustained spiritual understanding of any observation, experience or teaching is the infusion of that insight with loving kindness and its grounding in the humility of sincere faith. This way of being – this alternative to worldly strife, striving and worry – is for me the real legacy of Christ and the eternally viable *logos*, allowing Christians to appreciate the spiritual worth of the Old Testament more abundantly. Such a destination can be achieved via many different roads, but it is a great gift to our soul however we can arrive there. That progressively minded people have so frequently been alienated from Christ's message by a religious conservatism rooted in ignorance, tribal enculturation and fear is truly tragic, because the door to spirit that Jesus offers is as unabashedly liberal as it is liberating. The Old Testament does contain a great deal of legalistic prescription, confusing stories and convolutions of Divine wrath. But it also contains encouragement, poetry, wisdom and joyous laughter. Once our minds are opened, spirit can enrich us.

Other External Fonts of Spiritual Wisdom

As a Perennialist mystic, I believe Divine wisdom weaves itself into many different religions throughout history. I also believe that it requires discipline and discernment to differentiate edifying sources from those that distract us from authentic spiritual nourishment. In the Christian tradition, a wealth of spiritual source materials outside of the New Testament is available that reinforces many of the progressive themes we have discussed so far. From apocryphal texts to Gnostic writings to writings of the Church Fathers to the musings of Christian philosophers, poets and mystics over the centuries…there is an endless amount of art, literature, music and film that strengthens, encourages and comforts Christian believers. And just as Matthew, Mark, Luke and John offer slightly different perspectives on the life of Christ and difference emphasis in his teachings, the works of these other devoted believers provide powerful insight into different ways of navigating the Christian faith.

Among the earliest Christian writings I have found both interesting and enlightening are the *Gospel of Thomas*, the *Gospel of Peter*, the *Shepherd of Hermas*, the *Epistle of Barnabas*, the *Didache*, Justin Martyr's *First Apology* and *Second Apology*, the *Epistle of Mathetes to Diognetus*, and a smattering of Gnostic texts. Most of these writings date back to the second century, and some are as old as the oldest surviving New Testament documents themselves. Within their pages we find many of the same progressive themes in the New Testament repeated, clarified and even amplified – helping put to rest any questions of selective interpretation. I have also encountered enriching Christian material that was created much later as well. This would include the works of C.S. Lewis, Maura Eichner, Thomas Merton, Thomas Aquinas, Catherine of Sienna, W.H. Auden, Meister Eckhart, Hildegard van Bingen, Søren Kierkegaard, Anna Akhmatova, George Eliot (Mary Anne Evans), Wendell Berry, John of the Cross, Franky Schaefer, Immanuel Kant, Marilyn McCord Adams, Hans Küng, Linda Zagzebski, Gottfried Leibniz, Pseudo-Dionysius, René Descartes, Justus Lipsius, Theresa of Avila, John Bunyan, Albert Schweitzer and countless others.

Am I suggesting that the creative efforts of these and other Christians are equivalent to New Testament scripture in their spiritual value? Actually, I would say that sometimes they are equivalent, sometimes inferior, and sometimes superior to New Testament writings. Not because these later efforts are either more or less Divinely inspired, but because where the New Testament captures the milk of Christian beliefs – the basic foundations of Christ's message, love and sacrifice – works in later times often explore the solid food of the Christian spiritual experience; they wrestle with the deeper depths and broader breadths of a spiritually directed mind, heart and life. Sometimes people accomplished this brilliantly, and sometimes they fumbled in the dark, but their efforts are always additive in that they provoke our heart, mind and spirit to respond to issues of spiritual substance.

Yet far more important than any such external validations of Divine wisdom – more crucial than what other people have accomplished in the spirit – is the indwelling power of Divine truth within every human being, a power which indeed created these works and is expressed in many wisdom traditions. In this sense, the most progressive element of the Christian spiritual experience is the ongoing availability of insight, knowledge, understanding and wisdom through holy spirit in concert with intuition, conscience and other felt realities. That this spiritual understanding and skillfulness can expand and mature is something the Apostle Paul discusses at length in nearly all of his epistles – either by encouraging such growth, by praising its evidence in the Church, or by chastising believers for not growing swiftly enough in Christ. And how does this maturation occur? Through welcoming Divine guidance and insight and taking each insight to heart, through disciplined application of spiritual instruction in daily life, and through relinquishing ego and willfulness in favor of loving attitudes of willingness, devotion and service. To what end? A continuous transformation, first of self and all relationships, and then of the world at large. By becoming agents of positive change and conveyors of persistent blessing, Christians bear the spiritual fruits of Christ in the perpetual present.

As a mystic, I of course would like to promote a mystical perspective on a progressive unfolding of insight and wisdom as well. Consider this experience described by the Apostle Paul (NIV):

> "I know a man in Christ who fourteen years ago was caught up to the third heaven. Whether it was in the body or out of the body I do not know — God knows. And I know that this man — whether in the body or apart from the body I do not know, but God knows — was caught up to paradise and heard inexpressible things, things that no one is permitted to tell. I will boast about a man like that, but I will not boast about myself, except about my weaknesses."
>
> *2 Corinthians 12:2-4*

Now what is the point of having such decidedly mystical experiences, experiences which seem as fantastical as they are indescribable, if they are not spiritually beneficial in some way? In this context, Paul includes this event as part of a broader spiritual lineage – a verification of his closeness to God, though one he would not boast about. And that is the conviction that most mystics report of their own peak experiences: a validation of access to a spiritual realm, of insight into ineffable truths, of increased proximity to the Divine, and of abject humility. And, as I contend in my other writings (*Essential Mysticism, The Vital Mystic, True Love,* etc.), such experiences are accessible to everyone, because everyone shares a spiritual essence, a Divine Spark that illuminates their innermost landscape. For a Christian, indwelling holy spirit promises a gateway to these transcendent encounters, and there is no reason every believer should not avail themselves of that invitation. In this sense, Mystical union and Divine revelation are as progressive as every other theme we have examined: they are available to all, are constantly expanded and renewed, and always seek the good of the whole above the opportunistic advantage of the few.

But regardless of how we access or encounter spiritually edifying information, questions remain as to how we should evaluate and integrate that information in the course of faith. For Christians, if the New Testament helps establish a baseline by which to measure all subsequent revelation, then what resonates well with the values and themes represented there will be fairly easy to embrace. But what if new spiritual information departs from that baseline in some way? What if, just as Jesus' new covenant of *agape* superseded Old Testament commandments, a deeper understanding of the law of love seems to renovate New Testament principles? I think existing scripture provides us with guidance for this situation as well, especially in its discussion of knowledge and wisdom, so let's examine how it treats those concepts.

Gnosis: A Tool for Free-Thinking Skeptics

Among many self-described progressives I have known, the whole idea of religiosity is often at odds with progressive thinking. For them, only science and reason can deliver humanity from its own errors, and no amount of faith in spiritual realities could enhance human existence. Meaningful evaluation must therefore be logical and analytical. All too often, however, these attempts to establish a foundation of truth upon a few categories of narrowly defined evidence inadvertently exclude whole realms of viable human experience. For example, it has been well-established for some time that emotional centers in the brain play a critical role in decision-making, and that when these centers are impeded or damaged, people find it very difficult – often impossible – to make a "logical" choice about anything. The research and writing of Antonio Damasio has extensively documented this effect. It is also increasingly well-understood that an individual's ability to interpret facial expressions, social cues and complex emotional contexts can afford them greater success in their interpersonal relationships and in navigating society in general. The idea of *emotional intelligence* was made popular by Dan Goleman's book by that name, which promotes a particular EI model based on learned emotional competencies. There is also a scientifically validated test for emotional intelligence called the MSCEIT, which was developed using a different EI model based on what are presumed to be innate abilities.

In addition to emotional intelligence, there are also learning capacity, genetic memory and experiential knowledge embedded into different systems of the human body – somatic or embodied knowledge – which express themselves in physical appetites, intuitions and responses where causal relationships are not always clearly understood. Strong physiological instincts, urges, reflexes and conditioning are some of the more pronounced manifestations of embodied knowledge, but the body's learning and expressions of information can be much more subtle as well. Various bodywork modalities and body-centered psychotherapies have been exploring this process for decades, leading to a number of effective therapeutic techniques. Some of these techniques are grounded mainly in Western medicine and psychology, and others are Eastern traditions that draw upon centuries of successful implementation. I myself have experienced the benefits of Hakomi, Craniosacral Therapy, Myofascial Release, Shiatsu, Hathe Yoga and several others. For a helpful overview of such approaches, try Mirka Knaster's *Discovering the Body's Wisdom.* Also, in addition to therapeutic modalities, the study of aesthetic learning has recognized the importance of embodied knowledge and begun to better define the relationship between somatic experience and human understanding. Two books that explore this idea from different perspectives and disciplines are Elliot Eisner's *The Arts and the Creation of Mind,* and Per-Olaf Wickman's *Aesthetic Experience in Science Education.*

Following similar lines of reasoning into even deeper structures of being, mystics of various faith traditions contend that everyone also possesses the faculty to perceive and appreciate spiritual information – information that, like somatic knowledge and emotional intelligence, is helpful in navigating and constructing conclusions about our existence. They further warn us that relying solely on intellect, either to approach mystical awareness or interpret its peak experiences, will only cloud our understanding, creating barriers to both accessing and integrating spiritual information. Almost universally, mystical disciplines therefore encourage a gradual letting go of the routine consciousness and perception in order to make room for mystic activation. No matter what technique or underlying belief system is relied upon, the similarities of mystical experiences and their edifying and liberating potential is startling. For additional information, my books *Essential Mysticism* and *The Vital Mystic* explore this topic in greater depth.

What I am proposing, even to those skeptical of a spiritual dimension of existence, is that these other avenues of knowledge, these additional centers of intelligence, should simply be included in the modern, free-thinking skeptic's toolbox. In particular, I believe the activation of mystical faculties will provide a rich tapestry of information regarding otherwise inaccessible and ineffable realities. In effect, mystic activation can become a door into the realm of spirit. But why do I bring any of this up in the context of progressivism? Because, as I think most free-thinking skeptics would agree, I believe truly progressive thought is often constricted by external authorities and influences – whether these influences are prevailing memes of a secular culture or the religious edicts of a faith tradition. Any dogma, from any source, has a strong tendency to disrupt those subtle promptings from our innermost depths, our ability to discern the most skillful path ahead, our capacity for growth, and the clarity of mind and sensitivity of heart required to remain fully alert as we explore this amazing mystery called life.

So if our consciousness, memory and identity are comprised of many different input streams and dimensions of self, why would we ever want to exclude any of them in our attempts to understand the human experience? To reject any avenue of perception-cognition will either inhibit the breadth of that understanding or lead to incomplete conclusions. To rely solely on rational analysis is just as self-limiting as relying solely on emotional reasoning, or physically felt hunches, or divination rituals. None is so superior or refined in its apprehension of truth that it deserves to be elevated above all the rest. Yet this has been precisely the trend of human ideologies and institutions throughout the past few centuries: to compartmentalize and specialize each method of processing until they are unrecognizable or unintelligible to one another, even antagonizing and alienating each other. And this is how I believe many well-meaning folks – from liberal theologians to rationalist skeptics to empirical researchers – have overly narrowed the conversation about spirituality and the human condition throughout history and in current debates. They have, in effect, instituted a hyper-rational dogma that rejects other forms of evidence. So instead of drifting further in this direction, like many integral thinkers I would propose we include all of our innate faculties and capacities in exploring the spiritual realm.

But what does the New Testament have to say on this topic? We discussed in the chapter on *Spiritual Authority* how independent introspection is encouraged by scripture, and that avenues to understanding and activating Christ-like principles include consulting our own wisdom and knowledge. But is there any hope of finding scripture that supports a synergy of emotional intelligence, somatic knowledge, mystical awareness and analytical rigor? What follow are New Testament passages that touch on this synergy, addressing inner knowledge and wisdom specifically. The following verses either contain the words knowledge (γνῶσις) or wisdom (σοφία), or have a direct bearing on the same. These excerpts are quoted from the New Revised Standard Version (NRSV):

> 'For John the Baptist has come eating no bread and drinking no wine, and you say, "He has a demon"; the Son of Man has come eating and drinking, and you say, "Look, a glutton and a drunkard, a friend of tax-collectors and sinners!" Nevertheless, wisdom is vindicated by all her children.'
>
> *Luke 7:33-35*

> 'Woe to you lawyers! For you have taken away the key of knowledge; you did not enter yourselves, and you hindered those who were entering.'
>
> *Luke 11:52*

> 'And why do you not judge for yourselves what is right?'
>
> *Luke 12:57*

> Then some of those who belonged to the synagogue of the Freedmen (as it was called), Cyrenians, Alexandrians, and others of those from Cilicia and Asia, stood up and argued with Stephen. But they could not withstand the wisdom and the Spirit with which he spoke.
>
> *Acts 6:9-10*

I myself feel confident about you, my brothers and sisters, that you yourselves are full of goodness, filled with all knowledge, and able to instruct one another.

Romans 15:14

I give thanks to my God always for you because of the grace of God that has been given you in Christ Jesus, for in every way you have been enriched in him, in speech and knowledge of every kind— just as the testimony of Christ has been strengthened among you— so that you are not lacking in any spiritual gift as you wait for the revealing of our Lord Jesus Christ. He will also strengthen you to the end, so that you may be blameless on the day of our Lord Jesus Christ.

1 Corinthians 1:4-8

For it is written, 'I will destroy the wisdom of the wise, and the discernment of the discerning I will thwart.' Where is the one who is wise? Where is the scribe? Where is the debater of this age? Has not God made foolish the wisdom of the world?

1 Corinthians 1:19-20

Yet among the mature we do speak wisdom, though it is not a wisdom of this age or of the rulers of this age, who are doomed to perish. But we speak God's wisdom, secret and hidden, which God decreed before the ages for our glory. None of the rulers of this age understood this; for if they had, they would not have crucified the Lord of glory.

1 Corinthians 2:6-8

Now concerning food sacrificed to idols: we know that 'all of us possess knowledge.' Knowledge puffs up, but love builds up. Anyone who claims to know something does not yet have the necessary knowledge; but anyone who loves God is known by him. Hence, as to the eating of food offered to idols, we know that 'no idol in the world really exists', and that 'there is no God but one.' Indeed, even though there may be so-called gods in heaven or on earth—as in fact there are many gods and many lords— yet for us there is one God, the Father, from whom are all things and for whom we exist, and one Lord, Jesus Christ, through whom are all things and through whom we exist. It is not everyone, however, who has this knowledge. Since some have become so accustomed to idols until now, they still think of the food they eat as food offered to an idol; and their conscience, being weak, is defiled. 'Food will not bring us close to God.' We are no worse off if we do not eat, and no better off if we do. But take care that this liberty of yours does not somehow become a stumbling-block to the weak. For if others see you, who possess knowledge, eating in the temple of an idol, might they not, since their conscience is weak, be encouraged to the point of eating food sacrificed to idols? So by your knowledge those weak believers for whom Christ died are destroyed. But when you thus sin against members of your family, and wound their conscience when it is weak, you sin against Christ.

1 Corinthians 8:1-12

To each is given the manifestation of the Spirit for the common good. To one is given through the Spirit the utterance of wisdom, and to another the utterance of knowledge according to the same Spirit, to another faith by the same Spirit, to another gifts of healing by the one Spirit, to another the working of miracles, to another prophecy, to another the discernment of spirits, to another various kinds of tongues, to another the interpretation of tongues. All these are activated by one and the same Spirit, who allots to each one individually just as the Spirit chooses.

1 Corinthians 12:7-11

If I speak in the tongues of mortals and of angels, but do not have love, I am a noisy gong or a clanging cymbal. And if I have prophetic powers, and understand all mysteries and all knowledge, and if I have all faith, so as to remove mountains, but do not have love, I am nothing. If I give away all my possessions, and if I hand over my body so that I may boast, but do not have love, I gain nothing.

1 Corinthians 13:1-3

We want you to know, brothers and sisters, about the grace of God that has been granted to the churches of Macedonia; for during a severe ordeal of affliction, their abundant joy and their extreme poverty have overflowed in a wealth of generosity on their part. For, as I can testify, they voluntarily gave according to their means, and even beyond their means, begging us earnestly for the privilege of sharing in this ministry to the saints—and this, not merely as we expected; they gave themselves first to the Lord and, by the will of God, to us, so that we might urge Titus that, as he had already made a beginning, so he should also complete this generous undertaking among you. Now as you excel in everything—in faith, in speech, in knowledge, in utmost eagerness, and in our love for you—so we want you to excel also in this generous undertaking.

2 Corinthians 8:1-7

In him we have redemption through his blood, the forgiveness of our trespasses, according to the riches of his grace that he lavished on us. With all wisdom and insight he has made known to us the mystery of his will, according to his good pleasure that he set forth in Christ, as a plan for the fullness of time, to gather up all things in him, things in heaven and things on earth.

Ephesians 1:7-10

I have heard of your faith in the Lord Jesus and your love towards all the saints, and for this reason I do not cease to give thanks for you as I remember you in my prayers. I pray that the God of our Lord Jesus Christ, the Father of glory, may give you a spirit of wisdom and revelation as you come to know him, so that, with the eyes of your heart enlightened, you may know what is the hope to which he has called you, what are the riches of his glorious inheritance among the saints, and what is the immeasurable greatness of his power for us who believe, according to the working of his great power. God put this power to work in Christ when he raised him from the dead and seated him at his right hand in the heavenly places, far above all rule and authority and power and dominion, and above every name that is named, not only in this age but also in the age to come.

Ephesians 1:15-21

For this reason I bow my knees before the Father, from whom every family in heaven and on earth takes its name. I pray that, according to the riches of his glory, he may grant that you may be strengthened in your inner being with power through his Spirit, and that Christ may dwell in your hearts through faith, as you are being rooted and grounded in love. I pray that you may have the power to comprehend, with all the saints, what is the breadth and length and height and depth, and to know the love of Christ that surpasses knowledge, so that you may be filled with all the fullness of God.

Ephesians 3:14-19

For this reason, since the day we heard it, we have not ceased praying for you and asking that you may be filled with the knowledge of God's will in all spiritual wisdom and understanding, so that you may lead lives worthy of the Lord, fully pleasing to him, as you bear fruit in every good work and as you grow in the knowledge of God.

Colossians 1:9-10

For I want you to know how much I am struggling for you, and for those in Laodicea, and for all who have not seen me face to face. I want their hearts to be encouraged and united in love, so that they may have all the riches of assured understanding and have the knowledge of God's mystery, that is, Christ himself, in whom are hidden all the treasures of wisdom and knowledge.

Colossians 2:1-3

But solid food is for the mature, for those whose faculties have been trained by practice to distinguish good from evil.

Hebrews 5:14

If any of you is lacking in wisdom, ask God, who gives to all generously and ungrudgingly, and it will be given you.

James 1:5

Who is wise and understanding among you? Show by your good life that your works are done with gentleness born of wisdom. But if you have bitter envy and selfish ambition in your hearts, do not be boastful and false to the truth. Such wisdom does not come down from above, but is earthly, unspiritual, devilish. For where there is envy and selfish ambition, there will also be disorder and wickedness of every kind. But the wisdom from above is first pure, then peaceable, gentle, willing to yield, full of mercy and good fruits, without a trace of partiality or hypocrisy.

James 3:13-17

For this very reason, you must make every effort to support your faith with goodness, and goodness with knowledge, and knowledge with self-control, and self-control with endurance, and endurance with godliness, and godliness with mutual affection, and mutual affection with love. For if these things are yours and are increasing among you, they keep you from being ineffective and unfruitful in the knowledge of our Lord Jesus Christ.

2 Peter 1:5-8

Therefore, beloved, while you are waiting for these things, strive to be found by him at peace, without spot or blemish; and regard the patience of our Lord as salvation. So also our beloved brother Paul wrote to you according to the wisdom given to him, speaking of this as he does in all his letters. There are some things in them hard to understand, which the ignorant and unstable twist to their own destruction, as they do the other scriptures. You therefore, beloved, since you are forewarned, beware that you are not carried away with the error of the lawless and lose your own stability. But grow in the grace and knowledge of our Lord and Saviour Jesus Christ. To him be the glory both now and to the day of eternity. Amen.

2 Peter 3:14-18

The beast that you saw was, and is not, and is about to ascend from the bottomless pit and go to destruction. And the inhabitants of the earth, whose names have not been written in the book of life from the foundation of the world, will be amazed when they see the beast, because it was and is not and is to come. This calls for a mind that has wisdom: the seven heads are seven mountains on which the woman is seated; also, they are seven kings, of whom five have fallen, one is living, and the other has not yet come; and when he comes, he must remain for only a little while.

Revelation 17:8-10

From a place of suspended judgment, take time to meditate, pray, reflect upon and discuss the meaning of these verses taken as a whole before reading further. Is there a way you can practice any of the core principles in your daily life to gain a deeper understanding of the values and priorities reflected here?

What, then, are the central themes of these passages? How do they speak to inner knowing (*gnosis*) and wisdom (*sophia*), and their integration with other centers of knowledge? Do they reflect a progressive appreciation of what we might call the *spiritual interdependence* of every individual? Do they encourage an evolution of spiritual understanding? Or do they defer more strongly to tribal conformance and tradition? Do they reinforce freedom of thought, or enslavement to dogma? Do they integrate our interior centers of knowledge, or insulate them from each other? Here are the answers I believe this scripture offers us:

1. Knowledge and wisdom – indeed, as the Apostle Paul says in several instances, *all* knowledge and *all* wisdom – were available to the Christian community as gifts of the holy spirit. They were also understood to be innate capacities of mature believers in Christ, relied upon to make discerning choices and to interpret scripture. These capacities were so obvious and evident that they were called upon for mutual edification in the early Church – clearly without the involvement of Paul, the other apostles or any institutional authority.

2. Knowledge can make believers arrogant, even to the point of inadvertently harming other Christians. In such situations,

Christians should rely on love more than knowledge to guide them – for although their insight may be more mature or complete than another believer's (as in the case of food sacrificed to idols), what is more important in such situations is avoiding the distress and confusion of Christians who are less mature. In this loving consideration, the wisdom of right action is found. Thus, in this instance, *gnosis* is augmented with emotional intelligence to invoke *sophia*.

3. According to James, "wisdom from above" has many characteristics, among them being impartial, open to reason and willing to yield. That is, able to maintain neutrality of opinion while entertaining new or different ideas. Not only does this encourage freedom from dogma, but it integrates rational consideration of other perspectives and evidences with spiritual information and emotional intelligence, exemplifying a synergy of understanding.

4. The true evidence of such indwelling wisdom and knowledge are qualities of character and conduct. Being humble and peaceable, full of generosity and mercy, genuine and without hypocrisy. These are the "good fruits" of knowledge as moderated by love, and wisdom enhanced by faith. At the same time, skillful discernment is also perfected through practice – that is, we can condition our senses, our faculties of perception (αἰσθητήρια in Hebrews 5:14), through mental, emotional and physical discipline grounded in spiritual principles. In this way, the expression of faith in our physical being also contributes to our wisdom and knowledge; that is, we enhance our somatic intelligence at the same time, and thereby begin to integrate the multiple intelligences within.

I would therefore propose that free-thinking skeptics can subscribe to these New Testament principles using an integral model of knowledge and understanding. What this scripture seems to unambiguously communicate is that religious traditions and institutions should not be the governing influences in a person's spirituality and maturity. Instead, it is indwelling wisdom and knowledge – as moderated by faith, love, reason, practice, and the illumination of the holy spirit – that establishes and enhances all of these attributes. In Justin Martyr's *Second Apology*, he talks about the "implanted word" – the seed of truth that all people possess but which they can only partially understand and imitate – and the more complete wisdom and knowledge imparted by God's grace. We see similar sentiments throughout the *Gospel of Thomas,* where we read things like "There is light within a man of light, and he illuminates the whole world," and "If you do not know yourselves, then you dwell in poverty, and you are the poverty." In the *Epistle of Mathetes to Diognetus* we find: "Let your heart be your wisdom and your life be true knowledge that is properly received." Indeed I would say it is these powerful indwelling forces are intended to harmonize with each other and guide Christians into all truth, and that both inflexible prescriptions and institutional authority have no place at all in Christendom.

We can also find illustrations of how this orientation functions in the New Testament. One example is the story of Peter and Cornelius in Acts 10. Here is Acts 10:9-17 (NRSV):

> About noon the next day, as they were on their journey and approaching the city, Peter went up on the roof to pray. He became hungry and wanted something to eat; and while it was being prepared, he fell into a trance. He saw the heaven opened and something like a large sheet coming down, being lowered to the ground by its four corners. In it were all kinds of four-footed creatures and reptiles and birds of the air. Then he heard a voice saying, 'Get up, Peter; kill and eat.' But Peter said, 'By no means, Lord; for I have never eaten anything that is profane or unclean.' The voice said to him again, a second time, 'What God has made clean, you must not call profane.' This happened three times, and the thing was suddenly taken up to heaven. Now while Peter was greatly puzzled about what to make of the vision that he had seen, suddenly the men sent by Cornelius appeared...

At first Peter was puzzled about this mystical vision. But then, a little while later, we discover what he has concluded about his experience (NRSV):

> On Peter's arrival Cornelius met him, and falling at his feet, worshipped him. But Peter made him get up, saying, 'Stand up; I am only a mortal.' And as he talked with him, he went in and found that many had assembled; and he said to them, 'You yourselves know that it is unlawful for a Jew to associate with or to visit a Gentile; but God has shown me

> that I should not call anyone profane or unclean. So when I was sent for, I came without objection...
>
> Acts 10:25-29

Now consider that, according to the gospel accounts, Peter had already seen Jesus associate with Gentiles on several occasions. How could he have forgotten Jesus casting a demon out the Syrophoenician woman's daughter (Mark 7)? Or Jesus not only offering living water to the Samaritan woman at the well, but promising her that Samaritans would soon worship the Father in spirit and truth (John 4)? Or Jesus commissioning the apostles to make disciples of all nations (Matthew 28)? Or, perhaps most specifically of all considering Peter's vision, didn't Peter remember Jesus telling his disciples that all foods were already clean (Mark 7)? For whatever reason, Peter seems to have let this critical facet of Jesus' message slip his mind. So as he prays, he encounters a personal reminder of an established principle. Nothing new here, just a nudge back in the right direction. And how does Peter interpret the vision? At first he is confused, but then, when Cornelius' messengers arrive, Peter concludes that the vision of what has been "made clean" by God must include the Gentiles. How does he make this leap? Is there another vision with a detailed explanation? The account allows no time for this. Could it be that Peter intuits the truth within himself? Could he have comingled the mystery of his spiritual sight with reason, compassion and the immediate circumstances of human interaction to form his conclusions? I think this is a persuasive possibility, for this is precisely how *gnosis* evolves into skillful action.

To discard the power of *gnosis* and its synergy with other centers of intelligence also contradicts a crucial principle of Christ's message to humanity: that we contain Divinity. When Christian communications, leaders or institutions are relied upon for definitive edification and discernment, and the holy spirit, our capacity for love and our own native intelligences are given a back seat, this returns Christendom to the dogmatic legalism of the religious elite that Jesus so railed against, and destroys the holy temple that Jesus sacrificed his life to build within every believer (John 2:19, 1 Corinthians 6:19, 2 Corinthians 6:16, 1 John 4:13). Once again, there is no reason to reject any of the varied input streams sanctioned by New Testament scripture, and every reason to integrate them into a harmonized whole.

I think this provides a definitive answer to the question of how we should navigate any and all new spiritual information – even if that information hints at departure from established practice, or convicts us of evolutions in the law of love. This is how we can recognize that our own understanding is incomplete, and in fact the understanding of the Apostle Paul and other New Testament writers was incomplete in certain ways. At the same time, as we integrate *gnosis* with other centers of intelligence, we begin the journey from initial insight into mature wisdom. Eventually, the most spiritually profitable course of *agape* will become obvious, muddy water will settle and clear, the beast and its herder will vanish, and we shall behold the Divine face to face. Then, in all humility, we must recognize that our newborn truth is only with us for a little while, that we must be careful and considerate when sharing it with others, that we can only hold it lightly in our open hands, and that we will likely grow beyond it some day as our wisdom matures.

As a final thought regarding *gnosis*, I'd like to leave you with something attributed to the Apostle Paul. For me, this captures an important aspect of the spiritual interdependence and the source of insight and wisdom for all who follow Christ. It also suggests what we may be overlooking if we neglect spiritual awareness as a contributive avenue of insight and understanding:

> The animalistic man doesn't welcome things from the spirit of God, for they are foolishness to him and he isn't able to comprehend what is spiritually discerned. The spiritual person examines all, but is himself examined by no one. For who understood the mind of the Lord and who will instruct him? But we have the mind of Christ.
>
> *1 Corinthians 2:14-16*

"What If?" – Experimenting with an Alternate Canon

Despite the repeated encouragement we find in the New Testament that Christians should rely on interior *gnosis* for spiritual nourishment and mutual support, the Church's pattern during the last two thousand years has generally been to move in the opposite direction. Instead of emphasizing spiritual interdependence – an egalitarian fellowship of mortal temples for a living God – Christendom has for the most part endorsed, and sometimes violently enforced, dependence on institutional or hierarchical authority with its inevitably inflexible doctrine. Despite reform efforts that have sought to depart from such legalistic constraints, the Church has returned again and again to the assurance of externalized dependence. If it isn't deference to proclamations of the Holy See, then it's a claim that Divine revelation has ended and Christians must defer to the existing scriptural canon – or some other means of limiting both the importance of individual insight and the continuing power of the holy spirit.

There have been exceptions to this pattern of course, but those few flashes of Light have most often been marginalized or persecuted by mainstream authoritarian Christianity; they either did not survive into modern times or never gained enough momentum to pervade all of Christendom. Various Gnostic, Anabaptist and Behmenist movements could be grouped into this category, and of these the Religious Society of Friends (Quakers) seems to have had the most success in both surviving persecution and skirting the entrapments of dogma and externalized authority. Individual adherents to Christian mysticism can also be found within mainstream Catholic and Protestant denominations throughout history, but, with possible the exception of Jakob Böhme, they have seldom spawned successful shifts within the Church toward increased acknowledgement of the soul's strength, the powers of the spirit, or the Divinity within.

With all of this in mind, I would like to propose an experiment which may help us recognize how damaging reliance on external authorities can be. Let's consider for a moment what would happen if the New Testament canon were ever-so-slightly different than what the Church councils decided those many centuries ago. What would happen if we excised the 242 verses of the Pastoral Epistles – 1 and 2 Timothy and Titus? How would that have reshaped the Church over the past 1,700 years – a Church that has at times relied on quite a few of these verses to defend its doctrines?

First, let's discuss why we might choose the Pastoral Epistles for this exercise. What follow are brief summaries of tests for the inclusion of these epistles for my own spiritual edification, using the same hermeneutical tools outlined at the beginning of the book. Remember that these tools ideally include analytical, intuitive, experiential and participatory approaches. In the course of my research, I have drawn upon Werner Kümmel's *Introduction to the New Testament*, and A.H. McNeile's *An Introduction to the Study of the New Testament* among other sources. Here, then, are some of the major points gleaned from this research along with my own experiences, communal observations, and intuitive discernment:

1. The *Chester Beatty Papyri*, dating back to the early third century, did not contain any mention of 1 and 2 Timothy or Titus, and indeed did not have enough space to accommodate them among the missing pages. Also, although some of the Pastoral Epistles were referred to in passing by a number of 2nd century authors, the missives were not concretely quoted until Iranaeus in 170 A.D. It has further been argued that these epistles contain language and concepts too advanced for first century theology, and which are more reflective of developments in the second century Church – some scholars have even observed them to be similar in vocabulary and style to the writings of Polycarp (69 – 155 A.D.).

2. The overall language, vocabulary, themes and spiritual flavor of the epistles is not only quite different from the Apostle Paul's other writing, but directly contradicts his other epistles on several points. As just one example, the writer's hateful attacks of women are particularly strident and extreme, and are not in agreement with Paul's attitudes found in a preponderance of his epistles – and certainly not with the teachings and example of Jesus regarding women that we find earlier in the New Testament.

3. It seems overly convenient that influential Church Fathers Tertullian (160-225 A.D.) and Irenaeus (2nd Century to 202 A.D.) relied on the Pastoral Epistles to support their opposition to Gnosticism and Marcionism, which during their time appear to have been viable and perhaps even popular versions of Christianity. It can be argued that the Pastoral Epistles made a pronounced contribution to what later became a mainstream, authoritarian, traditionalized theology that forcefully contradicted these other schools of Christian thought. For their

part, Marcion (85-160 A.D.) rejected these epistles, and, according to the Christian scholar Jerome (347-420 A.D.), so did Basilides, a Gnostic who taught in Alexandria from 117 to 138 A.D.

4. From the very beginning of my own adoption of Christian beliefs and practices, something within me could not reconcile the rest of the New Testament with the tone and content of 1 Timothy in particular. In my struggles to incorporate its teachings into my faith experience, I first suspected that it had been written by Timothy as a means of self-justification. After all, how helpful it would have been to have the authority of the Apostle Paul behind phrases like "Don't let anyone disesteem you because of your youth..." (1 Timothy 4:12) After a time, however, I could no longer believe that Timothy was responsible for the epistle's frequent departures from the larger body of consistent thought I encountered elsewhere in the New Testament. After much prayer and reflection – and without knowledge of historical disputes over the epistle – my conscience could no longer entirely embrace 1 Timothy for my own edification. In the margin of my very first Bible, at the beginning of 1 Timothy, there is a note I wrote some twenty years ago that declares my conclusions: "Written by Timothy? No – a liar."

5. When we examine the theological significance of certain themes in the Pastoral Epistles – themes we cannot detect anywhere else in the New Testament – we are faced with a similar dissonance in how they have been expressed throughout Church history. We could even say that these unique ideas are in part responsible for many of the persistent problems within Christendom, and for particularly damaging consequences to Christian communities that have emphasized and prioritized them.

So these are some reasons why we might target the Pastoral Epistles for elimination from the canon altogether. But if we were to eliminate them, what impact might this have? Could removing just 3% (242/7956 verses) of the New Testament have altered the course of Church history or our current understanding of the Christian faith in substantial ways? To illustrate the unique and controversial contribution of these texts, here are some of the concepts we either find only in the Pastoral Epistles, or which are uniquely emphasized or expanded there:

1. If used appropriately, the religious law of the Old Testament is really a good thing, and should be used to deal with people who commit immoral, rebellious and sinful acts. After all, the Old Testament is inspired by God and can inculcate wisdom that leads to salvation, train people up in righteousness and good works, and reprove or correct others. (1 Timothy 1:8-11; 2 Timothy 3:14-17)

2. Women should dress plainly, never be allowed positions of authority over men, and they should never become teachers. Why? Because they were deceived by Satan in the Garden of Eden, and by implication are spiritually inferior to men. Their only hope of preservation in this fallen state is to bear children while demonstrating their belief in Christ. Not only should they be submissive to their husbands, but they should confine themselves to housework. (1 Timothy 2:9-15, 5:14; Titus 2:3-5)

3. Leaders (elders and deacons) in the Church must be married men, who are longtime believers and can manage their family well, whose children are Christians, who have certain other respectable characteristics (no alcoholism, avarice, or fits of anger, etc.), and who both conform to Church doctrine and are able to defend it. (1 Timothy 3:1-15; Titus 1:5-9)

4. During the apostasy, the great falling away from the faith, people will forbid marriage and promote abstaining from certain foods. They will mimic a kind of godliness but deny its real power, captivate weak women, and be perpetual learners who never recognize truth. They will reject Church doctrine and turn aside to myths, surrounding themselves with teachers who tickle their ears with things they want to hear. (1 Timothy 4:1-3; 2 Timothy 3:5-7; 2 Timothy 4:3-4)

5. Christians should avoid speculative debates and discussions of any kind, and especially about the Law of the Prophets. They should also never question the doctrinal pronouncements of the Church, and should not entertain any *gnosis* that contradicts this doctrine. (1 Timothy 1:3-7; 6:3-5,20; 2 Timothy 2:14,23; Titus 2:9-11; Titus 2:9-11)

There are of course many other principles in these same books that can be found elsewhere in the New Testament, and that is what perhaps makes it challenging to detect at first glance the unfortunate misdirection these epistles engender. But, once again, what makes the many ideas unique to these texts so troublesome is not just that they are different, but that they actively refute or antagonize the sentiments of a vast majority of other New Testament scripture on the same topics – even the reasoning Paul himself offers us elsewhere. According to the rest of the New Testament, Christians are no longer under Old Testament law, and are set free from its judgmental usage and from the constraints of all religious legalism; women are spiritually equal to men and as prophets and teachers and leaders should be honored and indeed relied upon to guide the Church; leaders in the Church are encouraged to remain single and devote themselves to God through celibacy, and marriage is considered a concession rather than proof of spiritual maturity; personal knowledge or *gnosis* of the Divine is celebrated and encouraged for the edification of the individual and the collective, while conformance to legalistic doctrine is discouraged…and so on. We have discussed these principles in detail throughout previous chapters. Yet, in 1 and 2 Timothy and Titus, we find strongly-worded opposition to them. Despite this fact, the aberrations in the Pastoral Epistles have nonetheless arguably shaped much of Christianity's evolution over the ensuing centuries.

So what if these departures from the dominant New Testament themes were eliminated from the canon? How might that have strengthened a different form of Christianity or altered the course of Church history? Imagine a Christendom where maturation of spiritual insight and discernment was encouraged through personal *gnosis*, while uniform Church doctrine took a back seat. Imagine a Church that viewed women as spiritual equals, exhorted them to teach and preach and lead, and honored them for these contributions. Imagine a culture of Christianity where intellectual and spiritual ideas were intensely debated and refined, and legalistic dogma was abandoned altogether in favor of trusting holy spirit and the law of love to guide believers into all truth. Imagine a world where Christians did not feel it was a spiritual imperative to procreate or view marriage as an avenue to confer greater spiritual authority. In other words, imagine a community of believers where people were permitted to marry or not to marry, to have children or not to have children, to seek knowledge of God and abide in the law of love, to challenge and revise Church doctrine, and which never reverted to the tenets of the Old Testament to control its adherents.

It is my belief that this is precisely the sort of Christianity that Jesus taught and exemplified in his time, and which were reinforced by apostolic missives to the different communities of early Christendom. It also reflects many of the beliefs found in the writings of Christian mystics and reformers throughout history. But, more importantly, this alternate manifestation of the kingdom of God expresses the pervasive attitudes and ideals of the New Testament itself. Although the Pastoral Epistles constitute only 3% of the canon, their influence has been as disproportionate as it has extraordinary. We touched on some of the reasons why this may have occurred in the last chapter, but in entertaining the idea of a world where these books were never part of the Bible, we begin to glimpse the disconcerting power deluding cultural influences can have on the evolution of religious institutions. As Galatians 5:9 warns: "A little yeast leavens the whole batch of dough."

In this light, should Christians – or anyone else for that matter – discard the Pastoral Epistles in their navigation of Christian faith? Of course not. As with everything discussed so far, I would encourage people to carefully and patiently consult their own inner Light instead; for Christians, such deliberation is a matter of conscience in concert with holy spirit. For me, although these books do contradict New Testament teaching on several points, they also contain practical wisdom and insight into Christianity that is encouraging and helpful. To reflexively discard them could potentially be as irresponsible as reflexively embracing them – which of course applies to all scripture. So, as is so often the case with spiritual matters, assessing the usefulness of the Pastoral Epistles is a process of discernment, application, reflection and maturation.

As an experiment, I think evaluating a Christianity sans the Pastoral Epistles has value. But given the legalistic tendencies inherent to an apostate Church, their removal may have made no difference at all to Christian history. And, of course, various reformers have promoted the exclusion or minimizing of various portions of the New Testament to little effect. For example, Martin Luther initially wanted to remove Hebrews, James, Jude and Revelation from the Biblical canon, but of course these books remain in Protestant Bibles. So instead of discarding or even reprioritizing, I think it behooves modern readers to err in the opposite direction, and instead include as much material as possible in their edification – and, as with so much else we have explored, avoid rigid formalization of what constitutes scripture and what does not. Personally, I found rich spiritual nourishment in my first exposure to Ecclesiastes, Proverbs, Psalms and the Gospel of John, so I am glad those hadn't been excised from the modern Bible when I first read it.

The Quagmire of Preference

There is a caveat here, however. For there is always a danger that we will be carelessly selective, conforming scripture to our own whims and fancies. I think we can be fairly confident that this is one reason why the Church initially canonized an authoritative list of texts, and why many Christians today are wary of departing from that canon. And yet we have seen how whims and fancies already intrude upon formalized scripture anyway. Whether dominant cultural memes, the emotional programming of our family of origin, the groupthink of our peers, or our particular stage of moral or spiritual development, the influences that shape the selectivity and preference in our interpretation and application of scripture are forceful, enduring and numerous. Some would even insist that these influences are inescapable, but I would not go so far. Instead, I would say what constitutes Divine prophecy, or what scripture can be conclusively classified as superior for edification, is an evolving process that relies on our spiritual interdependence and maturity. Most important, then, is what reliably contributes to the spiritual and cultural liberation of the individual, and to the maturation, the *taleios,* of both the individual and the collective.

For spiritual self-reliance and maturation are what ultimately refine the quality of edification we receive. As we grow, we learn to filter out distractions and influences that dissuade us from more interdependent forms of spirituality, relationship and community. Just as applying *gnosis* is enhanced through harmony with our various innate intelligences, growth and development are facilitated in part by practicing all the elements of our guiding hermeneutic. When we rely on a synthesis of reason, intuition, disciplined practice and communal dialogue to navigate the course of our spiritual journey, maintaining to whatever degree possible a neutral and non-judgmental outlook on whatever we encounter, we will naturally stimulate concurrent evolution in many areas of self. As we persist, we will evolve; and as we seek a more mature spiritual understanding, we will find it.

This is how believers and non-believers alike can both trust the spiritually enriching substance of the New Testament – or any other source of wisdom – and continually question it at the same time. Because what we are really learning to do is trust our more enlightened selves – that is, our spiritual awareness, our innate faculties of discernment, the wisdom of our experience, and our direct access to the Divine. As our understanding evolves, we will recognize the difference between the lures of whim and fancy and the evolutions of spirit. In recognizing that we will almost always be crowded on all sides by the pressures of conforming culture, and that these pressures may continue to color our understanding despite our best efforts, the only real freedom remaining for us is to look inward, to explore the essence of who we are and embrace that essence in our communion with spirit. Whatever our level of intimacy with *gnosis* and *sophia* – with inner knowing and wisdom – we can ground ourselves in that intimacy, have confidence in it, and bravely illuminate the deepest darkness with its warming Light.

CONCLUSIONS

Anyone who attempts to live by New Testament principles cannot gainsay the progressive implications of Jesus' example and instruction, and the equally liberal leanings of the majority of first century Christian teachings that have been canonized. If we subscribe to a conviction that arresting or reversing human population growth is a constructive and healing choice for both humanity and planet Earth, that conviction resonates strongly with the New Testament encouragement of celibacy. If we embrace pacifism and nonviolent responses to anger and conflict, we align ourselves perfectly with the directives and example of Christ and his apostles. When we preserve wilderness and protect wild animals and plants we are harmonizing with the preferences in New Testament accounts regarding where prayer, teaching, prophesy and other events critical to the evolution of the kingdom of God are intended to take place. If we advocate elements of socialism and Marxist ideology that support the economic good of everyone over a commercialist model of rewarding the cunning of an avaricious minority, we are advocating what was modeled by Christ and his followers in the early Church. Further, if we believe all available wealth should be channeled into relieving the suffering of the poor and the sick, and that the pursuit of wealth for our own comfort and self-importance is both distasteful and wasteful, we are simply conforming to Christ-like ideals.

As far as paying taxes are concerned, contributing to a progressive taxation model where those who earn more pay more of their income to the government could be argued as a natural intersection of New Testament instruction on the spirit of giving, the role of government and the necessity of taxes. Regardless of the specific tax structure, however, Christians should pay taxes without hesitation or complaint. In all of these arenas, where the imposition of Christian ideals on non-believers is concerned, a progressive view of tolerance and inclusion rather than judgmentalism or controlling behavior is the unquestionable preference of scripture; it is the responsibility of Christians to put their own hearts, houses and spiritual community in order, not to tamper with the lives of others – especially those who do not share their faith. So even though the New Testament is sociopolitically progressive, this does not necessarily translate into a Christian sociopolitical agenda. Rather, it exemplifies the nature of Christ-like lifestyle and interpersonal choices that Christians can make for themselves and promote within their spiritual community. Outside of the Church, the main focus of progressive Christian activism remains humble, self-sacrificing service to anyone in need.

In fact, one of the few potential stumbling blocks in the New Testament for a modern progressively-minded person might be the disaffection Jesus and his apostles seem to have had for political office or direct involvement in government. For me, political activism is an important part of my commitment to the well-being of this world and the people in it. And yet to have faith that spiritual forces will continue to accomplish good in the world without my involvement does not exclude my contributing to that good with my actions – so I vote, and I give, and I help, and I try to consume carefully – but I do not seek political office, and I would find it challenging to encourage anyone to do so for spiritual reasons. At the same time, I also meditate, pray and give thanks for the powers of good that work invisibly in concert with and beyond my individual will. My attitude of faith does not dilute my eagerness to be compassionately effective, but neither does it justify my setting myself up as God or wielding worldly authority over others. I fully trust that the arc of the universe bends towards equity and justice, that the Light of love and edification will prevail over ignorance and fear, but I also know that all equity and justice begins and ends in the love every individual expresses in their thoughts, words and immediate actions towards everyone around them – and my primary responsibility is therefore to embody that understanding in my own personal interactions and relationships.

Regarding Jesus' liberating attitudes towards women, modern society has only just begun to realize his radical vision of equality. We can declare with confidence that honoring and empowering women is both a progressive value and a Christian imperative. And even though the Apostle Paul seems to have been conflicted over this issue when offering his own opinions on the matter, even he had to admit (when speaking in the spirit) that women and men are equal in the eyes of God. Here we see that, as with hoarding wealth or waging war or lording it over others, the treatment of women as second class citizens is a worldly shortcoming. In the kingdom of God, all of these maladies, these imperfections of a non-spiritual life, are intended to attenuate until all Christians are living in peace, in harmony with each other and with society at large, and attending to the equalization of wealth and the well-being of everyone around them. This will be the enduring evidence of the holy spirit at work in the lives of believers as the kingdom of God matures. Ultimately, the community of Christ was never meant to be exclusive or judgmental, but to embrace, serve and love All that Is – whoever, whatever and wherever they are. As it says in several places in the New Testament (Matthew 19:28, Mark 9:12, Acts 3:21, Colossians 1:20, Revelation 21:5, etc.), God's ultimate purpose through Christ is to make *everything* new and restore *all things*. Christian attitudes about the feminine – and a championing of any other civil liberties – are among many intersecting currents in that all-inclusive ocean of transformation.

Such progressive implications can of course be disputed or avoided through skillful rationalization and denial, and we see such aversion routinely embodied in conservative Christian opinions, doctrines and behaviors. But conservatism is just a symptom – of the influence of constrictive cultural memes on society and individuals, of the apostate degradation of Christianity and the rise of antichrists described in scripture, of the need for balanced nourishment in every dimension of self, and of environmental and genetic barriers to well-being and transformative growth. Once again, such failings are not restricted to any one denomination or type of faith, but are pervasive throughout Christendom and all religious institutions. And although they seem to be in the minority, there are undoubtedly modern Christians who remain faithful to New Testament teachings among every denomination as well. Upon casual observation, it almost seems as though the most constructive embodiments of Christ's teachings are in fact distributed equally – but differently – across all variations of belief.

So in order to celebrate the original message of Christ, Christians must return to a spiritually progressive interpersonal activism that is grounded in a commitment to the priority of spiritual life in the kingdom of God, and to the consequent tolerance, compassion and self-sacrificing acts of service in the world. Many times over the scripture of the New Testament encourages believers to abandon all legalism, judgmental attitudes and fear, to avoid duplicating the darkened understanding of the religious elite of Jesus' day, and to favor the law of love. In addition, Christians are exhorted to refine their understanding, to graduate from the milk of the word to spiritually solid food, and to continually evolve their knowledge and wisdom in the spirit. This is the challenge that remains before the Church as a whole, and before every believer in Christ. It is also the only way conservative Christians can relieve the cognitive dissonance between their sociopolitical convictions and the progressive *logos* of the New Testament.

A Progressive Response to Conservative Christianity

I should point out that I have a number of conservative friends and acquaintances, some of whom identify as Christian, and we frequently have spirited discussions about many of the issues covered in this book. It has become clear to me over the course of such discussions that these conservatives often desire the best for their fellow human beings, they just advocate a different methodology than I do (at least much of the time…as I have, on occasion, also been known to agree with certain conservative-leaning approaches). So I want to be clear that this book is not an indictment of the genuine faith and compassionate intentions of these good folk. On the contrary, whenever loving kindness swells within the human heart, I'm certain the Divine is right there in the midst of it, regardless of what political views the mind might hold. What this book is really about is the spiritual efficacy of a given set of values as reflected by the instruction and examples of the New Testament itself. Conservative values, on the whole, just tend to be at odds with the values Christ demonstrated. So although beginning a Christian journey from a conservative vantage point is not inconceivable, maturing to any degree along the way requires letting go of worldly, traditional and institutional perspectives. Anyone may start their journey in a state of self-protective fear, and in fact fearful awe of the Divine may signal the onset of wisdom, but perfect love casts out all fear, and empathy and compassion carry spiritual understanding into its ultimate refinement.

What are the most constructive responses a progressively-minded person can have to a less evolved, less compassionate mindset? The New Testament itself offers several responses, and it seems appropriate to consult that document for insight. Some options might be:

> "But I tell you: Love your enemies and pray for those persecuting you..."
>
> *Matthew 5:44*

> "Be attentive to yourselves. If your brother sins, admonish him, and if he repents, forgive him. If he sins against you seven times in a day, and returns to you seven times saying 'I repent,' then you should forgive him."
>
> *Luke 17:3-4*

> But now I have written to you not to keep close company with anyone called a brother who is sexually immoral or avaricious, an idolater or a reviler, a drunkard or rapacious. Don't even to eat with such a person.
>
> *1 Corinthians 5:11*

> I don't want to overburden you, but if anyone has caused grief, he hasn't grieved me but all of you, at least in part. This admonition by the majority is sufficient for such a person; on the contrary, you should forgive and comfort such a person, so he isn't swallowed up by excessive sorrow. For this reason I exhort you to publically affirm your love for him.
>
> *2 Corinthians 2:5-8*

> Brothers, if a human being is overtaken in some transgression, you who are spiritual should restore such a person in a spirit of gentle humility, contemplating yourself lest you also be tempted. Bear one another's burdens, and in this way you will fulfill the law of Christ.
>
> *Galatians 6:1-2*

> Reject foolish, uneducated speculations, knowing they give birth to conflict. It doesn't behoove the lord's servant to quarrel, but to be affable towards everyone, able to teach, patiently enduring bad things, in gentle humility instructing those in opposition. Perhaps God will grant them repentance for a full recognition of the truth, and they may sober up out of the devil's snare where they were captured to do his will.

2 Timothy 2:23-25

> Is anyone suffering hardship among you? Let them pray. Is anyone cheerful among you? Let them sing praises. Is anyone incapacitated with disease among you? Let him call for the elders of the church, and let them pray over him, having anointed him with oil in the name of the lord. The prayer of faith will preserve the one who is sick, and the lord will raise him up; if he has committed sins, it will be forgiven. Confess your sins to one another, then, and pray on behalf of one another, so that you may be made whole. The supplication of the righteous has great power as it operates.
>
> *James 5:13-16*

Here we have an array of reactions to limited understanding and counterproductive behavior that is narrowed by a clear set of guiding intentions: to be loving and kind on the one hand, but also to be strong, resolute and disciplined on the other. To repeatedly forgive is not to enable or reinforce wrongdoing; being kind does not equate being indulgent. Promoting compassion and tolerance does not mean remaining silent or passive in the face of wrongdoing. Yet, at the other extreme, being strong or even forceful does not mean becoming hostile or violent. Having a more mature understanding does not encourage condescension or conceit. To rebuke in a spirit of gentleness is not the same as reviling in a spirit of vindictiveness. This is the balancing act that skillful compassion demands, and what I believe is the most effective way to care for Christian conservatives. Progressives can help conservative-leaning Christians become more aware of their error, contrasting and comparing their values to the values of Christ, and exemplifying a more enlightened way of thought and conduct for them to follow, but then we must let go. There is nothing more to be done than to forgive, bless, pray and love with sincere humility.

And when people persist in their error? For believers, scripture encourages them not associate intimately with fellow Christians who cannot recognize their mistakes, cannot confess their troubles, or who cannot invite forgiveness for wrongdoing. Believers are also exhorted to avoid a battle of wills with such people, and to once again trust in God and the power of prayer instead. This aligns perfectly with the nonviolence promoted by New Testament teachings, and also takes into consideration the probability of antichrists and an apostate Church. I think this good advice for any progressive-leaning person. It is pointless to debate a mind committed to obscuring Love, Light, Life and Liberation; there is no external remedy for willful rejection of the Divine, it can only be healed from within. Whether or not we believe in the existence of fallen angels who strive against the spiritual edification of humanity or who tempt people to cling to darkness, the reality of both inner and circumstantial conditions that disrupt our spiritual evolution cannot be ignored. That is, in fact, how I would define evil: anything within or without that persuades us to disregard the evolutionary imperative of growth and maturity, both individually and collectively, in any and all dimensions of being. And a progressive person doesn't respond to such evil with more disruption, condemnation or conflict, but overcomes evil with good – that is, with the intention and embodiment, to whatever degree possible, of ever-increasing Love, Light, Life and Liberation. I believe this is how all healing occurs in personal, interpersonal and transpersonal spheres of existence.

Aspiring to the Divine is a lifelong calling, and we should not be surprised at the ebb and flow of both individual and collective spiritual realization. That so many of those who self-identify as Christians in the U.S. have lost their way, becoming confused by the pressures of tribal conformance and distortions of Christ's teachings, should neither surprise us nor exclude Christianity as a compassionate and inspirational avenue of faith. It is the proven tendency of human institutions to dilute the power of spiritual experience, distance people from their Divine essence, honor the past above the present, and restrain progressive tendencies in favor of suppressive controls. After all, institutions are really more committed to perpetuating themselves than the values and methodology they purport to represent. So to whatever degree Christendom emphasizes codified religiosity above direct encounters with spirit, it demands renewal and recommitment to the law of love. That was the message Jesus had for the religious experts of his day, and a message that remains perpetually viable and potent.

> "Enter through the narrow gate, for the gate is wide and the road is broad that leads to destruction, and there are many going in through it. The gate is small and the road is narrow that leads to life, and the ones who find it are few. Beware of false prophets who come to you in the robes of sheep, but are greedy wolves on the inside. You'll know them by their fruits. People don't gather grapes from thorn bushes, or figs from thistles, do they? Likewise, every good tree produces good fruit,

> but a corrupted tree bears evil fruit. A good tree can't produce evil fruit, and a rotten tree can't produce good fruit. Every tree that doesn't produce good fruit is cut down and cast into the fire. Therefore, you will know them by their fruits. Not everyone who says to me 'lord, lord' will enter the kingdom of heaven, but only those doing the will of my Father who is in heaven. Many will say to me on that day, 'lord, lord, didn't we prophesy in your name and drive out demons in your name and perform many mighty works in your name?' And I will declare to them: 'I never knew you; you who work wickedness be gone from me!'"
>
> *Matthew 7:13-23*

The Mastery of Love

The implication woven throughout much of Jesus' teaching is that loving God, loving ourselves, loving our neighbors, loving our enemies, and loving our spiritual brothers and sisters is fundamentally and continually difficult. Such love requires tremendous effort, diligence, discipline, focus, integrity, honesty, insight and endurance. That human beings will sometimes fall short of this ideal is understandable and perhaps inevitable, but the opportunity to correct course and find a way back to the firmament of love is equally enduring. In the Parable of the Sower, "the seed on good soil stands for those with a noble and good heart, who hear the word, retain it, and by persevering produce a crop." (Luke 8:15) Will there be storms that wash away a believer's best efforts? Of course. Will there be times a Christian forgets to tend the fields of spirit, and the harvest languishes into nothing? Undoubtedly. Will there be long dark nights where the sun of Divine love seems like a distant memory, leaving a faithful heart to wither in despair? Yes. I have spent more time than I wish to recount in such spiritual deserts. But the only barriers to my returning, to being consciously grounded in the Source, are my own persisting ignorance, arrogance, willfulness and conceit. Once I let go of these intrusions and begin to seek again, with humility and openness, the sacred garden flourishes within once more.

Additionally, once I wholeheartedly embrace my own spiritual activism and my own accountability to the call of love, the failures of others become irrelevant. The fact that an apostate Church trumpeting hypocrisies has so come to dominate U.S. culture and politics does not dilute the positive vision of Christ's life I have included in my journey, nor has it disrupted my commitment to be a proponent of progressive values. Legalism has never held the spiritual authority it claims, but the convictions of my conscience and the insights of my heart do – and always will. If I can hold fast to those, if I can remember and rely upon the Divine gift that resides within me, then I will find the knowledge and wisdom I need to navigate the trials of this life, and I can forgive every deficiency or failure within and without. I believe this to be the orientation of mature compassion, the perfection that arrives when the imperfect is accepted and embraced unconditionally.

Recently, an acquaintance posted a question about the nature of love on his Facebook wall. The responses came from all over the world, from many different cultures and spiritual persuasions, and were inspiring and humbling to read. Indeed I felt the resulting dialogue spoke to the versatility and richness of social networking as an avenue for participatory spirituality. Scrolling down my computer screen, I encountered the clear and unmistakable stamp of Divinity, the essence of spiritual wisdom, and the aroma of Christ. Here is my own contribution to that discussion, which for me represents an eternal standard against which a life of spirit perpetually evolves, and within which the tumultuous history of the Christian Church can be most accurately understood:

> "I intuit love to be the question at the core of being which constantly seeks an answer to itself, only to discover that the answer *is* itself. But this takes time. And, as love becomes more self-aware, it changes; it evolves through different stages and expressions, until, at last, there are no conditions, no differentiations, no possessions, no conceptions of giving, taking or sacrifice. In the end, there is only the infinite intimacy of love fully comprehending and being itself, of unconditionally embracing its own essence in all things.
>
> There are many manifestations of love along the way, of course. Many incomplete or partial loves. In all of these the love can be felt, can provide insight, can offer pleasurable satisfaction and contentment – and, as the many relationships and synergies love develops with itself grow and mature, there can be culmination in profound harmony and wisdom. Whenever dissonance, failure or abuse result from actions and attitudes that someone believes to be love, this is merely love not fully knowing itself, but attempting nevertheless to be – that is, to be imperfectly expressed. But I do not think love can be separated from

> any of these incomplete manifestations. Love is part of everything we encounter and express as it seeks to know itself and be known. This is why forgiveness, letting go of judgment and the acquiescence of our willfulness and ego arise naturally throughout love's journey, because the complete welcomes the incomplete. This is how love, light and liberation ultimately become one and the same."

At this time in history, progressives have a wonderful opportunity to reshape progressive spirituality, and progressive Christians have a wonderful opportunity to reshape Christendom. The teachings of the New Testament offer vibrant substance to the spiritual seeker regarding the nature and practice of radical compassion, a Light that has been obscured by dogmatic religiosity over the ages, but which can nevertheless be amplified by everyone who decides to embrace it. Certainly this Light bears patiently with those who cling to an incomplete understanding of Christ, reminding them of forgotten truths at every opportunity, while at the same time always ready to forgive and console without judgment. Even as progressives offer stern rebukes to their conservative brothers and sisters, they must yearn for healing, reconciliation and harmony with the same. But far more important than concern over phases of spiritual understanding is the attitude of loving service among and between progressives and the Church on behalf of the good of All. Concern and caring for anyone suffering in the world should transcend all other priorities. Love is action in ever-widening arenas, a persistent affection that enacts the greatest and most immediate good for everyone. Love defines what true progress looks and feels like. Regardless of someone's political or religious leanings, it is devotion to compassionate, self-sacrificing service that most clearly evidences the Divine, most unfailingly demonstrates the relevance of Christian faith, and most effectively embodies an enduring progressive ideology.

NT Translation & Early Christian Literature Resources

Print

Willis Barnstone, Editor, *The Other Bible,* Harper San Francisco, 1984, ISBN 00062500309

F. Wilbur Gingrich & Frederick Danker, *A Greek-English Lexicon of the New Testament & Other Early Christian Literature* (Translated from Walter Bauer's 5th Edition, 1958), University of Chicago Press, Second Edition, 1979, ISBN 0226039323

Everett Harrison, Geoffrey Bromiley & Carl Henry (Editors), *Baker's Dictionary of Theology,* Baker Book House, 1975, ISBN 0801040426

Wesley Perschbacher (Editor), *The New Analytical Greek Lexicon,* Hendrickson Publishers, 2006, ISBN 0943575338

Paul McReynolds (Editor), *Word Study Greek-English New Testament,* Tyndale House Publishers, 1999, ISBN 9780842382908

G. Abbott-Smith, *A Manual Greek Lexicon of the New Testament,* T&T Clark, 1964

Alfred Marshall, *Nestle-Marshall Interlinear Greek-English New Testament,* Zondervan, Second Edition, 1976

The Analytical Greek Lexicon, Zondervan, 1970

Web

bible.cc

bible.oremus.org

www.biblegateway.com

www.bible-researcher.com

www.earlychristianwritings.com

www.ancienttexts.org

Other

Frederick Henry Ambrose Scrivener (Editor), *Interlinear Greek New Testament Bible* (Kindle Edition), ASIN B003TFE5CM